CONTENTS

HEALTH-RELATED RESOURCES FOR BLACK AND MINORITY ETHNIC GROUPS

Acknowlegements

The HEA would like to thank the following for providing illustrative material for this book:

- Derbyshire Family Health Services Authority (Apni sehth)
- Birmingham Family Health Services Authority (Children's colds)
- Refugee Action (A guide to living in Britain for refugees from Vietnam)
- Cinenova (The haircut – a film by Veronica Martel)
- Sickle Cell Society (Let's talk sickle)
- Bolton Centre for Health Promotion (Menopause, Weaning)
- West Midlands Fire Service (Sapna jal giaa)
- London Borough of Hammersmith and Fulham (Self defence? Common sense!)
- Northern Visions (Travelling people)
- Cancerlink (What is cancer?)

© Health Education Authority, 1994
Hamilton House
Mabledon Place
London WC1H 9TX
ISBN 0 7521 0033 5
Typeset by DP Photosetting, Aylesbury, Bucks
Printed by The KPC Group, London and Ashford, Kent.

FOREWORD

The Chief Medical Officer's report (1991) drew attention to the health needs of black and minority ethnic groups. In 1993 the publication *Ethnicity and health* further reinforced the Government's commitment to the provision of appropriate and accessible services. It also highlighted the need for relevant information and resources.

We have an ongoing commitment to improve the health of people from black and minority ethnic groups. In 1988, as part of this commitment, Ministers identified funding specifically for the production of health promotion materials targeted to these groups. This stimulated organisations to work in partnership to produce a wide range of new initiatives.

The Health Education Authority held a series of viewing days to promote these and other initiatives which relate to the health of black and minority ethnic groups. At these viewing days a clearly expressed need was identified for a central source of information.

In response to this, the Health Education Authority has set up a central database of nationally available resources. We welcome this database and also this publication as a tangible contribution to improving much needed and easily accessible information.

We look forward to further initiatives from the Department of Health, the Health Education Authority and the National Health Services Ethnic Unit working together in a newly formed partnership.

Baroness Cumberlege
Parliamentary Secretary for Health

PREFACE

This timely publication and database is one of a number of long term Health Education Authority initiatives which reflect a strategic focus to reducing inequalities in health. The Health Education Authority and the National Health Service Ethnic Health Unit are working closely together to promote the health of black and minority ethnic groups. We consider that provision of information plays a key role in the development of national and local partnerships.

This is the hard copy of a national database of health-related resources for black and minority ethnic groups. It is the result of a national search and will be of benefit to both purchasers and providers. The database highlights what is nationally available for use by the providers of services and identifies gaps in provision which will be useful for those involved in commissioning new resources.

The database will be updated on a regular basis to ensure it continues to provide an overview of the national picture. The Health Education Authority, in partnership with the King's Fund, is setting up an electronic link between the two centres. This shared approach will lead to a more effective use of quality information services by NHS bodies.

The provision of a central and accessible source of information will enable and support the development of local activity. A number of the resources demonstrate effective ways of consulting and working in partnership with local communities. Some local agencies have used this process to build a continuing dialogue with local communities to help develop appropriate and effective services. These initiatives are to be welcomed. We commend this health education resource database to all users, particularly within the health authorities and trusts, primary and secondary care and in the voluntary sector.

Dr Michael Chan
Director, NHS Ethnic Unit

Paul Lincoln
Key Relationship Director, HEA

INTRODUCTION

This book aims to inform those who are concerned with commissioning, purchasing or providing healthcare services for black and minority ethnic groups. A wide search was undertaken in England in 1993 to identify as many health-related resources as possible. The results of that search are contained in this book.

- Information is presented about a range of health-related resources produced for black and minority ethnic groups. This includes resources which:
  — promote healthy lifestyles
  — inform about health services and how to use them
  — are concerned with particular conditions and diseases.
- Some resources have been produced for health professionals to assist them in assessing the needs of black and minority ethnic groups and how those needs may be met appropriately. Other resources have been produced to support those involved in training health professionals. These identify:
  — examples of good practice
  — key issues for specific communities
  — key issues for service provision
  — training needs of healthcare professionals.

The book can be used flexibly. It could be used as a reference to identify suitable resources for target communities or to inform healthcare service provision and training. Gaps in resource provision can be identified and may serve to guide those concerned with commissioning and producing resources, preventing duplication and encouraging the development of new resources to fill existing gaps. Overall it is hoped it will save time for those working in the field of health as resources can be quickly identified. Also, the reviews will facilitate effective decision making concerning suitability and appropriateness.

Definitions and terminology

In this publication the term 'black and minority ethnic groups' has been used. The rationale for this term is described in the quotation below taken from the report *Action not words: a strategy to improve health services for black and minority ethnic groups* (1988). The report was produced by the NAHA Working Party on Health Services for Black and Minority Ethnic Groups.

> The use of terms to describe different groups in the community is an extremely sensitive issue. The Working Party considered this at length and decided to use the term 'black and minority ethnic groups'. The word increasingly used by people of African/Afro-Caribbean and Asian origin is *black*. This term underlines a unity of experience of discrimination and inequality among people whose skin colour is not white. At the same time there are many people from minority communities in Britain who do not identify themselves as black but who, because of their ethnic origin, language, cultural or religious differences share a common experience.

There is no intention to cause offence to those who find this term unsatisfactory or who would prefer not to include themselves in such a description.

Throughout 'health professional' has been used to describe anyone who may be involved in providing health care in a professional capacity including health promotion activities within the voluntary and statutory sectors.

The term 'resources' has been used to describe a variety of formats. A wide range of different formats are included – video, audio-cassettes, manuals and guides, booklets, training packs, posters and models. Many resources are available in community languages. Items such as medical text books, journal articles, local reports and theses have not been included. The focus is on resources which have a practical application to health promotion activity rather than items which provide background reading or specialist medical information.

Leaflets have not been included because of the difficulties in providing accurate, up-to-date information about them. Often leaflets are locally produced containing local contacts and information. They may be short-lived because of funding or other constraints. The quality of production and durability is variable, ranging from glossy with colour illustrations through to photocopied text on flimsy paper. However some information regarding leaflets can be found in the list of resource directories (Appendix 5). Local health promotion units (now known as agencies) often produce leaflets for their local communities.

Background to the black and minority ethnic groups (BMEG) resources database project

The black and minority ethnic health resources database project was developed in response to an expressed need from a wide range of people involved in health promotion in both the voluntary and statutory sectors. The Health Education Authority (HEA) has always received significant numbers of inquiries about resources for black and minority ethnic groups.

The need for the database was also identified in a project which disseminated a series of resources funded by the Department of Health and managed by the HEA. In order to disseminate information about the new resources and others which had been recently produced, the HEA organised a series of national viewing days in London in September 1991. Health promoters and people with an interest in health from statutory and voluntary services were invited. The days were oversubscribed. Participants were impressed with the quality of the resources and requested further information about similar resources. In response to the demand a series of eight viewing days was organised around the country in partnership with regional and district health authorities. These took place between November 1991 and June 1992. They were also oversubscribed and resulted in more requests for up-to-date information about resources for black and minority ethnic groups. It seemed to be difficult for people to find out about new resources (which were perhaps not widely publicised) and there was a reticence to purchase items with often only the title as a guide to its contents and suitability for a particular audience. The black and minority ethnic health resources database was developed to try and meet these needs.

A national search was undertaken in early 1993 to try and identify as many health-related resources for black and minority ethnic groups as possible. Over 4000 letters were sent out explaining the purpose of the project and requesting information about resources. The letter was accompanied by a simple form to return with any details about known resources. Letters were sent to a wide range of statutory and voluntary services in England concerned with health, including:
– health promotion units (agencies)
– voluntary and community groups concerned with health
– district directors of public health
– district dental officers
– district health education officers
– district specialists in community medicine
– community dietitians
– primary healthcare facilitators
– environmental health officers
– AIDS co-ordinators
– directors of education
– directors of social services
– producers and distributors of health promotion resources
– professional organisations concerned with health.
In addition requests for information were included in a number of publications and newsletters.

Over 800 individual written responses were finally received in response to the search. These varied from 'no information to share' through to catalogues and printouts of information from databases. A large number of phone calls were received from people who wanted information and who requested searches on particular topics or in specific languages. Many of the written responses took the same form and asked for a copy of the completed database. It quickly became apparent that this was an area health professionals and others wanted information about.

The responses themselves were interesting. Many health promotion units (agencies) sent catalogues of their resource collections which contributed to an overview of available resources. Some were using resources which were dated and some had almost no relevant resources in their collection. Some units (agencies), particularly in areas with large numbers of specific communities, were well resourced and were involved in producing resources themselves often working with the target communities. A few units (agencies) responded that they had no need of such resources – sometimes this was explained by the respondents as due to there being few people from black and minority ethnic groups in their locality. However some units (agencies) in areas with large numbers of different communities seemed not to be proactively meeting their needs and one deputy district health promotion officer responded 'We have never had any requests for such materials'.

Over 90 new resources and 19 forthcoming resources were identified as a result of the search plus books and reports about local needs and services. The new resources were varied and are included in this publication.

The black and minority ethnic resources database can be accessed via the HEA's Health Promotion Information Centre (for further details see page 15). New resources will continue to be added as they become available and information about new resources will be welcome.

What the search revealed

The resources identified by the search were varied in terms of health topics covered, the communities they addressed and target audience. The resources included on the database had to be nationally available.

Previous research on the availability and coverage of resources for health promotion with black and minority ethnic groups identified a number of issues and observable patterns. Bhopal and Donaldson's analysis of health promotion resources for the period 1977 to 1987 revealed that 'the priorities for health education have been birth control, pregnancy and child care'.[1] They noted a lack of resources addressing topics such as prevention of chronic diseases, smoking and alcohol education. (It should be noted that Bhopal and Donaldson's study included leaflets. The figures quoted in this introduction do not include leaflets.)

This research was developed further by Bhatt and Dickinson[2] who compared resources available for black and minority ethnic groups with the findings of Bhopal and Donaldson. Bhatt and Dickinson used the *Health education for ethnic minorities* resource list produced by

[1] R.S. Bhopal and L.J. Donaldson, 'Health education for ethnic minorities – current provision and future directions', *Health Education Journal* 1988; **47**; 137–40.
[2] A. Bhatt and R. Dickinson, 'An analysis of health education materials for minority communities by cultural and linguistic groups', *Health Education Journal* 1992; **51**(2); 72–7.

the Health Education Authority in 1990, comparing it to the previous list published in 1987, to identify 'shifts in emphasis in health education for minority communities'. They noted that a wider range of resources had become available. More resources had been produced in the areas of women's health, use of health services, 'heart health', HIV and AIDS and provision for carers. There was little provision for African-Caribbean or Chinese communities. The absence of any resources relating to hypertension was noted with concern.

The results of the search undertaken by the HEA for the black and minority ethnic resources database (1993) has also reflected new directions, developments and gaps in resource provision. Table 1 (page 10) indicates the number of resources available for each of the language groups/communities. This includes all formats *except* leaflets and all were currently available at the time of going to press.

It can be seen that more resources have been produced for Bengali communities than any other. Gujarati-, Punjabi-, Urdu- and Hindi-speaking communities follow respectively. At the present time it is not clear why so many resources have been produced for Bengali communities in comparison with other communities. A pragmatic reason might be the contribution of a large number of resources from a few producers who have become skilled and confident in the production of health resources for and with their local Bengali communities.

Resources targeting Chinese communities have increased since Bhatt and Dickinson's analysis and this is closely followed by the number of resources for Vietnamese communities. However it must be remembered that the total number and topic coverage of resources for each community is still extremely small and limited in comparison to the number, range and quality of those produced for the majority population.

African-Caribbean communities are, according to 1991 Census data, the second largest ethnic population in the UK. However, the number of resources targeted at these communities does not reflect this. There may be several reasons for this. Previous commentators have speculated that because people from African-Caribbean communities speak English they are deemed to be served by resources produced for the majority (white) population. Many recently produced resources make determined efforts to reflect and appeal to a multiracial and multicultural community and perhaps producers consider this includes and meets the needs of African-Caribbean communities. Yet the effectiveness of these resources as opposed to the effectiveness of resources developed to target African-Caribbean communities directly has not really been tested. Evaluation of new resources for these communities and of multiracial resources will have implications for the future resource development.

Small numbers of resources have also begun to appear for communities not previously directly addressed by health promotion resources. These include resources in Turkish, Greek, Arabic, Somali and Yemeni plus resources for travelling communities.

Table 1 **Number of resources available by languages/communities**

Languages/communities	Posters only	Other formats
African (resources in English targeting African communities)	3	14
African-Caribbean	2	17
Arabic	3	8
Bengali (incl. Sylheti)	14	91
Chinese/Cantonese	4	35
Greek	2	13
Gujarati	10	69
Hindi	9	48
Hindustani or Hindi/Urdu*	0	14
Japanese	0	2
Polish	0	4
Punjabi	9	63
Somali	2	7
Spanish	0	1
Swahili	2	2
Travellers	0	8
Turkish	5	17
Urdu	10	62
Vietnamese	1	10
Yemeni	1	4

* The resources referred to here are described by the producers as available in Hindustani or Hindi/Urdu.

Notes
Several resources are counted more than once as the same resource may be available in several languages.
Almost all resources listed are also available in English or with English translations.
'Other formats' includes video, audio-cassettes, multimedia packs, booklets, training guides, manuals and packs, etc.

Table 2 (see opposite page) refers to the health topics covered by the resources. Many items are counted more than once as they may address more than one topic. It is always difficult to categorise topics as many overlap. This topic list was drawn up according to the contents of the resources. It is an attempt to list topics accurately and logically and to reflect current health concerns such as Health of the Nation key areas.

A significant development has been the increase in the number of resources relating to professional development. Many seek to inform health professionals about different communities, their health needs and how to work appropriately and acceptably with people from different communities. Resources about cultural identity, access to health services and communication have also increased.

This may reflect a move to try to improve service provision for black and minority ethnic groups – a direction noted in the Chief Medical Officer's report *On the state of the public*

Table 2 **Health topics covered by the resources**

Topic	P	O/F	Topic	P	O/F
Access to health services	—	25	Learning difficulties	—	5
Alcohol	—	6	Mental health	—	17
Ante- and postnatal care	—	20	Nutrition	3	26
Arthritis	—	1	Older people	1	13
Asthma	—	1	Oral health	—	7
Cancer	—	1	Parent/Child health	—	24
Coronary heart disease	—	4	Physical activity	—	7
Communication	—	14	Physical disability	—	3
Community	—	25	Professional development	—	44
Contraception	—	4	Refugees	—	6
Cultural identity	2	28	Religion	—	11
Cystic fibrosis	—	2	Safety	1	8
Death and dying	—	6	Screening	—	8
Diabetes	—	15	Sexual abuse	—	3
Down's syndrome	—	1	Sexual health	7	13
Eczema	—	1	Sickle cell	1	8
Education	—	19	Smoking	1	2
Environmental health	—	9	Solvents	—	1
Equal opportunities	4	38	Tay Sachs	—	1
ESOL	—	11	Technology	—	1
Female genital mutilation/	—	4	Thalassaemia	1	5
Female circumcision			Travel	—	2
HIV and AIDS	9	24	Travellers	—	10
Immunisation	1	5	Women's health	1	26
Infant feeding	—	6	Work and the workplace	—	6

Key   P = posters only; O/F = other formats: video, audio-cassettes, multimedia, booklets, training guides, manuals and packs (no leaflets).

Note   Many resources are counted more than once as some resources deal with more than one topic.

health 1991, part of which addressed the health needs of black and minority ethnic groups, concluding

> . . . people working within the health service need to be aware of the differences, both in terms of disease patterns and lifestyle, and to consider how these differences need to inform appropriate service provision.

The Patient's Charter may have been a further stimulus, stating that patients have a right to 'respect for privacy, dignity, and religious and cultural beliefs' and to 'be given detailed information on local health services'. A range of resources now exist for training and supporting health professionals to identify and meet the needs of black and minority ethnic groups.

In terms of response to Health of the Nation key areas (coronary heart disease and strokes, cancers, mental illness, accidents and sexual health) and the other key areas identified in *Ethnicity and health – a guide for the NHS* (diabetes, infant health, haemoglobinopathies and access to health services)[1] the picture is uneven.

No resources specifically on hypertension or strokes have been brought to our attention. Coronary heart disease is slowly being taken on board, however. For example a recent video about exercise and physical activity for women from Asian communities informed viewers about the prevalence of coronary heart disease in Asian communities. Much of the information in resources about healthy eating is concerned with the prevention of coronary heart disease.

The national search has also not revealed many resources about cancer although resources about breast and cervical screening have been produced for some communities. Like many other resources about diseases and conditions, the only resource specifically about cancer that we are aware of has been produced by a voluntary group.

There has been a gradual increase in resources related to mental illness which tend to fall into two categories: those which inform about services available to people who are mentally ill; and those which question the differential rates of mental illness and varying quality of treatment for people from black and minority ethnic groups. Newer resources seek to make users of services aware of their rights and to present users' viewpoints.

Accident prevention is an area which has seen limited growth particularly in relation to children, safety in the home and on the roads. These almost exclusively target Asian communities.

In relation to sexual health, the number of resources on HIV/AIDS has increased, confirming a trend noted in Bhatt and Dickinson's work. The number of new resources exclusively about contraception has declined. This may be because contraception (in terms of safer sex and condom use) is now often discussed in the context of HIV/AIDS education.

There has been a recent increase in resources about diabetes, but those available are almost exclusively for Asian communities and focus on dietary advice based on a traditional diet. Diabetes is four to five times more prevalent in Asian communities than in non-Asian communities and twice as prevalent in Caribbean communities as in white communities.[2] This is not reflected in the number of resources available which support health professionals advising people how to manage and control diabetes.

Antenatal and postnatal care still feature significantly but the newer resources have been developed for communities not previously catered for such as Chinese communities. Some deal with new topics such as promoting breastfeeding or information about home birth choices. Many of the older resources now need updating to reflect changes in ante- and postnatal care.

[1] *Ethnicity and health – a guide for the NHS* (Department of Health, 1993).
[2] *Ethnicity and health – a guide for the NHS*, p. 44.

Resources about haemoglobinopathies are still almost entirely produced by voluntary groups. Few new resources have appeared in recent years, which seems surprising given the significance of these conditions and the developments made in availability of genetic screening. The newest resource targets health professionals and seeks to raise their awareness of the need for and value of screening. Most other resources are for the general population aiming to inform about the existence of sickle cell and thalassaemia. Notable exceptions are those targeting children who have the conditions and which aim to help the child understand the illness and treatment.

As has been noted earlier, resources related to improving access to health services for black and minority ethnic groups have seen some increase. These resources include those for training health professionals and those directly targeting the communities themselves.

There are still very few resources which deal with alcohol, smoking, solvent and drug abuse. One resource has been drawn to our attention which specifically focuses on smoking and another resource which contains a section on smoking cessation.

Formats of resources and the development process

It is mainly in the last ten years or so that health-related resources have been developed targeting specific communities but in this time a body of skill and experience has been built up. Changes have occurred in how resources are developed and produced and in the formats chosen.

The most noticeable change has been the increased use of video. No doubt this reflects that we now live in a society where almost everyone has access to or is familiar with the medium of video. It is a way of taking a message directly into the home. There are indications that some communities prefer health promotion information in this medium. It is also an accessible medium irrespective of the literacy level of the audience.

Video is a medium often used when information is given in a language other than English. Many videos use a drama/soap opera format to open up a topic for discussion, particularly if it is a controversial area such as HIV/AIDS.

In older videos the script was usually written first in English and then translated into the chosen language or more often several languages and then dubbed. This was not always satisfactory as the script did not have a natural flow, often seeming clumsy or overly academic. A new development has been separate scripts and separate filming (with different actors and locations, etc.) for each language version so that the people in the video and the script are authentic for that particular language and cultural group (for example *Teeth for life*, see page 171). Increasingly scripts are being developed and written in the chosen language of the resource rather than translated from English.

There is a growing awareness of the need to involve target communities in resource development at an early stage. Some producers have begun to work with target communities at the beginning of the process rather than show them the finished product and ask for comments. This makes it much easier to incorporate suggestions and avoid costly mistakes. It also increases the chances of developing an appropriate and therefore effective resource and it enables health educators and communities to discuss health priorities and needs.

Many of the videos produced recently are of broadcast quality. Some videos are being developed for use in waiting areas and others have been designed to support routine consultations with health professionals. Others have been made available for free loan from video hire shops.

One of the difficulties of video as a medium is that it can date quickly. People are used to sophisticated imagery on screen and changes in fashions etc. can become very noticeable. Many of the older videos have a dated feel about them and it is difficult to known what difference this makes to the viewers and their receptiveness to the information. Also if information or advice changes it can mean a video can only be used with a facilitator to ensure the correct information is included (for example when immunisation schedules changed many resources needed supplementary information to ensure they were up to date and accurate).

The national search has confirmed that more resources are becoming available for black and minority ethnic groups. Improved quality and provision of resources for black and minority ethnic groups must be welcomed as they can enhance appropriate and effective services.

- A broader range of health topics and health concerns is being addressed
- More attempts are being made to tailor resources to health needs as defined by the communities themselves
- Lessons are being learnt about how to consult with and involve communities in the development and dissemination of health resources
- Producers are becoming more skilled in resource production and making more use of popular mediums such as video
- Resources have been developed to inform health professionals about working more effectively in a multiracial society and meeting the health needs of all sections of the community
- Resources have been developed to support the training needs of health professionals.

The resources

All resources included in this publication or on the database are nationally available for purchase or hire. Inclusion of a resource in this publication or the black and minority ethnic groups resources database does *not* imply recommendation.

Each resource included in the main body of this publication is accompanied by a review.

This aims to give a snapshot view of the resource and enable more informed choices to be made about the purchase and use of resource. The review is not an evaluation but a description of several aspects of the resource:

- who it is for
- who produced it
- what it covers and any accompanying support material
- how information is conveyed
- any additional information required or omissions in the resource
- how the resource could be used
- involvement of target communities in its development and/or testing.

The accuracy and acceptability of language translations has *not* been evaluated. Posters and models have not been reviewed and are listed separately in Appendix 1. Late and forthcoming resources in Appendix 2 do not have reviews and it is advisable to check with producers and distributors for further information.

Critical readers

In order to ensure the reviews were useful a number of people from around the country were asked to comment critically on some pilot reviews. These critical readers represent a wide range of health interests, skills and experience. Many thanks are extended to the critical readers who contributed their time despite being very busy and who were so encouraging about the development of the database. A list of the readers can be found in Appendix 3.

The critical readers were asked to read and comment on a review of a resource with which they were familiar and a review of a resource completely new to them. A questionnaire was provided for responses (see Appendix 4). All readers found the amount and type of information provided to be useful and reviews of resources they were familiar with were considered to be accurate. Some minor changes were suggested which were incorporated into the review structure.

Sources of further information

As new resources and information appear all the time it is important to keep up to date. The following will be helpful to health professionals and others interested in the health of black and minority ethnic groups who want to keep in touch with new developments. Please also see Appendix 5 which lists resource directories.

(a) Health Promotion Information Centre

Housed at the HEA in London, the Health Promotion Information Centre holds the national collection of information about health promotion and related issues. The collection consists of journals, articles, books, training materials and audio-visual resources. The information centre's catalogue is held on the Unicorn Database which can identify relevant information items quickly and efficiently thereby producing up-to-date and targeted searches. A link between the King's Fund Centre library and the Health Promotion Information Centre has been developed recently, enabling wider searches to be undertaken on the catalogues of both centres.

The black and minority ethnic health resources database is part of the Unicorn Database and can be accessed in the same way. All resources in the black and minority ethnic resources database have been purchased and are available for viewing. It is possible for searches to be undertaken on a range of health topics for a specific group in the community and in a specific language.

The Health Promotion Information Centre is available to health professionals and others working in the field of health. The centre is open to visitors, by appointment only, and preview facilities are available. Searches can be requested by telephone or in writing. Resources advisers at the centre can also be consulted about the use and development of health promotion resources.

Health Promotion Information Centre
Health Education Authority
Hamilton House
Mabledon Place
London WC1H 9TX
Tel: 071 413 1995

(b) SHARE

The SHARE project provides a wide range of information on health and black and minority ethnic populations. The project is funded by the Department of Health and is based at the King's Fund Centre in London. SHARE can provide information about projects, services and research; details of relevant published material; support for service development and information for policymakers. A regular newsletter is produced with information about new projects and initiatives.

SHARE
King's Fund Centre
126 Albert Street
London NW1 7NF
Tel: 071 267 6111

(c) Health and Ethnicity Programme database

The Health and Ethnicity Programme of North East, North West Thames Regional Health

Authority aims to 'record and disseminate information in the domain of transcultural healthcare'. The database contains 3000 plus references on all aspects of health and ethnicity, with published literature forming the backbone of the database. The information held is of national relevance and includes local information. The database can provide literature searches on specialist areas, including lists of relevant contacts, names and organisations and details of continuing research. The service is free to those working for the NHS in the NE/NW Thames Regional Health Authority. A charge of £10 per search is made for those working outside the NHS or outside the region.

Health and Ethnicity Programme database
NE/NW Thames Regional Health Authority
40 Eastbourne Terrace
London W2 3QR
Tel: 071 725 5357

(d) Ethnic Minorities Health – *Current awareness bulletin*

The aim of the *Current awareness bulletin* is to index information relating to all aspects of the health of minority groups. Most items listed are journal articles but conference proceedings, theses, books and other items such as audio-visual resources may also be included. The main emphasis relates to British practice but some international references are included if relevant. The quarterly bulletin is available on subscription.

Ethnic Minorities Health – *Current awareness bulletin*
Medical Library
Field House Teaching Centre
Bradford Royal Infirmary
Bradford
West Yorkshire BD9 6RJ
Tel: 0274 364130

(e) Local health promotion agencies

Health promotion agencies (formerly known as health promotion units) are a valuable source of information and support and, because they are local, are more easily accessible. Many agencies have large collections of resources available for loan plus libraries for reference. They can supply leaflets, posters and other kinds of health promotion resources. They are staffed by health promotion specialists and can provide information and advice about health promotion strategies and resources. They will also have information about initiatives and interests within local communities. The phone number of your local agency will be listed in the telephone book under your local health authority.

Important texts

The following documents and reports are of national relevance and have been published within the last two years. They draw attention to the health needs of black and minority ethnic groups and have implications for needs assessment, service development and provision. They will be of interest to commissioners, purchasers and providers of all healthcare services.

Ethnic health bibliography. G Karmi and P McKeigue. North East, North West Thames Regional Health Authority, 1993.

Ethnicity and health – a guide for the NHS. Department of Health, 1993.

Equality across the board: *report of a working party on black and ethnic minority non-executive members.* NAHAT and King's Fund Centre, 1993.

Guidelines for the implementation of ethnic monitoring in health service provision: *a complete guide for setting up ethnic monitoring.* North East, North West Thames Regional Health Authority, 1992.

Health for all our children: *achieving appropriate health care for black and minority ethnic children and their families.* Action for Sick Children, 1993.

'Health of black and ethnic minorities' in Department of Health *On the state of the public health*: *the annual report of the Chief Medical Officer of the Department of Health for the year 1991.* HMSO, 1992.

The patient's charter. Department of Health, 1992.

Race, gender and drug services. Institute for the Study of Drug Dependence, 1993.

Report of a working party of the Standing Medical Advisory Committee on sickle cell, thalassaemia and other haemoglobinopathies. HMSO, 1993.

Safety and minority ethnic communities: *a report on the home safety information needs of Asian, Chinese and Vietnamese communities.* Royal Society for the Prevention of Accidents, 1993.

How to use this book

- The resources in this book are listed alphabetically by title ignoring definite and indefinite articles such as 'The' and 'A'.
- Entries for each resource include information about the target audience, the cost, the producer and date of production and the distributor's name.
- The address and telephone number of each distributor is listed in Appendix 6.

- All information was correct at the time of going to press (August 1994). Details such as price may change over time. Items may be withdrawn or no longer be produced so it is advisable to check information with the distributor.
- Indexes: two indexes are used, which include all resources reviewed and the posters and models listed in Appendix 1.

  Topics index

  Languages/Communities index

  We have used the producers'/distributors' descriptions in drawing up this index. We have therefore organised this index by both languages and communities.
- Appendices:
  1. Posters and models
  2. Late and forthcoming resources
  3. Critical readers
  4. Questionnaire
  5. Directories of resources
  6. Distributors

  Appendix 2 contains resources which we were not able to review because they arrived after the final date. This is not the fault of the producer or distributor, but the resources may not have come to our attention until a late stage of the project. Other resources listed in this appendix were forthcoming but not necessarily available at the time of publication.
- It is not always necessary to purchase resources as they may be held by your local health promotion agency and available for loan. Alternatively if they do not hold the resource they may consider purchasing it if asked. Some items can be obtained from the distributor and previewed for a small charge which is refunded if the item is purchased. All resources listed in this book can be previewed at the Health Promotion Information Centre at the HEA (see page 15).
- *Always* preview a resource yourself before using it to ensure you are familiar with the issues it raises and have any additional information required. If you are working with linkworkers and interpreters it will be helpful to ensure they are familiar with the resource too.

We would like to thank everyone who has contributed to and supported the work of this project. We would also like to thank the staff of the Health Promotion Information Centre and particularly Bren Davies and Chandy Perera for their assistance in producing this book.

Claudette Edwards
Catherine Herman
Mary Ryan
Project Team

TOPICS INDEX

Community

Pack

Black community care charter *English* **58**
Call for care *Bengali, English, Gujarati, Punjabi, Urdu* **64**
Computers and Asian languages *English* **74**
Double discrimination *English* **84**
Equal chances *English* **89**
A guide to living in Britain for refugees from Vietnam *Cantonese, English, Vietnamese* **98**
HIV/AIDS: a guide for carers of young children *English* **110**
HIV, homelessness and local authority housing *English, Hindi, Portuguese* **113**
Interpreters in public services *English* **118**
Positive action *English* **144**
Report and reflections on the challenging racism course for white community workers *English* **150**
Settling in the United Kingdom *Cantonese, English, Vietnamese* **160**
Where to from here? *Cantonese* **181**
Working with Chinese carers *English* **185**

Video

According to need *English* **45**
Asian carers *English, Hindi* **52**
AWAAZ *Bengali, English, Gujarati, Hindi, Punjabi, Urdu* **53**
Britain's forgotten elders *English* **63**
An environment of dignity *English* **88**
Facing the challenge *English* **92**
Housing for the ethnic elderly *Bengali, Cantonese, English, Greek, Gujarati, Hindi, Punjabi, Turkish* **115**
My mum thinks she's funny! *English* **134**
The right to be understood *English* **151**
A welcome break *English, Punjabi* **177**
Zara dhyan dein *Hindi (with English subtitles)* **190**

Contraception

Pack

Health information for women *English, Gujarati, Urdu* **104**
Your guide to family planning *Bengali, English, Hindi, Punjabi, Urdu* **187**

Video

To plan a family *English, Bengali, Hindi* **142**

Cystic fibrosis

Audio-cassette

Cystic fibrosis *Gujarati, Urdu* **80**

Video

From chance to choice *English* **95**

Death and dying

Pack

Caring for Hindus and their families *English* **66**
Caring for multicultural clients *English* **67**
Caring for Muslims and their families *English* **67**
Caring for Sikhs and their families *English* **68**
Death with dignity *English* **81**
Patient's charter standard *English* **140**

Diabetes

Pack

British Diabetic Association information pack *English* **64**

Down's syndrome

Eczema

Education

Environmental health

Equal opportunities

Pack

Poster

Video

English for speakers of other languages (ESOL)

Audio-cassette

Pack

Video

Female genital mutilation/ circumcision

Pack

Video

HIV/AIDS

Audio-cassette

Multimedia

Pack

Poster

Video

Immunisation

Pack

Poster

Video

Rubella *Bengali, Hindi (with English subtitles)* **153**
Zara dhyan dein *Hindi (with English subtitles)* **190**

Infant feeding

Audio-cassette
Breastfeeding *Sylheti (Bengali)* **61**

Pack
Weaning *English, Gujarati, Urdu* **176**

Video
Asian weaning photograph album *(no text)* **53**
Breastfeeding *Bengali (with English subtitles), Sylheti* **61**
Growing up strong *Bengali, Hindi* **97**
A healthy start *Bengali, English, Gujarati, Hindi, Punjabi, Urdu* **109**

Learning difficulties

Pack
Double discrimination *English* **84**
Information pack for parents *Arabic, Bengali, Cantonese, English, Gujarati, Punjabi, Spanish, Urdu* **117**

Video
AWAAZ *Bengali, English, Gujarati, Hindi, Punjabi, Urdu* **53**
One way history *English* **138**
Physical and mental handicap in the Asian community *Bengali, English, Gujarati, Hindi/Urdu, Punjabi* **142**

Mental health

Multimedia
Shanti stress pack *Bengali, English, Gujarati, Hindi, Punjabi, Urdu* **161**

Pack
Crisis card *Bengali, English, Urdu* **77**
A cry for change *English* **79**
Mental health and Britain's black communities *English* **131**
Schizophrenia *Bengali, English, Punjabi, Urdu* **157**
Understanding schizophrenia *Bengali, English, Gujarati, Hindi, Punjabi, Urdu* **174**

Video
All in the mind *English* **48**
Black community care charter *English* **58**
Depression in ethnic minorities *English* **82**
Don't know where to turn *Bengali, Cantonese, English, Hindustani, Punjabi, Somali, Turkish, Vietnamese* **83**
A fearful silence *English* **92**
Mistaken for mad *English* **132**
Postnatal depression *Bengali, English, Hindi* **145**
Silent in the crowd *English* **163**
Zara dhyan dein *Hindi (with English subtitles)* **190**

Nutrition

Model
Afro-Caribbean pack (replica foods) *(no text)* **191**
Replica Asian foods *(no text)* **194**

Multimedia
Snax teaching pack *English* **165**

Pack
British Diabetic Association information pack *English* **64**

Older people

Oral health

Parent and child health

Pack
Everybody's hair *English* **91**
HIV/AIDS *English* **110**
Guidelines for the evaluation and selection of toys and other resources for children *English* **97**
Play with confidence *English* **143**

Video
AWAAZ *Bengali, English, Gujarati, Hindi, Punjabi, Urdu* **53**
Care in cold weather *Bengali, English* **63**
Child development *Bengali, English, Gujarati, Hindi, Punjabi* **71**
Children's colds *Bengali, English, Gujarati, Punjabi, Urdu* **72**
Four mothers *English* **94**
The haircut *English* **99**
Happy, smiling, healthy children *Bengali, Punjabi, Urdu (with English subtitles)* **100**
The home medicine box *Sylheti (Bengali)* **114**
Inside out *English, Urdu* **118**
My mum thinks she's funny! *English* **134**
Play *Bengali, Cantonese, English* **143**
A sound start for your baby *English* **166**
Talk, play and learn *English, Gujarati, Punjabi, Urdu* **168**
A welcome break *English, Punjabi* **177**
What to do about headlice *Bengali, English* **179**
Your baby's hearing *Bengali (with English subtitles)* **186**
Your children's teeth *Bengali (without English subtitles), Punjabi, Urdu (with English subtitles), English* **186**

Physical activity

Multimedia
Shanti stress pack *Bengali, English, Gujarati, Hindi, Punjabi, Urdu* **161**

Pack
Big Bert does P.E. *English, Punjabi, Urdu* **56**

Video
Amar dil *English, Bengali, Gujarati, Punjabi* **49**
Keep active, keep healthy *Bengali, English, Gujarati, Hindi/Urdu, Punjabi* **121**
Growing older, keeping well *Cantonese (with English sub-titles)* **96**
Self defence? Common sense! *English* **159**
Zara dhyan dein *Hindi (with English subtitles)* **159**

Physical disability

Video
AWAAZ *Bengali, English, Gujarati, Hindi, Punjabi, Urdu* **53**
Physical and mental handicap in the Asian community *Bengali, English, Gujarati, Hindi/Urdu, Punjabi* **142**
A welcome break *English, Punjabi* **177**

Professional development

Multimedia
Meeting Hindu families *English* **128**
Meeting Muslim families *English* **128**
Meeting Sikh families *English* **129**

Pack
Caribbean food and diet *English* **65**
Caring for everyone *English* **66**
Caring for Hindus and their families *English* **66**
Caring for multicultural clients *English* **67**
Caring for Muslims and their families *English* **67**
Caring for Sikhs and their families *English* **68**
Checklist health and race *English* **70**
Child protection and female genital mutilation *English* **71**
Context cards *English* **75**

Safety

Poster
Fireworks safety campaign *Bengali, English, Gujarati, Punjabi, Urdu, Welsh* **192**

Video
Day to remember: the wedding *Hindustani dialogue with Bengali, English, Gujarati, Punjabi, Urdu voiceover commentaries* **80**

Firewatch *Bengali, Cantonese, English, Gujarati, Punjabi, Hindi/Urdu, sign language and subtitles* **93**

Inside out *English, Urdu* **118**

Sapna jal giaa (The dream that went up in flames) *Hindi* **155**

Think safe, be safe *Bengali, English, Hindustani* **172**

Your move *Bengali, English, Gujarati, Hindi, Sylheti, Urdu* **188**

Zara dhyan dein *Hindi (with English subtitles)* **190**

Screening

Audio-cassette
Breast-screening *Arabic, Bengali, English, Urdu* **61**

Pack
Health information for women *English, Gujarati, Urdu* **104**

Video
The breast self-examination and the gynaecological examination *Cantonese (with English subtitles)* **62**

The cervical smear test *Bengali, English, Gujarati, Hindi, Punjabi, Urdu* **69**

From chance to choice *English* **95**

The gynaecological examination *Bengali, Cantonese, English, Greek, Hindi, Turkish and signed and subtitled version* **99**

Mrs Khan goes for breast screening *Bengali, English, Gujarati, Hindi/Urdu, Punjabi* **133**

Zara dhyan dein *Hindi (with English subtitles)* **190**

Sexual abuse

Model
Teach-a-bodies playpeople *(no text)* **195**

Pack
Black girls speak out *English* **59**

Secrets *English* **158**

Sexual health

Multimedia
Safer play – safer sex *Bengali, English, Gujarati, Hindi, Punjabi, Turkish, Urdu* **154**

Pack
The black male's sexuality and relationships social education pack *English* **59**

Health information for women *English, Gujarati, Urdu* **104**

Religion, ethnicity and sex education *English* **149**

Sex education *English* **160**

Poster
Black by popular demand *English* **191**

Don't think about it: use it! *Bengali, English, Gujarati, Hindi, Punjabi, Turkish, Urdu* **192**

Fact: you're never too old to enjoy sex *English* **192**

Safer sex is good sex *Bengali, English, Gujarati, Hindi, Punjabi, Turkish, Urdu* **194**

Safer sex *English (for African-Caribbeans)* **194**

Safer sex *English (for Asians)* **194**

What's so tough and manly about risking your partner's life? *English* **195**

Travel

Pack
AIDS and mobility *English, French, German* **111**

Video
HIV and AIDS information for seafarers *English, Polish, Portuguese, Spanish, Tagalog* **113**

Travellers

Pack
Moving on *English* **132**
Rommaneskohna *English* **153**

Video
Partnership 2000 *English* **140**
Travelling people *English* **174**

Women's health

Audio-cassette
Breast-screening *Arabic, Bengali, English, Urdu* **62**
Women's health *Sylheti (Bengali)* **184**

Multimedia
Shanti stress pack *Bengali, English, Gujarati, Hindi, Punjabi, Urdu* **161**

Pack
African women's health issues *English* **45**
Child protection and female genital mutilation *English* **71**
Female genital mutilation *English* **93**
Health information for women *English, Gujarati, Urdu* **104**
Listen my sister *English* **124**

Menopause: a time to look forward *English, Gujarati, Urdu* **130**
The menopause: coping with mid-life change *Bengali, English, Gujarati, Hindi, Punjabi, Urdu* **131**

Poster
If a blood sample is being taken *Arabic, Bengali, Cantonese, English, Greek, Gujarati, Hindi, Punjabi, Turkish, Urdu* **193**

Video
Another form of abuse *English* **49**
The breast self-examination and the gynaecological examination *Cantonese (with English subtitles)* **62**
The cervical smear test *Bengali, English, Gujarati, Hindi, Punjabi, Urdu* **69**
A fearful silence *English* **92**
Four mothers *English* **94**
Great expectations *English* **96**
The gynaecological examination *Bengali, Cantonese, English, Greek, Hindi, Turkish and signed and subtitled version* **99**
Hysterectomy *Bengali, English, Gujarati, Hindi/Urdu, Punjabi* **115**
In their own words *English* **117**
It's hard being a woman *English* **119**
Keep active, keep healthy *Bengali, English, Gujarati, Hindi/Urdu, Punjabi* **121**
The menopause *Bengali, Cantonese, English, Gujarati, Hindi/Urdu, Punjabi, Somali, Turkish, Vietnamese* **129**
Mrs Khan goes for breast screening *Bengali, English, Gujarati, Hindi/Urdu, Punjabi* **133**
Self defence? Common sense! *English* **159**
Silent tears *English* **163**
Zara dhyan dein *Hindi (with English subtitles)* **190**

Work and the workplace

Pack
Training: implementing racial equality at work *English* **173**

Video

LANGUAGES/COMMUNITIES INDEX

Almost all of these resources have an English version or translation – please see individual listings

Chinese (Cantonese-speaking)

Audio-cassette

Pack

Poster

Video

Poster

Video

Hindi (see also Hindustani)

Audio-cassette

Multimedia

Pack

Somali

Spanish

Swahili

Vietnamese

Yemeni

RESOURCES

According to need: services for older people in a multiracial society

FORMAT: Video, 34 mins; with 16-page trainers' guide

LANGUAGE: English

TARGET AUDIENCE: Older people, service providers

PRICE: £45.00 inc.

PRODUCER: Albany Videos and Age Concern, 1989

DISTRIBUTOR: Age Concern England

This training video is aimed at service providers and describes how services can be developed and improved for older people from black and minority ethnic groups. It was made by the Department of Health and Age Concern. It describes a range of statutory and voluntary services provided for Asian, African-Caribbean, Polish and Vietnamese people (lunch clubs and day centres, a self-help group, home care and residential homes). Services are explored from the providers' and users' points of view, and the mix of interviews is lively and interesting. Older people state clearly what they value about these services. Providers (from managers to home helps) describe the development of services, equal opportunities policies and the recruitment and training of staff which have resulted in good practice. Dealing with problems such as racism from other service users is discussed. The accompanying trainers' guide suggests introductory and follow-up training exercises. The video can be viewed as a whole or in sections to enable discussion of issues in more depth. Enough material is provided for several sessions and could help service providers identify starting points for change. It is a useful training resource which challenges providers to consider how well their service meets the needs of all members of the community. Discussions of how to deal with racism are practical and may be a helpful way of opening up this area with all members of staff.

African women's health issues

FORMAT: 12-page booklet

LANGUAGE: English

TARGET AUDIENCE: Women

PRICE: 20p

PRODUCER: Positively Women, 1992

DISTRIBUTOR: Positively Women

This booklet is for African women and aims to provide clear information about HIV/AIDS. It was produced by Positively Women with support from Westminster Council. The booklet has nine short sections which cover: HIV testing and research, Looking after yourself, Confidentiality, Safer sex, Rights in hospital, Pregnancy and children, Practical support, Benefits and grants, Rights of refugees and other immigrants. The information is concise and clear and is most relevant to women who are HIV positive. Advice is given about further sources of help and support. The booklet does not deal with what HIV is or how it is transmitted. It is a useful reference for women and encourages them to seek the support of others who are in a similar situation. Women from the African Women's Support Group at Positively Women contributed to the booklet.

AIDS and mobility: a manual for the implementation of HIV/AIDS prevention activities aimed at travellers and migrants

FORMAT: 64-page manual

LANGUAGE: English, French, German

TARGET AUDIENCE: Health professionals

PRICE: Free

PRODUCER: National Committee on AIDS Control, European Project: AIDS and Mobility, 1993

DISTRIBUTOR: National Committee on AIDS Control

This manual describes various HIV/AIDS prevention activities targeting international travellers and migrants. It aims to share information about health education activities in a range of countries and raise awareness of the need for education programmes aimed at travellers and migrants. The manual was funded by the Commission of the European Communities, the World Health Organization and the Ministry of Welfare in the Netherlands.

Travellers in this resource are defined as people who engage in international movement, such as holidaymakers and business people. Migrants are defined as people who change residence from one country to another with the intention of engaging in paid employment and/or staying for a long period of time. They have a sociocultural and linguistic background which is significantly different from the majority of the population in the new country of residence. Of the health education activities described, six target travellers and eight target migrants. The description of each activity includes objectives, involvement of target group, cost, evaluation and follow-up. Some are described in more detail than others and a contact address is given for each.

The kind of work described includes posters, leaflets, peer education, radio broadcasts and theatre groups. Some full-colour examples of images used in some of the activities are included at the end. Those involved in planning health education programmes may be interested to find out how other countries have approached the topic of HIV/AIDS for different groups within the community.

Alcohol awareness: towards a transcultural approach

FORMAT: 50-page manual

LANGUAGE: English

TARGET AUDIENCE: Primary healthcare teams, trainers

PRICE: £16.95

PRODUCER: London Boroughs' Training Committee: Training for Care and Greater London Association of Alcohol Services, 1991

DISTRIBUTOR: Pavilion Publishing

This training manual aims to enable trainers to facilitate a two-day training course for primary care workers who are directly involved with people who have alcohol problems. The training course aims to encourage useful and sensitive transcultural approaches in working with users from black and minority ethnic groups. The manual was produced by the Alcohol Training Project of the London Boroughs' Training Committee and was funded by the Department of Health. The introduction provides background information and covers the aim, objectives, rationale and principles of the manual. The second part is an outline of a one-day training course for trainers of primary care workers. It aims to familiarise trainers with the manual and its materials so that they can proceed to use it confidently. Part three describes and outlines a two-day course for primary care workers including materials for activities (such as case studies etc.). It is stressed that the course does not provide basic information about alcohol and participants need to have this knowledge already. The course is discussion based with some role play activities. It is designed to encourage exploration of stereotypes and find new ways of working. It contains action planning elements and examines how agencies can meet the needs of black and minority ethnic groups.

The manual is clearly written and well laid out. Activities and photocopiable materials are easy to follow. There is a short bibliography. It is a practical resource and trainers will find it a useful starting point. The training course for primary care workers was piloted with two groups and changes incorporated as a result of this. An advisory group was established to contribute to the manual and consisted of a wide range of advisers and counsellors from alcohol agencies.

Alcoholism in the Asian community

FORMAT: Video, 30 mins.

LANGUAGE: English, Hindi

TARGET AUDIENCE: General public

PRICE: £29.90 inc.

PRODUCER: N Films, 1987

DISTRIBUTOR: CFL Vision

This video was made to inform Asian communities about alcoholism. It was produced as part of the Asian Mother and Baby Campaign, funded by the Department of Health and supported by the Royal College of Nursing.

A mixture of documentary and drama is used to explore the effects of alcohol abuse. A voice-over informs of the dangers of alcohol to the body, relationships, family and working life. The drama follows a man who has begun to drink excessively as a result of unemployment. He attends a rehabilitation unit and receives counselling afterwards. His family are pleased and supportive. The drama is optimistic and does not deal in any depth with the difficulties of giving up alcohol. Drinking alcohol is presented as dangerous and leading to loss of dignity. Interviews with a psychiatrist and counsellor are used to provide some information about the effects of alcohol on the body and the system of alcohol 'units'. The diversity of Asian communities is not reflected in the video. This video attempts to deal with a complex issue and was one of the first such resources to tackle this subject within Asian communities.

All about ... AIDS

FORMAT: 32-page booklet

LANGUAGE: English

TARGET AUDIENCE: 16- to 19-year-olds, general public

PRICE: £2.00 inc.

PRODUCER: International Planned Parenthood Federation, 1993

DISTRIBUTOR: International Planned Parenthood Federation

This booklet for a general African-Caribbean audience (young people and adults) aims to inform about HIV and AIDS and how to protect against infection. It was produced with financial support from the Overseas Development Administration of the UK.

The illustrated booklet covers a wide range of HIV and AIDS issues – transmission, testing, symptoms, other STDs, safer sex and contraception. There is a short story about a man who acquires HIV but does not discover this until after he is married. It touches upon many difficult issues such as informing his partner and living with HIV. The information about safer sex is explicit and condoms are strongly promoted. There is a discussion of how to talk about safer sex with a partner. Some of the advice differs from current UK advice about safer sex (e.g. partners who are sure they are HIV negative can enjoy any sexual activity without precautions). The illustrations are line drawings and depict young people from the Caribbean. The booklet will be of interest to people who are sexually active. Parents and teachers may also find it a useful resource to support teaching and discussion with young people. It can be used as a stand-alone resource for people to read alone or with a partner. It could be used to trigger discussion and information sharing in group settings. The booklet has been pre-tested in Trinidad, Tobago and Grenada and focus groups from these countries contributed to its development.

All in the mind

FORMAT: Video, 30 mins; with 25-page trainers' notes

LANGUAGE: English

TARGET AUDIENCE: Healthcare professionals, mental health teams, social workers

PRICE: Video, £84.60 inc. notes (entitled *Mosaic* year 1 notes) £7.50 + p&p

PRODUCER: BBC, 1989

DISTRIBUTOR: Video: BBC Videos for Education and Training; notes: BSS (*Mosaic*)

This video and accompanying trainers' notes are of interest to health professionals and others working in the field of mental health. The video examines the discriminatory treatment people from black and minority ethnic groups receive from mental health services. It was produced as part of the BBC's Continuing Education Mosaic Project which addresses issues of equality in a multicultural society.

The video examines how people from black and minority ethnic groups come into contact with mental health services and what sorts of diagnosis and treatments they receive. Four people talk about their experiences of mental health services. Professionals such as psychiatrists, psychotherapists, probation officers and health service managers describe how mental health services and staff work from a Eurocentric viewpoint and adhere to stereotyped notions of black people. This leads to misdiagnosis (including under- and over-diagnosis) and inappropriate treatment. Two services which are successfully meeting the mental health needs of black and minority ethnic groups are shown (an intercultural counselling service and a supported housing scheme).

The accompanying training notes include discussion-based exercises for use in group settings. The exercises encourage participants to examine the information and views presented in the video and consider the implications for the service they work in. Some statistical information would benefit from updating to include research findings since the video was made. However these findings do support the statistics referred to in the video and notes. The video is useful trigger material as it raises a number of important issues; trainers and others interested in mental health may find it helpful in initiating discussion about the mental health needs of black and minority ethnic groups.

All you need to know about thalassaemia trait

FORMAT: 13-page booklet

LANGUAGE: Bengali, English, Gujarati, Hindi, Punjabi, Urdu

TARGET AUDIENCE: General public, health professionals

PRICE: 35p inc.

PRODUCER: United Kingdom Thalassaemia Society, 1987

DISTRIBUTOR: UK Thalassaemia Society

This booklet aims to provide information for people who have thalassaemia trait. It was sponsored by the World Health Organization.

The booklet reassures that thalassaemia trait is not an illness but that there may be implications if a person with thalassaemia trait has children. The difference between thalassaemia trait and thalassaemia major is outlined. Simple graphics are used to explain the chances of a child inheriting either thalassaemia trait or major. People from certain parts of the world are advised to have a blood test prior to conceiving and to seek advice from a genetic counsellor if the test is positive for thalassaemia trait.

The booklet is well designed and presents information in an accessible way. People are encouraged to take the booklet with them when they visit their GP. Health professionals may find it a handy reference, particularly when explaining the genetic information about thalassaemia and the likelihood of a child being born with the trait or disease itself. It is a helpful booklet for people to take away after discussion with a health professional.

Amar dil

FORMAT: Video, 50 mins; with 10-page booklet

LANGUAGE: English, Bengali, Gujarati, Hindi and Punjabi (10 mins each language)

TARGET AUDIENCE: General public

PRICE: £25.00

PRODUCER: Leicestershire Health Authority, Health Education Video Unit, 1991

DISTRIBUTOR: Leicestershire HA Video Unit

This video aims to inform Asian communities about prevention of coronary heart disease. It was produced by Leicestershire Health Authority as part of the Look After Your Heart campaign.

Graphic illustrations and numerous visuals of people in everyday situations at home, at work and in the community, are used with a voice-over format. Descriptive sections explain about angina, heart attacks, and coronary heart disease. Advice is given on a healthy lifestyle, such as the importance of diet, exercise and giving up smoking. The video is upbeat and has a catchy jingle about a healthy lifestyle. It presents a lot of specific information and encourages people to take action to prevent coronary heart disease. The accompanying booklet briefly recaps the main information points from the video including suggestions about how to eat a more healthy diet and tips for coping with giving up smoking. The changes in lifestyle suggested are realistic and acceptable to Asian communities.

Asian communities in Leicester were involved in the production of this resource. A mixture of actors and members of the community took part in the video and most of it was shot in community venues. It has been extensively trialled within Asian communities. People were very interested and many commented they were not aware of some of the information before. The upbeat approach was particularly appreciated. It is excellent trigger material and likely to be of interest to any audience in any setting but may well strike a chord with people approaching middle age.

Another form of abuse: the prevention of genital mutilation

FORMAT: Video, 20 mins

LANGUAGE: English

TARGET AUDIENCE: Health professionals, teachers, social workers

PRICE: £15.00

PRODUCER: Foundation for Women's Health (FORWARD), 1992

DISTRIBUTOR: Foundation for Women's Health

This training video is for policy makers, practitioners and specialists in areas of community health development and child protection. It aims to raise awareness about genital mutilation and so prevent the practice. It was funded by the Department of Health. The video commences with the director of FORWARD stressing that genital mutilation is a form of physical abuse and that the term 'circumcision' can give a misleading impression about the practice. Different forms of genital mutilation are explained with the aid of computer graphics and the law regarding female circumcision is briefly outlined. The video examines health problems, sexual problems and problems with childbirth which result from the practice. The interviews with women who have been circumcised include young women who have been taken out of the UK for the operation. Community leaders explain why they have chosen not to have their daughters circumcised and the view that it is an 'Islamic obligation' is challenged. The video directly addresses teachers, health visitors and social workers, emphasising that it is a child protection issue. A social worker refers to a case where action was taken to prevent a girl being circumcised. How to work with families is tackled with suggestions about counselling and informing people of the law and risks of female circumcision. This is a challenging video about a practice which is controversial within many communities and an issue of which many people outside those communities are unaware. It is useful trigger material for training as it highlights many complex issues as well as informing its audience about the prevalence and effects of female circumcision.

Antenatal care for you and your baby

FORMAT: Cassette, 15 mins (copyright free); with leaflets and A2 poster

LANGUAGE: Cassette available in Bengali, Cantonese, English, Gujarati, Hindi, Punjabi, Urdu, Yemeni. Poster captioned in same languages. Leaflet available in Bengali/English, Cantonese/English, Hindi/English, Urdu/English

TARGET AUDIENCE: Women

PRICE: Cassette £35.00. Various price packages available for posters and leaflets

PRODUCER: South Birmingham Health Authority, 1993

DISTRIBUTOR: Birmingham Maternity Hospital

This resource is targeted at women who do not speak English and aims to increase awareness and understanding of routine antenatal care, some common screening procedures in pregnancy and the use of foetal movement charts.

A female presenter talks in a friendly and informal manner to the listener. She explains the purpose of antenatal care, outlining what happens at a booking visit and the choices available in antenatal care. Some information is described in detail (ultrasound, amniocentesis, CVS, smoking and passive smoking). The tapes state that women will be given a kick chart. This is standard procedure in Birmingham but may not be elsewhere, so presenters should check this and advise women accordingly. Mention is made of language barriers and the availability of interpreters and linkworkers but no advice is given on how to arrange these. This will need to be considered when women are given the tapes. Women may also be interested in antenatal classes in their language as the cassette promotes attendance at classes. They will also need information about choices in antenatal care available locally. Leaflets in some of the languages accompany the cassettes and briefly reinforce the main points. The print on the leaflets and the poster is quite small. The poster advertises the cassettes and is designed to encourage women to ask for them. Women who do not speak English will find the cassettes encouraging and informative, but they are only an introduction to antenatal care and will need to be supported by health professionals who can communicate with women either directly or through interpreters/linkworkers. The cassettes have been piloted in all languages and women were very positive in their response to them, valuing the opportunity to have some information in their mother tongue. They were developed by midwives and linkworkers.

Apni sehth (Our health)

FORMAT: Video, 12 mins; with notes and leaflets

LANGUAGE: Punjabi. Leaflets in English, Punjabi, Urdu

TARGET AUDIENCE: General public

PRICE: £40.00

PRODUCER: Derbyshire Family Health Services Authority, 1991

DISTRIBUTOR: Derbyshire FHSA

This video was developed for Punjabi communities and this is reflected in the language used, clothes and food featured. However, the promotion information states it would be relevant to all groups from the Indian subcontinent.

Focusing on obesity and healthy eating patterns, it uses a lively drama-type story about an ordinary family (parents, children and grandmother). The father suffers some chest pain and consults his GP who advises him to lose weight to stay healthy. A visit to a dietitian is followed by changes in the family eating patterns which are discussed and demonstrated. The video realistically portrays family life and deals with some of the arguments commonly raised against healthier eating patterns ('it won't taste the same', 'I like cola', 'we've always cooked that way', etc.). The suggested changes in eating and cooking patterns are achievable and respect tradition and culture.

The accompanying leaflet is attractive and colourful. It has tips and suggestions for cooking traditional foods with less fat and more fibre. The video was made to be used in group settings by any group interested in health issues. It is also suggested that it can be viewed at home by families so that key family members can be reached. This is an excellent trigger film and will certainly spark much discussion about what is healthy eating and how this can be achieved.

Are you good enough for you?

See *Counselling and sexuality*

Are you a racist?

FORMAT: Video, 50 mins

LANGUAGE: English

TARGET AUDIENCE: General public

PRICE: £106.00 + VAT

PRODUCER: BBC, 1985

DISTRIBUTOR: BBC Videos for Education and Training

This video was made for television as part of the BBC Horizon series. Using a 'fly on the wall' technique the camera follows eight people through a week of intensive group discussion about racism. The participants are four black people who have experienced racism and four white people who say they are racists. They spent a week living together sharing views and opinions. A (white) facilitator worked with the group.

The racists are vociferous and dogmatic in their views. This makes painful viewing as they seem impervious to the distress and anger they cause to the black participants. The film ends with one white participant changing her views but the others remaining entrenched. Those involved in providing training may find the video helpful for examining how to facilitate honest discussion about such a sensitive and difficult issue. It may also be useful in illustrating how widespread and deeply rooted racist views are and how hard it is to challenge those views. The film was made prior to the development of much racism awareness and anti-racist training. Many would now question the decision to involve black people in challenging white racists, seeing this as a further expression of racism.

Asian carers: caring and sharing

FORMAT: Video, 20 mins; with 26-page booklet

LANGUAGE: Video in English, or Hindi with English subtitles. Booklet in English, Gujarati

TARGET AUDIENCE: Carers, trainers

PRICE: £25.00 inc.

PRODUCER: Penumbra Productions, 1988

DISTRIBUTOR: Leicester Council for Voluntary Services

This video and accompanying booklet aim to inform and advise Asian carers about the range of services and help which may be available to them. The video was commissioned by the Informal Caring Programme of the King's Fund and was funded by the Department of Health and the Health Education Authority. The video was jointly produced by Leicester Council for Voluntary Service and SCOPE.

Through a series of interviews carers explain what their life is like and how frustrating and stressful it can be at times. Most of the carers are women, but one father talks at length about caring for his son who has learning difficulties. The carers also describe services and support such as respite care, day centres, residential homes, community nursing service, occupational therapy, sit-in services and social workers. Some of the services are shown in the video. Carers explain how sometimes services are not designed with Asian people in mind, how they may have felt reluctant to use them because of guilt or anxiety or because they simply did not know about them. Some services shown have appointed Asian workers in order to take on board the needs of Asian communities and this could be a useful discussion point with carers and service providers.

The booklet is densely packed with information which mostly refers to the Leicester area. As it was published in 1988 some details about places and times etc. may be out of date, but it does provide a framework of the kind of information people want. The print is very small.

Carers from Asian communities will find this an interesting and at times emotional video as people talk of the sadness and frustration of their lives. It directly addresses carers and people talk of how helpful they have found various services. Some of the services are clearly examples of good practice from which others could learn. This video could also be used for training service providers as it challenges the notion that Asian communities always have close-knit families to provide support. It could be used in group settings followed by discussion or viewed at home by individuals. Presenters would need to ensure viewers are provided with up-to-date information about the services and benefits which are mentioned.

Asian weaning photograph album

FORMAT: Pack containing 32 colour photographs

LANGUAGE: English

TARGET AUDIENCE: Parents, health professionals

PRICE: £49.95 inc.

PRODUCER: South Glamorgan Health Authority, 1992

DISTRIBUTOR: South Glamorgan HA

This A4-size photograph album is to support health professionals who are advising mothers from Asian communities about weaning. It was produced by the Health Promotion and Education Unit and Community Nutrition and District Dietetic Department of South Glamorgan Health Authority.

The album consists of 32 laminated photographs in a permanent ring binder. The photographs show the types of food, preparation methods and utensils which may be helpful for weaning. Care has been taken to show foods which are culturally appropriate as well as well-known brands of commercial vegetarian baby foods. One photograph shows a mother breastfeeding. Some show foods such as salt and sugar which are not recommended and these have a cross through them to indicate this. A guide to the photographs is included, which simply states what each photograph represents. There is no guidance about how to use the photographs.

They could assist when a health professional and a mother do not share a common language or communication is limited. However they cannot replace direct communication or ensure the information is understood or questions are answered. They may be most helpful when used to aid communication between a health professional and mother via a linkworker or interpreter.

AWAAZ: help for parents of children with special needs

FORMAT: Video, 53 mins; with 39-page guidance notes and 22-page booklet

LANGUAGE: Bengali, English, Gujarati, Hindi, Punjabi, Urdu

TARGET AUDIENCE: Health professionals, parents, social workers

PRICE: £15.99 + 10% p&p (English version), £13.99 + 10% p&p (other languages)

PRODUCER: Penumbra Productions, 1990

DISTRIBUTOR: Manchester Council for Community Relations

This video and accompanying booklets (information booklet for parents and guidance notes for presenters) are for Asian parents of children with special needs. They aim to provide parents with information about benefits and services and to empower them to make use of what is available. The film-makers consulted with over 60 parents in the Manchester area. Parents talk powerfully about their experiences of having a child with special needs and their struggle to receive information and services. Issues in the film are raised first from a parent's point of view and in their own words, so the film reaches out directly to parents.

The parents who are interviewed vary in age, size of family and age of the child with special needs. Some parents speak in English and others speak in their first language with subtitles. All of them stress the need to ask for assistance and some recount experiences of challenging authorities in order to obtain services. The range of services is covered thoroughly. As the video aims to make parents aware of what is available, presenters need to have local supplementary information to hand (e.g. leaflets to claim benefits, local addresses). Some of the information in the video is now out of date (e.g. Independent Living Fund has changed) and presenters need to ensure that any supplementary information given to parents is up to date.

The video and booklet can be used with individual families in their own homes or with groups of parents. The guidance notes suggest how to structure both settings and how to improve communication. The video is helpfully broken down into smaller sections dealing with specific topics such as education. Groups could view the film in this way over a series of weeks. The video would also be of interest to professionals and health visitors. It points out strongly that parents may not know what is available and that services often do not reach those who are entitled to them.

Badelte riste (Changing relationships)

FORMAT: Video, 28 mins; with notes

LANGUAGE: Gujarati or Urdu with English subtitles

TARGET AUDIENCE: General public, health professionals

PRICE: £70.00

PRODUCER: Health Wise Productions, 1990

DISTRIBUTOR: Health Wise Productions

This video has been produced for Urdu- and Gujarati-speaking Muslim communities and aims to encourage discussion about HIV and AIDS. It was produced by Dewsbury Health Authority in consultation with the Asian Muslim community. It is accompanied by notes for educators which explain the aim of the video, give some information about the Muslim way of life and Islam, as well as guidance for effective use of the video. A dramatic approach is used with a style and imagery which will be familiar and interesting to the target audience. The story unfolds as Sharif finds he is HIV positive as a result of a

blood transfusion following an accident ten years ago. The supportive family doctor (also Muslim) encourages Sharif to tell his wife, Namja. Before Sharif can do so, Namja happily reveals she is pregnant. Deeply distressed they turn to their doctor for help. He is supportive throughout, as is an Asian woman counsellor and the imam. However, the wider family and community display a range of attitudes (mainly misinformed) which leave the couple isolated. The emotional distress of the couple and their immediate family is vividly acted out.

The makers chose not to focus on sexual transmission in order to enable educators to raise the issue of HIV and AIDS without causing offence. Sexual transmission is briefly referred to (Sharif says he has never been promiscuous). The notes recommend a cautious approach to identifying sexual transmission. Throughout Sharif and Namja are advised by their GP to 'take precautions' to protect themselves and the imam encourages them to follow medical advice – it is not made clear what the precautions should be. They are told clearly how HIV cannot be transmitted. Some commentators have noted that the lack of clear information about sexual and other forms of transmission is an omission which is cause for concern.

The focus on transmission via blood products may be confusing, as it is also stated that all blood products are now screened. This may leave some people thinking there is no risk now of HIV and AIDS. Equally, those who have had transfusions in the past may be left worried about HIV transmission. Educators will need to be aware of this and provide advice and reassurance. An animated sequence which explains the difference between HIV and AIDS is clear and informative. It does highlight how lack of information about HIV and AIDS can lead to prejudice and may well spark discussion about how people treat each other, especially men and women. The video is well made and has won several awards nationally and internationally.

Balancing diet for health

FORMAT: Video, 17 mins

LANGUAGE: Dubbed Bengali, Hindi, Punjabi or Urdu with English subtitles

TARGET AUDIENCE: Parents, carers

PRICE: £18.75 inc.

PRODUCER: Cygnet, 1992

DISTRIBUTOR: Cygnet Limited

This video is for mothers from Asian communities and deals with the importance of a balanced diet, especially in relation to children. The video was produced for Wycombe Health Authority School Nursing Service and was funded by Look After Your Heart, Wycombe Health Promotion Service and the Department of Health.

The video uses still shots of foods and cartoon-type animations to explore the subject. The need for a balance of foods is stressed and food groups are illustrated (proteins, dairy produce, carbohydrates, fruit and vegetables), with suggestions about the number of servings required per day from each group. A low fat, low sugar and high fibre diet is recommended. A traditional diet is reflected throughout. Examples of packed lunches for children are shown with close-ups of the food being prepared and the completed meal. This part of the video is likely to be the most interesting to parents/carers and may be a useful starting point for discussion, sharing of views and experiences. The video was made in response to concern by school nurses about children receiving nutritionally balanced meals.

Be prepared, be happy

FORMAT: Video, 20 mins

LANGUAGE: Bengali, English, Gujarati, Hindi, Hindi/Urdu, Mirpuri, Punjabi

TARGET AUDIENCE: Parents, health professionals

PRICE: £35.50 inc.

PRODUCER: DHSS and Save the Children Fund, 1984

DISTRIBUTOR: CFL Vision

This video is for Asian communities and aims to inform about what to expect from antenatal care. It was made as part of the Asian Mother and Baby Campaign by the Department of Health and Save the Children.

The video is dramatised and follows a young couple expecting their first child. The woman is unsure about what to expect and first visits her GP with her mother-in-law and then the hospital for a booking appointment with her husband. A voice-over explains how antenatal care is arranged in the UK. Routine questions and checks are demonstrated (such as taking blood samples, weight checks, urine and blood pressure, etc). At the hospital the husband translates for his wife and during an examination she is unable to speak with the doctor as they do not share a common language. Mention is made of free prescriptions and dental treatment during pregnancy and taking any unprescribed medication is advised against. Dietary advice is given, vitamin and iron supplements are recommended. This video does seem quite dated now and although the information given has not changed significantly, antenatal care has become more informal and client led. The video would be useful in training health professionals as it illustrates well the difficulties health professionals and patients face when they cannot communicate.

Being white

FORMAT: Video, 30 mins; with 20-page booklet

LANGUAGE: English

TARGET AUDIENCE: Trainers

PRICE: £45.00

PRODUCER: Federation of Community Work Training Groups, 1987

DISTRIBUTOR: Albany Video

This video, for white people, aims to encourage awareness and understanding of how being white affects their life, culture and relationships with people who are not white.

The video records a group of white men and women, from various backgrounds, discussing what being white means to them. The discussion covers Irish, Jewish and working class backgrounds. White culture including Christianity and white exclusiveness is openly discussed. The participants explore how as white people they contribute knowingly and unknowingly to personal and institutional racism. They describe how they have begun to challenge this and acknowledge that racism is a problem for white people and thus needs to be tackled by white people. The accompanying booklet contains discussion points for groups to use before and after watching the video and a list of further resources. The video was designed to prepare people for further work on anti-racism and equal opportunities. It is a thoughtful video which may be helpful to use with people for whom this area of personal development is very new.

Big Bert at the health centre

FORMAT: Pack; set of 29 A4 cards

LANGUAGE: English

TARGET AUDIENCE: Key Stage 1 (5–8), Key Stage 2 (8–12), teachers

PRICE: £1.50

PRODUCER: St Paul's Community Project, 1985

DISTRIBUTOR: Language Alive

This black-and-white photo pack for use with children, aims to stimulate their spoken language (in both English and their mother tongue). The pack was produced by the St Paul's Language Development Project with help from various charities. It is the fourth educational resource produced in this series.

The photographs feature big Bert – a clown – and a multiracial group of children with the school nurse. The photographs depict situations which primary school children will encounter during routine visits by the school nurse, doctor and dentist. The location used is a modern health centre. The producers suggest the photographs are used not only to stimulate language development, but also as preparation and reassurance about potentially worrying situations such as dental treatment or having injections. The photographs can be used in sequence or selected appropriately. They could also be included in cross-curricular work (for example, children weighing and measuring each other).

Big Bert does P.E.

FORMAT: Pack; set of 19 A4 cards

LANGUAGE: English, Urdu, with Punjabi written phonetically

TARGET AUDIENCE: Key Stage 1 (5–8), Key Stage 2 (8–12), teachers

PRICE: £1.50

PRODUCER: St Paul's Community Project, 1984

DISTRIBUTOR: Language Alive

This black-and-white photo pack aims to support and reinforce work on prepositions. The pack was produced by the St Paul's Language Development Project with help from various charities. It is the second educational resource produced in this series.

The photographs are spiral bound and feature Big Bert – a clown – and a multiracial group of children. They depict activities and objects commonly used in primary school physical education work which will be familiar to most children. Each photograph is accompanied by a short simple sentence describing it and containing a preposition. The text is in English with a parallel text in Urdu script and Punjabi written phonetically to enable use by English-speaking teachers. It has been designed so that the pictures can be used alone, with the English text or with the Urdu script and phonetic Punjabi. The prepositions chosen are in common use, especially in directions and instructions.

The pack will be of use to those teaching English to children who are speakers of other languages. Many children will find the photographs amusing.

Bilingual health pack for speakers of Bengali
Bilingual health pack for speakers of Chinese
Bilingual health pack for speakers of Gujarati

FORMAT: Pack; 4 cassettes and workbook in each pack

LANGUAGE: Bengali, Chinese, English, Gujarati

TARGET AUDIENCE: Teachers, lecturers

PRICE: £53.00 inc. each pack

PRODUCER: ESOL, Adult Education in Northamptonshire, 1991

DISTRIBUTOR: Northampton College

This audio cassette and workbook are designed for speakers of other languages who want to learn English at home on their own. It was produced by the ESOL (English for Speakers of Other Languages) Department of Adult Education in Northamptonshire.

The pack tackles four situations – making an appointment with a doctor, talking to the doctor, changing an appointment, and making an emergency call for the doctor to visit at home. A brief and realistic script covers many of the questions and phrases which may arise. The tape plays the conversation in English first, then English and Bengali (or Chinese or Gujarati as appropriate), then in English only and with a gap for the student to practise one half of the conversation. The workbook contains the script of the tape in English and the relevant language with instructions about how to work through it. There are also a few useful social interaction phrases at the end. The idea is that students can stop and rewind the tape as much as they want and work through at their own pace. The language used is simple and covers many common phrases such as 'What is your name and address?'

The pack could be used in a group setting as part of an English class but some people may prefer to practice alone at home.Although the producers do not say the pack is for women the speakers in the script are women and the situations are ones which women will find useful. The pack has been independently evaluated by ESOL tutors.

Black and ethnic minority clients: meeting needs

FORMAT: Video, 60 mins

LANGUAGE: English

TARGET AUDIENCE: Health professionals, primary healthcare teams, trainers, service providers, commissioners

PRICE: Not for sale – available for preview at viewing centres nationally

PRODUCER: Healthcare Productions, 1993

DISTRIBUTOR: Healthcare Productions

This video for nurses, midwives and health visitors aims to inform about the need for, and role of linkworkers and advocates in assisting communication between health professionals and patients. It was made for the *Update* series which is part of the Royal College of Nursing's Continuing Education Project for nurses, midwives and health visitors and is supported by the Department of Health.

A dramatised sequence demonstrates how difficult it is for patients and health professionals to communicate if they do not share a language. Linkworkers and advocates explain their role and the contribution they make to effective communication. How to work with a linkworker is explored. Issues such as matching linkworkers and patients appropriately, planning, body language during

consultations, directing questions to the patients, allowing enough time for linkworkers to explain as well as translate are covered. Consultations involving linkworkers are seen in action with the linkworkers explaining cultural, religious and other factors to health professionals and explaining agency systems and practices to patients. It stresses linkworkers are trained professionals who can contribute to uptake of services and compliance with treatment as well as help ensure a more equal service for all.

The video is not for sale but can be seen at viewing centres around the country. Health professionals will find this an informative video and linkworker schemes may wish to use it with health professionals to explain what a linkworker can do and how to work together.

Black community care charter

FORMAT: 14-page booklet

LANGUAGE: English

TARGET AUDIENCE: Mental health teams, primary healthcare teams, social workers

PRICE: £5.00 inc.

PRODUCER: National Association of Race Equality Advisers, 1993

DISTRIBUTOR: National Association of Race Equality Advisers

This charter aims to 'remind institutions of their responsibilities from a black perspective and inform individuals as service users and carers of their rights under the Community Care Act'. The charter is for service providers such as social services departments and health authorities. It is also relevant to policymakers and training authorities.

The charter lists individuals' and carers' rights with a helpful checklist. Key responsibilities for purchasing/provider agencies are listed and the charter deals with needs assessment, design of care packages, development of contracting and purchasing, quality, complaints and monitoring. It is emphasised that black voluntary organisations can be considered as means of meeting needs appropriately and should be consulted. It addresses what needs to be achieved (for example, 'registration officers should target the black voluntary sector to ensure they realise their potential and become eligible for registration').

The charter is a useful starting point for service providers to ensure services are appropriate and sensitive to the needs of all sections of the community. The charter was drawn up by a steering group of participants from health authorities and social services departments around the country.

Black girls speak out

FORMAT: 26-page pack, illustrations

LANGUAGE: English

TARGET AUDIENCE: Women, social workers, counsellors, health professionals

PRICE: £3.00 + 45p p&p

PRODUCER: The Children's Society, 1991

DISTRIBUTOR: The Children's Society

This booklet is for girls and young women. It was written by two young women who describe themselves as Caribbean and Anglo-Asian and is about their experiences of surviving sexual abuse.

The booklet is a collection of writing by the two young women plus some drawings. The writing is reprinted as it was written so it looks like handwriting. This coupled with the very personal nature of the writing make it accessible to young people. The young women describe why they felt they couldn't tell anyone of the abuse, why they did eventually tell, what happened then and how they felt about participating in a group for young women survivors. The impact of race and colour on the young women's experiences is a central theme. For example, they touch on not

wanting to be proud of being black because a black person had abused them, being blamed and rejected by the Asian side of the family, being the only black person in the survivors' group. The booklet is not about the abuse itself but focuses on the young women's feelings and how they were treated after they had told.

The young women state they wrote the booklet in the hope that it would help 'you to talk about your feelings with someone you feel you trust'. The booklet will be of great interest to young women who have been or are being sexually abused. It is also relevant to professionals who may be working with young people, as it raises important issues about the extra difficulties black young people can experience in seeking help if they are being abused and the kind of support they may need and find helpful. It is one of the few resources produced on this topic for young people by young people.

The black male's sexuality and relationships social education pack

FORMAT: Pack; with one 57-page and one 25-page manual

LANGUAGE: English

TARGET AUDIENCE: (Key Stage 4 (14–16), young people (16-plus), youth workers, teachers

PRICE: £7.95 inc.

PRODUCER: North East Mitcham Community Centre, 1993

DISTRIBUTOR: Mitcham Community Centre

This pack aims to provide materials for groupwork with young men, exploring issues to do with sexuality, racism and relationships. It was the product of a group which met with a youth worker and sexual health worker at the North East Mitcham Community Centre in London.

One of the manuals consists of a copy of the materials used with the group (questionnaires, agree/disagree statements sheets, case studies, outlines of activities to trigger discussion, etc.). The other includes notes and comments from the facilitators about the group's progress and the planning of the sessions. The facilitators had planned a full and challenging programme and they describe some of the difficulties they faced in establishing the group. They also report the views of the group on many issues, some controversial, some predictable and many thoughtful.

The group sparked much discussion about issues which previously were not talked about seriously and provided opportunities for sharing information and views. The pack is direct in the way it tackles the subject matter and facilitators are frank in their discussion of the group. The material could be used in many informal settings with young men to promote discussion about sexuality. It will be of particular interest to youthworkers and teachers.

Blood disorder not disease

FORMAT: Video, 15 mins

LANGUAGE: English

TARGET AUDIENCE: General public, health professionals

PRICE: £15.50 inc.

PRODUCER: Verité à Tous, 1989

DISTRIBUTOR: Verité à Tous

This video is suitable for general audiences and aims to raise awareness of and understanding about sickle cell anaemia. It was made by a young man, Ashu Egbe, who is living with sickle cell anaemia.

A variety of techniques are used to explore the subject – interviews with people in the street about what they know about sickle cell, people with sickle cell explaining what a crisis feels like, a sickle cell support group in action, an interview with a health professional who specialises in treatment of sickle cell, an interview with an employer about an employee with sickle cell, a simulated scene of a crisis and Mr Egbe telling the viewer about living with sickle cell anaemia. The video will also be of interest to people who have sickle cell, their families and friends. Health professionals will also find it useful to hear what kind of support people with sickle cell want from them.

Blood ties

FORMAT: Video, 8 mins

LANGUAGE: English

TARGET AUDIENCE: General public, health professionals

PRICE: £25.00

PRODUCER: United Kingdom Thalassaemia Society, 1987

DISTRIBUTOR: UK Thalassaemia Society

CORPORATE AUTHOR: United Kingdom Thalassaemia Society

This video for a general audience aims to raise awareness of the serious nature of thalassaemia major and the need to screen for thalassaemia. It was produced by the United Kingdom Thalassaemia Society.

The short video focuses on two young women who have thalassaemia major. They describe what life is like for them living with the condition. Both young women must use a subcutaneous pump for twelve hours a day, five days a week plus regular hospital check-ups and blood transfusions. The women talk of how their life is affected by the need for such constant medical treatment but acknowledge that without it they would die. They talk about family members and friends who have chosen not to continue with the treatment and have died. A father explains how the first time he heard of the condition was when his newborn son was diagnosed with thalassaemia major. The video notes the importance of screening.

It is accompanied by the booklet *All you need to know about thalassaemia* which provides further information about thalassaemia major and minor.

This is a useful video for raising awareness about thalassaemia. It also raises the difficult issue of young people choosing not to continue with treatment and could be used with young people who have the condition to trigger discussion about how they feel about their treatment. People may need additional information about how to access local screening and genetic counselling services.

Breastfeeding

FORMAT: Cassette, 12 mins; with 3-page script

LANGUAGE: Sylheti

TARGET AUDIENCE: Women, health professionals, primary healthcare teams

PRICE: £1.50 inc.

PRODUCER: Culture Waves for Bloomsbury and Islington Health Authority, 1992

DISTRIBUTOR: Camden and Islington Health Authority

This cassette is for women from Bengali (Sylheti-speaking) communities and aims to encourage new mothers to breastfeed their babies. The cassette is the first in a series of three health information tapes for women from Bengali communities.

The cassette adopts a radio drama approach and we hear Sufia discussing how to feed her new baby with her sister-in-law and mother-in-law and later with the health visitor. The Bengali-speaking health visitor confirms that mother-in-law is right and breastfeeding is best for babies – 'the old way from our country is also the modern way'. The cassette is short and interesting as the different points of view emerge from each character. It ends with the health visitor listing information points about breastfeeding.

This cassette may be helpful to midwives and health visitors who are seeing new mothers and

is an interesting way of raising the issue. It could also be used antenatally to spark discussion about feeding choices. As it is so short it can be listened to during a home visit or left for a woman to listen to with or without other family members. The cassettes are designed to be available, free of charge, in lending libraries, GPs' surgeries, clinics and community centres. It is good value for money. The cassette was produced in close consultation with the local Bengali community.

Breastfeeding: the best way to feed your baby

FORMAT: Video, 26 mins

LANGUAGE: Bengali with English sub-titles. Sylheti dubbed version available

TARGET AUDIENCE: Women, health professionals

PRICE: £12.77

PRODUCER: Tower Hamlets Health Promotion Service, 1991

DISTRIBUTOR: East London & City HPS

This video for mothers from Bengali communities aims to increase women's confidence in their ability to breastfeed. It also provides information about problems which may occur, how to overcome them and sources of help. It is not a 'how to' guide to breastfeeding, and women are not shown breastfeeding. It was produced by Tower Hamlets Video Production Unit in collaboration with the Maternity Services Liaison Scheme and the Midwifery Health Promotion Service.

Using a documentary-style approach, with actors playing all the main roles, it examines breastfeeding from a mother's point of view. Mothers talk about their experiences and explain problems they encountered and how they overcame them. A midwife outlines the benefits of breastfeeding and an older doctor explains why she chose to breastfeed her children. Breastfeeding is stressed as a natural and traditional method of feeding and grandmother adds her point of view.

There are nine short sequences which could be viewed independently over a number of sessions. Midwives may find it a useful way of providing information about, and of promoting, breastfeeding. It could be viewed by women during their stay in hospital, at home or at antenatal visits. Ideally if viewed with a health visitor there would be opportunity for further discussion. The video has a gentle pace and lots of visuals of mothers with babies and infants. The presentation of breastfeeding from a mother's point of view is refreshing and different from many of the other sources available on this topic. It deals sensitively and practically with everyday concerns women may have, such as feeding in public or with the family. The local Bengali communities and Bengali health workers were involved in the production of the video which developed out of a local infant feeding project and health authority feeding campaign.

Breast-screening: your questions answered

FORMAT: 4 cassettes, 10 mins each; with 3-page English transcript

LANGUAGE: Arabic, Bengali, English, Urdu

TARGET AUDIENCE: Women, health professionals

PRICE: £2.50 each cassette. Discounts available for quantities

PRODUCER: Salford Health Promotion Centre, 1991

DISTRIBUTOR: Salford Health Promotion Centre

These cassettes are for women in the 50 years-plus age group and aim to inform and reassure them about the breast-screening process.

The process is explained in the form of an information talk given by a female presenter. It is stressed that the radiographer will be female and that the screening takes place in private. The recall and assessment procedure is also explained. Care is taken to reassure women that the process is not harmful or painful and breast-screening is presented as a sensible health choice. Women may need more information such as how to arrange to have an interpreter or linkworker present. Some women may wish to talk with a health worker, particularly if there is a family history of breast cancer, as they may be more worried than most about the possible outcomes of breast-screening.

Many women will find it useful to listen to a cassette in the privacy of their home prior to screening. It may be helpful for women who have literacy problems, are partially sighted or blind or if literature is not available in their language. The phone number for further advice is local to the Salford area so listeners elsewhere will need a local contact address and phone number. The cassettes are good value and could easily be loaned from GPs' surgeries, clinics, community centres and libraries. The cassettes have been piloted by local women in the Salford area.

The breast self-examination and the gynaecological examination

FORMAT: Video, 20 mins

LANGUAGE: Cantonese with English subtitles

TARGET AUDIENCE: Women, health professionals

PRICE: £35.25 inc.

PRODUCER: Healthcare Productions for London Chinese Health Resources Centre, 1990

DISTRIBUTOR: Healthcare Productions

This video is for women from Chinese communities who speak Cantonese. It was funded by the Department of Health. It aims to inform and reassure women about breast self-examination and the gynaecological examination. The video will be of most interest to women who have never had an examination before; it also addresses particular concerns women may have such as the language barrier and seeing a woman doctor. In the first section a woman is shown by a nurse how to examine her breasts. Advice about this has changed since the video was made and now women are encouraged to be 'breast aware'. However, much of the information given by the nurse is still relevant as she identifies the kinds of changes women need to be aware of. This section of the video could be omitted if desired but may be useful in discussions with women about the importance of recognising any changes at an early stage. It could also be supported with further information about the breast screening programme. The second section thoroughly explains and demonstrates the gynaecological examination. It begins with a discussion with the (woman) doctor and is followed by examination with a speculum, taking a cervical smear and a bi-manual examination. The examination is shown twice, the second time showing the actual time it takes. This may be very reassuring to women who are anxious about the procedure. Throughout the video women of a variety of ages talk about having examinations, initial fears and embarrassment, worries about language and so on. One woman is shown visiting the doctor with a linkworker to assist with translating.

Some women may find this an embarrassing video to view as women are shown partially naked and the examinations are shown explicitly. Viewers need to be prepared for this. It is probably best viewed by women individually or in small groups. If this could be done with a health professional any questions could be answered, local information about services be provided, and some discussion of what happens if something abnormal is identified could be included. This is an informative video which deals honestly and sensitively with the subject. It may be particularly useful for women who are anxious about examinations as it does give a realistic idea of what to expect.

Britain's forgotten elders

FORMAT: Video, 30 mins

LANGUAGE: English

TARGET AUDIENCE: Older people, service providers

PRICE: £29.00

PRODUCER: Skyline Film and Television for SCEMSC, 1986

DISTRIBUTOR: SCEMSC

This video for service providers aims to raise awareness of the needs of older black and minority ethnic people.

The video explores why older black and minority ethnic people do not use existing provision and identifies how appropriate provision can be developed. Four different services in the London area are shown – a day centre for Asian elderly, a Caribbean club, a Chinese community centre and an Asian community centre. Older people explain why they prefer this provision and how it contributes to their enjoyment of life. Community workers and staff from SCEMSC stress the importance of older people being able to have opportunities for social and leisure activities with others who share their language/culture/beliefs/religion, etc. Older people talk too of how they do not feel welcome in many mainstream services.

The video will be of interest to those involved in service provision for older people and may encourage discussion of how well the needs of all older people in the community are being met. The video also questions why mainstream provision has not taken on board the needs of older black and minority ethnic people and why this has been left to the voluntary sector.

British Diabetic Association information pack

FORMAT: Pack; 12 looseleaf sheets

LANGUAGE: English

TARGET AUDIENCE: Health professionals, primary healthcare teams

PRICE: £1.50 inc.

PRODUCER: British Diabetic Association, 1993

DISTRIBUTOR: British Diabetic Association

This pack aims to inform health professionals about African-Caribbean diet and appropriate advice for people with diabetes. It was compiled by members of the British Diabetic Association's Afro-Caribbean Working Party.

The pack consists of a folder containing information sheets about: traditional African-Caribbean diet, providing dietary advice for African-Caribbean people on diabetes, African-Caribbean recipes, tips on how to adapt a traditional diet for people with diabetes, information about educational resources and an up-to-date bibliography of journal articles about diabetes and the African-Caribbean communities. The pack is almost exclusively for health professionals but the recipes and tips sheets could be used directly with patients. This is a practical resource which will enable health professionals to provide more relevant and culturally appropriate dietary advice for African-Caribbean people with diabetes.

Call for care

FORMAT: 64-page book

LANGUAGE: Bengali, English, Gujarati, Punjabi, Urdu

TARGET AUDIENCE: Carers

PRICE: £1.95 + 80p p&p

PRODUCER: Health Education Authority with King's Fund Centre, 1991

DISTRIBUTOR: Health Education Authority

This short book, produced by the HEA and King's Fund for Asian carers of older people, provides information about sources of help and support for carers and tackles more difficult issues such as emotions and death.

The book begins by defining 'carers'. Services which may be available to help carers, including welfare benefits, are described. Consideration is given to communication difficulties, and sample letters in English requesting interpreting services are included. Much of the advice is practical, with addresses and suggestions about how to take action, case studies, and comments from carers illustrating points throughout. The book notes how carers may have mixed feelings about the person they care for and may have to cope with difficult behaviour. Some carers may find it a relief to read that other people feel the same way too. Stereotypes of Asian families as always close-knit and supportive are challenged and there is advice about how to campaign for more equal services which respond to the needs of Asian communities.

Carers will find this a useful and interesting book. Those who are unsure of what they can ask for or are entitled to will find it a useful guide, as will those who work with carers.

Care in cold weather

FORMAT: Video, 8 mins; with 4-page notes; also available as a cassette

LANGUAGE: Bengali, and Bengali with English dubbing (on one video)

TARGET AUDIENCE: General public

PRICE: £11.92

PRODUCER: Tower Hamlets Health Promotion Service, 1992

DISTRIBUTOR: East London & City HPS

This short video for Bengali communities aims to give simple, practical advice on keeping warm and healthy during cold weather.

In five sections it covers: warm clothing for children, warm clothing for adults, heating in the home, warm food and drink and protecting your skin. Each section uses the same actors, featuring a mother and father and two school-age children. The clothing suggested is culturally acceptable and emphasis is placed on adequate clothing for wear outdoors. Moisturisers and lip salve are recommended, with several common brand names shown. The video will be of most use to those who are newly arrived in Britain and unused to cold weather.

The video has been designed to stand alone and be used without the support of a health professional. It is suitable for viewing in group settings or for individual home viewing. It could also be used in waiting areas. The video was produced in consultation with members of local Bengali communities.

Caribbean food and diet

FORMAT: 56-page booklet, illustrations

LANGUAGE: English

TARGET AUDIENCE: Primary healthcare teams, health professionals

PRICE: £5.95 + £1.00 p&p

PRODUCER: National Extension College, 1987

DISTRIBUTOR: Sandwell HPU

This booklet is part of a training series for health professionals who may need to give dietary and nutritional advice. It seeks to inform about African-Caribbean food and diet and enable health professionals to give appropriate advice to people from African-Caribbean communities. This booklet was originally produced as part of *Food and diet in a multi-racial society* published by the National Extension College.

The booklet provides background information about African-Caribbean communities in the UK and about dietary patterns of African-Caribbean communities in the UK. How to give appropriate advice is covered with sample menus and diets for specific conditions such as hypertension. Each section includes discussion points and activities about the information presented. These aim to reinforce the information presented and to encourage awareness of the nutritional value of traditional diets. A number of case studies are provided at the end for health professionals to practise providing dietary advice. A reference section and bibliography provide more detailed information. This booklet introduces health professionals to the background, dietary beliefs, and other factors which affect the diet of African-Caribbean communities in the UK. It was designed to be used as part of a structured learning experience in a group setting and will be of most benefit if used in this way. However it can also contribute to individual study. The booklet is based on research undertaken in Trinidad, Barbados and Jamaica.

Caring for everyone: ensuring standards of care for black and ethnic minority patients

FORMAT: 17-page booklet

LANGUAGE: English

TARGET AUDIENCE: Health professionals, service providers

PRICE: £5.95 inc.

PRODUCER: National Extension College, 1991

DISTRIBUTOR: National Extension College

This booklet is for health professionals and managers of health services at all levels. It addresses the issue of equal access to health care and how this can be made a reality. It was funded by the Department of Health.

The booklet defines equal access, identifies what racism is and why it must be challenged. It examines caring for people from different communities. Practical aspects of care (e.g. diet, religious observances, using names correctly) are covered and issues relating to interpreting are explored. It is written in an accessible style with brief quotes from patients and staff to illustrate points. Each section includes a series of questions for readers to consider in relation to their service – these could easily be incorporated into training sessions on ensuring equal access. Staff are encouraged to reflect on how people feel in hospital and how people from different communities may experience health care designed for white people.

The booklet pinpoints what needs to be done within health services to initiate equal access and gives some guidance about how to begin.

Suggestions for change are specific and practical such as how to work with interpreters and ensuring the hospital shop has a range of snacks suitable for all patients. The booklet does not give detailed information on provision for particular communities but suggests staff find out this information from the local communities themselves. There is a useful reference section at the end. Short and readable, clear and to the point, the booklet encourages health professionals to examine closely the services they offer and identify areas for improvement. There is a companion booklet for patients entitled *Coming into hospital*, also produced by the National Extension College.

Caring for Hindus and their families: religious aspects of care

FORMAT: 83-page manual

LANGUAGE: English

TARGET AUDIENCE: Health professionals, service providers, carers, trainers

PRICE: £10.95 inc.

PRODUCER: National Extension College for HEC, DHSS and King Edward's Hospital Fund for London, 1983

DISTRIBUTOR: National Extension College

This manual is one of a series of three (the others are *Caring for Sikhs* and *Caring for Muslims*). Written for health professionals, it aims to inform about religious beliefs and practices of Hindus with particular reference to provision of health care, especially in hospital.

The manual explains the Hindu philosophy of life, beliefs and religious practices. Traditional diet, family duties, practical care (e.g. dress and washing), naming systems, birth, marriage and death ceremonies, festivals, attitudes to contraception, abortion and infertility are all dealt with. Notes are included for trainers, with brief suggestions for training sessions. An appendix lists various Hindu terms with meanings in English and approximate guides to pronunciation.

Although written in accessible language the quantity of information presented is considerable. The manual notes that there may be many variations among people about adherence to religious practices and advises health staff to talk to patients about their needs. The section on naming systems may be particularly helpful as it indicates how to address someone correctly.

This manual may be helpful to trainers who are providing training for staff about different cultural and religious groups in Britain as it presents a lot of information succinctly. However, additional information would also be needed about the range of beliefs and practices among Hindus today, as for many people the traditional way of life may have changed and Hindus are not a homogeneous group. The manual was written with the cooperation of a number of people from Hindu communities.

Caring for multicultural clients

FORMAT: 52-page manual

LANGUAGE: English

TARGET AUDIENCE: Health professionals, primary healthcare teams

PRICE: £5.50 inc.

PRODUCER: Midwifery Unit, St Thomas's Hospital, 1993

DISTRIBUTOR: St Thomas's Hospital

This manual aims to provide information and guidance about the care of patients from black and minority ethnic groups, with particular reference to midwifery settings. It was written by a midwife at St Thomas's Hospital in London who was concerned about the need for health professionals to have an understanding of patients' cultures, traditions and religious beliefs. The first part is a general introduction to caring for patients from different cultures. Issues such as use of interpreters, communication with a patient whose first language is not English, and coping with bereavement, are covered. Health professionals are encouraged to consider all aspects of their interaction with patients and to learn more about patients' cultural and religious observances in order to offer appropriate care. The second part is a description of the main beliefs and practices of a number of black and minority ethnic groups, with specific reference to pregnancy and birth. Topics such as naming the new born, attitudes to blood tests and transfusions, preferences at birth and traditional confinement practices, are included.

The manual is a useful reference source for maternity staff and could also be used in midwifery, medical and GP training. It is easy to read and offers practical guidance. The author consulted widely with health professionals and representatives of the various communities.

Caring for Muslims and their families: religious aspects of care

FORMAT: 86-page manual

LANGUAGE: English

TARGET AUDIENCE: Health professionals, service providers, carers, trainers

PRICE: £10.95 inc.

PRODUCER: National Extension College for DHSS and King Edward's Hospital Fund for London, 1982

DISTRIBUTOR: National Extension College

This manual is one of a series of three (the others are *Caring for Hindus* and *Caring for*

Sikhs). Written for health professionals, it aims to inform about religious beliefs and practices of Muslims with particular reference to provision of health care, especially in hospital.

The manual explains the beliefs and duties of Muslims including information about Islam, the Holy Qur'an and the mosque. Family duties, practical care (e.g. dress and washing), diet, Muslim names, birth and childhood ceremonies, festivals, marriage, divorce, contraception, abortion, infertility and death are all dealt with from a traditional point of view. Notes are included for trainers with brief suggestions for training sessions. An appendix lists various Muslim terms with meanings in English and approximate guides to pronunciation. Although written in accessible language the quantity of information presented is considerable. The manual notes that there may be considerable variation about adherence to religious practices and advises health staff to discuss with patients their needs. The section on Muslim names may be particularly useful as it indicates how to address a person correctly.

The manual may be helpful to trainers who are providing training for staff about different cultural and religious groups in Britain as it presents a lot of information succinctly. However, additional information would also be needed about the range of beliefs and practices among Muslims today as for many the traditional way of life may have changed and Muslims are not a homogenous group. The manual was written with the cooperation of a number of people from Muslim communities.

Caring for Sikhs and their families: religious aspects of care

FORMAT: 69-page manual

LANGUAGE: English

TARGET AUDIENCE: Carers, trainers, health professionals, service providers

PRICE: £10.95 inc.

PRODUCER: National Extension College for DHSS and King Edward's Hospital Fund for London, 1983

DISTRIBUTOR: National Extension College

This manual is one of a series of three (the others are *Caring for Hindus* and *Caring for Muslims*). Written for health professionals, it aims to inform about the religious beliefs and practices of Sikhs with particular reference to provision of health care, especially in hospital.

The manual explains the Sikh way of life including how Sikhism began, the five signs of Sikhism and the role of the gurdwara (Sikh temple). Family duties, practical care (e.g. dress and washing), diet, naming systems, birth and childhood ceremonies, festivals, marriage, divorce, contraception, abortion, infertility and death are all dealt with from a traditional point of view. Notes are included for trainers with brief suggestions for training sessions. An appendix lists various Sikh terms with meanings in English and approximate guides to pronunciation. Although written in accessible language the quantity of information presented is considerable. The book notes that there may be much variation among people about adherence to religious practices and advises health staff to discuss with patients their needs.

The section on naming systems may be particularly useful as it indicates how to address someone correctly. This book may be helpful to trainers who are providing training for staff about different cultural and religious groups in Britain as it presents a lot of information succinctly. However, additional information would also be needed about the range of beliefs and practices among Sikhs today as for many people the traditional way of life may have changed and Sikhs are not a homogenous group. The manual was written with the cooperation of a number of people from Sikh communities.

Catering for who? A documentary about careers and education for Bangladeshi men

FORMAT: Video, 30 mins

LANGUAGE: English, Sylheti

TARGET AUDIENCE: Parents, teachers, lecturers, youth workers, young people (16-plus)

PRICE: £25.00 (maximum: prices vary according to purchaser)

PRODUCER: Bengalis with Attitude, 1992

DISTRIBUTOR: Asian Community Media

Produced by a group of young Bengali men from Mossley, Thameside, this documentary video uses interviews with group members and professionals to question why so many Bangladeshi young men (86 per cent) end up working in the catering trade.

The young men challenge the assumptions and expectations they feel society has about them and candidly explain their experiences of the education system, their parents' views, and the need for them to contribute economically to the family. They also discuss the lack of positive role models for Asian young people and the effects of racism. The interviews and group discussions give the young men a voice which is rarely heard, as they challenge the assumptions and expectations they feel society has about them.

The video was made with the support of the Thameside Metropolitan Borough Council, Community Languages and Arts Centre, and Black Youth Work Leisure Services. The group produced the video entirely by themselves and although the technical quality, particularly the sound, can be distracting at times, it examines a difficult issue with confidence and feeling. This video could be used in a range of settings such as youth groups, schools and parent/teacher associations. It provides a useful trigger to explore issues of racism, expectations and equal opportunities and could also be a useful contribution to training teachers, youth workers and others in contact with young people.

The cervical smear test

FORMAT: Video, 11 mins; with 6-page leaflet

LANGUAGE: Bengali, English, Gujarati, Hindi, Punjabi and Urdu on one video. Leaflet in same languages

TARGET AUDIENCE: Women, health professionals

PRICE: £20.00

PRODUCER: Leicestershire Health Authority, Health Education Video Unit, 1988

DISTRIBUTOR: Leicestershire HA Video Unit

This video for women from Asian communities seeks to inform about the cervical smear test and encourage women to attend for screening. It was produced with financial support from the Department of Health. A voice-over is used to explain what the smear test is and who should have one. There is a very brief description of how the test is done and a woman is seen lying on a couch and talking with a female doctor.

Women are advised about how long results take and what may happen if the result is abnormal. Information is given about where the test may be carried out, but the guidance about how often tests should be done has now changed and so women need to be advised accordingly. The video was made before call-

and-recall systems were established and so viewers would need to be informed about this. The accompanying leaflet is a transcript of the video. The video has a practical and reassuring tone, stressing that having regular smear tests is a way of maintaining good health.

It would need some input from a health professional or community worker to update the information and perhaps discuss in more detail what the test involves. It was based on information provided by the Women's National Cancer Control Campaign.

Challenging racism

FORMAT: 36-page pack, illustrations, tables

LANGUAGE: English

TARGET AUDIENCE: Key Stage 4 (14–16), teachers, young people (16-plus), youth workers

PRICE: £15.95 + p&p

PRODUCER: The Chalkface Project, 1993

DISTRIBUTOR: CEDC

This pack is for use with Key Stage 4 students and young people. It aims to provide opportunities for young people to explore their perceptions of, and attitudes towards, people from different cultures and races. It was produced by the Chalkface Project. The pack consists of 28 activities designed for personal and social education and English classes but which can also be used for humanities and as tutor work. Each one-page activity is illustrated and photocopiable. Most are designed to be completed in a single lesson and there are suggestions for homework and extension activities. The activities encourage students to develop more thoughtful attitudes and to challenge racism. They range from less risky to more risky and offer a mix of individual and small group work. The teachers' notes advise awareness of the students' attitudes before using the pack and suggest they may be more appropriate for a mature group with whom the teacher/presenter has a good relationship. A section at the end provides

more information for teachers/presenters about each activity.

Although designed for classroom use this pack could be used in many other settings such as youth clubs. It is a flexible resource which could be used completely or selectively according to time available etc. The producers note in the introduction that classes in which one racial or cultural group are a minority will need careful management, guidance is not offered about how to do this apart from brief comments in the teachers' notes.

Checklist health and race: a starting point for managers on improving services for black populations

FORMAT: 39-page manual

LANGUAGE: English

TARGET AUDIENCE: Health professionals, primary healthcare teams, service providers, commissioners

PRICE: £12.00 inc.

PRODUCER: King's Fund, 1993

DISTRIBUTOR: Bournemouth English Book Centre

This manual is for managers within health services at all levels and aims to provide guidance about making services more appropriate for, and accessible to, black and minority ethnic groups. It was prepared by the King's Fund Centre with advice from the NHS Management Executive and funding from the Department of Health.

The manual consists of detailed checklists which can be used to review and develop race equality policy and practice in service provision. The checklists target local issues, commissioning and purchasing issues, providers' issues and service provision (such as catering and dietary services). Two annexes address particular service provision (e.g. for disabled people) and health conditions. The checklists can be used selectively to address various or particular issues. Managers may find the checklists a focused way of examining how well services are meeting the needs of black and minority ethnic groups and of establishing baselines for service provision. A short bibliography refers to up-to-date publications and research reports which address equality issues. This is a practical manual which thoroughly examines provision of health services in a tangible and quantifiable way.

Child development

FORMAT: Video, 23 mins

LANGUAGE: Bengali, English, Gujarati, Hindi/Urdu, Punjabi

TARGET AUDIENCE: Parents, health professionals

PRICE: £29.90 inc.

PRODUCER: N Films for Asian Mother and Baby Campaign, 1987

DISTRIBUTOR: CFL Vision

This video, for both parents and carers of babies and toddlers, aims to inform about the developmental milestones most children achieve. It also covers developmental checks in the early years and encourages parents to talk and play with their children. The video was funded by the Department of Health and was supported by the Health Visitors Association, the Royal College of Nursing and the British Paediatric Association. The video follows three children at two different ages so that six developmental stages are covered. These are birth and 6 weeks, 8 months and 10 months, 18 months and 2 years. Throughout, children are seen with their parents and families in their own homes. Parents discuss the child's development and enjoy each new achievement such as the first smile. Mothers attend baby clinics for regular checks and discuss

vaccination with doctors and health visitors (the immunisation schedule has now changed and viewers need to be updated about this). Parents are encouraged to consult their doctor if they have any concern about their child.

Safety and accident prevention are stressed and demonstrated at all ages.

This is an informative video which parents will enjoy. Health visitors may find it particularly useful. It may be viewed in home or group settings to trigger discussion about child development. As people are usually interested in what their child will do in the next few months, it is probably best viewed in sections selected according to the child's age. The format of the video aids this approach.

Child protection and female genital mutilation: advice for health education and social work professionals

FORMAT: 32-page manual

LANGUAGE: English

TARGET AUDIENCE: Primary healthcare teams, social workers, health professionals

PRICE: £3.50

PRODUCER: Foundation for Women's Health Research and Development (FORWARD), 1992

DISTRIBUTOR: Foundation for Women's Health

This manual is for any professional concerned with the welfare and protection of children. It aims to provide guidelines for professionals who are working with communities where female genital mutilation is practised. The publication was produced with support from the Department of Health.

The manual outlines what female genital mutilation is, including physical and medical complications. There is a discussion of which communities may practice female genital mutilation and why. The legal context is explained and suggestions about how to use child protection procedures are included. The need for professionals to work sensitively with families is stressed and a case history highlights the difficulties professionals may face including fears of being labelled racist. The manual firmly asserts that female genital mutilation is a child protection issue. It also notes the changes being made in African and Asian nations where the practice is being eradicated and has been made illegal in many countries.

This practical manual provides factual information and guidelines based on the Children Act 1989. Professionals not familiar with female genital mutilation will find the advice from a social worker about working with families supportive. The manual was written with advice from community leaders and comments from a wide range of professionals.

Birmingham *family* **Health** *services*

Children's Colds

An Asian language video for parents

The video shows, in story form and explanatory interludes with illustrative graphics, how a Punjabi family copes with a cold as it goes through the family. It emphasises that colds are self limiting and that parents can take simple measures to relieve symptoms. It clarifies the role of the doctor, when to seek help, what parents should expect from the doctor and that advice on simple treatments is also available from the pharmacist.

- Filmed with Asian actors, with dialogue in Punjabi
- Voice-over story line and commentary in five language versions (English, Bengali, Gujerati, Punjabi and Urdu)
- Backed by specially commissioned research
- High quality, professionally produced video
- For use in waiting rooms, clinics, health centres and for home viewing
- Support pack for structured use by health workers
- VHS tape, 20 minutes running time

How to order - complete the order form overleaf and return with your payment to Video Sales at Birmingham FHSA.

Children's colds: an Asian languages video for parents

FORMAT: Video, 20 mins; with 15-page booklet, 9-page notes and script

LANGUAGE: Video in Bengali, English, Gujarati, Punjabi, Urdu. Booklet in Bengali/English

TARGET AUDIENCE: Parents, health professionals, primary healthcare teams

PRICE: £49.50 inc. (£25.00 inc. for additional language copies)

PRODUCER: Birmingham Family Health Services Authority, 1992

DISTRIBUTOR: Birmingham FHSA

This video is for parents from Asian communities and aims to help them become more aware of appropriate treatment for children's colds and coughs, when they should consult their GP and what they should expect from the consultation.

The video tells the story of how a Punjabi family with three school-age children cope with a cold as it spreads through the family. The storyline is in Punjabi with a voice-over. The management and treatment of colds at home is demonstrated. Animated graphics explain cold viruses and how the body builds up resistance. Family life is portrayed realistically with both parents and grandmother caring for the children. Guidance notes are included for showing the video in group settings with suggestions for discussion and key points noted.

The video can be used in a variety of settings such as waiting areas in GPs' surgeries, group viewing with a health professional or community worker or home viewing. Short, clear and practical, it will inform parents and encourage them to feel more confident about dealing with minor illnesses. The video was made as a result of GPs' concern about the difficulties Asian families experienced in coping with colds and the different prescribing practices noted among GPs for Asian families. Research was then undertaken into the health beliefs and practices of Asian parents, and was used to ensure the video tackled parents' concerns and information needs appropriately. The research data is also available to those interested.

Close to home: a drama about HIV and AIDS

FORMAT: Video, 32 mins; with 6-page booklet

LANGUAGE: Punjabi with English

TARGET AUDIENCE: General public, healthcare professionals

PRICE: £25.00 inc.

PRODUCER: Wolverhampton Primary Health Care Unit, Health Promotion Department, 1992

DISTRIBUTOR: Wolverhampton Health Promotion

This video for Punjabi communities was made to support HIV/AIDS education within the Asian communities. It takes the form of a social drama which has something to say to all age groups in the community.

The story opens with a young student worried he may have HIV because he has 'taken a risk'. Unable to discuss the problem with his family, he seeks help from a college counsellor. His parents find out he is worried about HIV and family life falls into disarray. Eventually the young man chooses to have a HIV test with his parents' support. Methods of transmission are described and sources of help and support clearly explained.

The accompanying booklet suggests questions for follow-up discussion and provide some

basic information about HIV/AIDS. The video can be used as trigger material to spark discussions and share information. Presenters may find it helpful to have local information about sources of help such as GUM clinics and family planning clinics. The video does not focus on prevention in detail but simply advises condom use and use of clean needles, etc. Presenters may wish to expand on this information. It does touch on the risk from unscreened blood transfusions in countries where blood screening does not exist and some viewers may want more detailed information about this.

Code of practice for interpreters

FORMAT: 15-page booklet

LANGUAGE: English

TARGET AUDIENCE: Health professionals, social workers, service providers

PRICE: £3.50

PRODUCER: Ethnic Study Group, Coordinating Centre for Community and Health Care, 1991

DISTRIBUTOR: Ethnic Study Group, Coordinating Centre for Community and Health Care

This booklet aims to provide clear guidelines on the principles of good practice for the provision of interpreting skills within the healthcare system. The code was prepared by committee members and staff of the Ethnic Switchboard following wide consultation with others.

The guidelines refer to terminology, professional settings where interpreting may be needed, guidelines for conducting the interpreting session, confidentiality and advocacy. They seek to clarify the boundaries of what an interpreter should and should not do, or be expected to do. A useful section deals with special situations such as what to do if the patient is unhappy with the interpreter, the service or medical procedure. In most cases of uncertainty the interpreter is advised to consult with their line manager. This concise booklet will be helpful to those providing and using interpreting services as it highlights potential areas of difficulty and establishes some boundaries for professional interpreting services.

Coming into hospital: an information book for patients

(Includes copy of *Caring for everyone: ensuring standards of care for black and ethnic minority patients*)

FORMAT: Pack

LANGUAGE: *Coming into hospital* available in Arabic, Bengali, Chinese, English, Greek, Gujarati, Punjabi, Turkish, Urdu, and Vietnamese. *Caring for everyone* available in English.

TARGET AUDIENCE: Health professionals, service providers, primary healthcare teams, commissioners

PRICE: £15 inc. per language; complete set £99 inc.

PRODUCER: National Extension College, 1991

DISTRIBUTOR: National Extension College

This pack of booklets is for patients coming into hospital who need information about hospital procedure in their first language. It was funded by the Department of Health.

The pack consists of laminated master sheets which can be used to photocopy the booklet in the relevant language. This means the booklet can be reproduced cheaply when needed. The booklets explain what to expect when someone is admitted to hospital. Issues covered include transport to hospital, what to bring with you, food in hospital, visitors, and hospital staff. Consent to treatment is explained; what to do if you need an interpreter, how to complain and confidentiality are also dealt with.

Generally, the booklets give an overview and more detailed local information would need to be supplied, for example about visiting hours on a ward, interpreting arrangements available.

The booklets are simply written, well laid out and easy to follow. Each page has some multiracial illustrations which make it visually more interesting. An English version is available for English-speaking staff so that they are aware of what information people have. The English version is also suitable for English-speaking patients. It is recommended that people receive the booklet before they come into hospital and that the booklets should be held in appropriate places such as the admissions departments and GPs' surgeries. Bloomsbury Patient Advocacy Service were consultants in the development of this pack. A companion booklet for staff is also available *Caring for everyone: ensuring standards of care for black and ethnic minority patients*.

Computers and Asian languages: a guide for community organisations on computing in the languages of the Indian sub-continent

FORMAT: 68-page manual

LANGUAGE: English with guide to programs in Bengali, Gujarati, Hindi, Punjabi, Tamil and Urdu

TARGET AUDIENCE: Community workers, teachers, lecturers

PRICE: £10.00 inc. (individuals and community groups), £20.00 (institutions and local authorities)

PRODUCER: Oldham Resource and Information Centre, 1991

DISTRIBUTOR: Oldham Resource and Information Centre

This manual is the result of research into wordprocessing and desktop programs in the languages of the Indian sub-continent. The guide aims to enable groups and community organisations with limited funding to make informed choices about the most suitable programs for their needs. The research project was funded by the British Library Research and Development Department.

Twenty-six programs are listed with information about distribution, cost, computer and printer compatibility, type of program and facilities, scripts available. Samples of scripts have been included for most programs. Information is also provided about difficulties in producing satisfactory scripts for some languages such as Urdu. There are suggestions about alternative ways of producing scripts and a useful glossary of languages and scripts.

This guide will be useful to those considering producing written material in any of the languages of the Indian sub-continent. The information about the programs is concise and practical. It is also easily understood by those who are not computer experts, but want to make use of new technology. Schools, community groups and any organisation which needs/wishes to produce material in these languages will find the manual helpful.

Context cards

FORMAT: Pack; with 10 × A5 cards (5 sets) and 1 page of notes

LANGUAGE: English

TARGET AUDIENCE: Teachers, lecturers, trainers

PRICE: £8.00 (5 sets)

PRODUCER: Leicestershire Education Committee, Centre for Multicultural Education, 1993

DISTRIBUTOR: Leicestershire Education Committee

This series of training materials is for use in INSET training about multicultural and anti-racist education.

The five sets of cards are designed to be used by groups of four to six, with the assistance of a facilitator or trainer. The cards aim to enable participants to examine their theoretical understanding of anti-racism within a practical and realistic setting. Each card poses a dilemma for the group to consider and, if possible, to determine a response. The dilemmas have been selected from real situations and relate to the whole school, i.e. parents, governors, and non-teaching staff as well as pupils and teachers. Each pack contains enough cards for 2–3 hours' discussion. There are some notes for facilitators on how to use the cards.

This pack offers a way of examining how teaching staff can put anti-racism and multiculturalism into practice. It provides an opportunity to discuss the difficulties staff may experience in developing and adhering to such policies as well as a chance to share strategies for successful implementation. The pack has been trialled successfully with groups of education staff from a variety of backgrounds.

Copyart

FORMAT: Pack, illustrations

LANGUAGE: No text

TARGET AUDIENCE: Teachers, lecturers, youth workers, community workers

PRICE: £29.95 + £2.00 p&p

PRODUCER: ILEA Learning Resources Branch, 1987

DISTRIBUTOR: AMS Educational

This is a collection of photocopiable illustrations which can be used by anyone involved in preparing materials for use in education and in the wider community. It was produced by a large group of educationalists working within the Inner London Education Authority.

The illustrations are black-and-white line drawings on A4 stiff card and held in a ring binder. Each illustration is provided in five sizes and there is also a series of borders and outlines etc. The multiracial drawings depict men, women and children of all ages engaged in a wide range of traditional and non-traditional activities and in a variety of situations. The illustrations seek to reflect people as realistically as possible, so for example people wear glasses, portray a range of emotions, it includes people with disabilities, people of different sizes and shapes, etc. The pack was designed to provide images which redress imbalances in much imagery available and shows the full range of people who make up society. This is a flexible and practical resource which will enhance the production of materials such as leaflets or posters.

Counselling and sexuality

FORMAT: Videos × 4; with 140-page manual

LANGUAGE: English

TARGET AUDIENCE: Trainers, health professionals, primary healthcare teams

PRICE: £49.95 inc. each; £160 inc. set

PRODUCER: Hygia Communications for International Planned Parenthood Federation, 1992

DISTRIBUTOR: Hygia Communications

This training resource is for health professionals and others working in family planning settings who wish to develop counselling skills and address a broader range of issues to do with relationships and sexuality. The resource was funded by the Ford Foundation.

The video dramas are set in a family planning centre and follow a trainee counsellor observing counselling in action. The resource provides an introduction to counselling skills and issues to do with the provision of counselling. It is recommended for those who are new to counselling.

In the videos the counsellor is a trained professional, but all the others are actors, reflecting a multiracial community. The videos were unscripted – the actors were given a role and a problem situation and were then allowed to improvise. The situations and problems covered are common difficulties which people face all over the world and which are likely to arise in family planning settings. The first video *You're talking to me now*, is a compilation of selected sequences from the other three videos.

In the video *Are you good enough for you?* A female counsellor sees a young woman for premarital counselling. She is 17 years old and soon to be married to a partner chosen by her family and whom she has not met. The young woman finds the counselling session difficult as she is unused to being asked her opinion. The counsellor offers her the opportunity to participate in a group with other young women in a similar situation. The group session focuses on self-esteem with the counsellor skilfully enabling discussion about their anxieties. These include worries about not being accepted by their partners' family, fear about the wedding night and differing views about contraception. The video can be used to raise a number of issues such as working with groups, counselling people unused to having control over their lives and the importance of acknowledging and respecting societal and cultural values. The counsellor and the young women are from Asian communities.

The video *I've got gonorrhoea?* features a female counsellor telling a young mother who came for a routine appointment that she has got gonorrhoea. She has been infected by her husband and the counsellor subsequently sees them together. The counsellor demonstrates a variety of counselling skills and techniques including breaking bad news and dealing with anger and distress. Many complex issues about relationships and sexuality are raised such as the effect of the birth of a child on a couple's relationship and the importance of communication between partners. The counsellor and the couple are African-Caribbean.

The video *Let's go back a little* is about a middle-aged married couple who are experiencing relationship and sexual difficulties. This is picked up when the man objected to the woman being fitted with a coil and insisted that she should have it removed. They see a female doctor together. The man then sees the doctor alone. This is followed up by a joint counselling session several months later. Initially the man refuses to acknowledge or discuss their difficulties. The video raises a number of issues such as violence in relationships, the difficulty of discussing sexual problems and the denial of the existence of problems. The counsellor demonstrates skills and techniques which enable the man to talk about his feelings and behaviour. The counsellor and the couple are from Middle Eastern communities.

The accompanying training guide is in six parts. Part 1 is for managers and policymakers and explores the development and support of a counselling service in a family planning setting. Part 2 consists of training activities to enable people to examine their own feelings and beliefs about sexuality. Part 3 is a series of activities for the development of counselling skills including models and techniques demonstrated in the *You're talking to me now* video. Part 4 is a scene-by-scene synopsis of the video and contains activities to explore issues raised about counselling. Part 5 provides guidance about counselling people with sexual problems using the PLISSET model. Part 6 provides activities to examine counselling skills in more depth, referring to the process and content of the other three videos.

This resource provides enough material for either a complete course or several selected training sessions on counselling. Activities are discussion based and there are opportunities for role playing and practising counselling techniques. The videos can also be used to raise awareness and encourage debate about the need for and value of counselling in family planning and other settings. The resource, which is designed for group settings, requires a skilled counsellor and facilitator.

Crisis card

FORMAT: Pack

LANGUAGE: Bengali, English, Urdu

TARGET AUDIENCE: Mental health teams, health professionals, primary healthcare teams, general public

PRICE: Enquire for details

PRODUCER: International Self Advocacy Alliance, 1991

DISTRIBUTOR: Survivor Speakout

Crisis card is an information card for those experiencing mental health difficulties. Crisis cards are for people who may have a mental health emergency and be unable to explain their wishes. It guides professionals as to what would be useful to the bearer

The cards carry personal information completed by the carrier. They were produced by the International Self Advocacy Alliance funded jointly by Rochdale Social Services and Rochdale Health Authority.

Each card includes the person's name and address, a nominee who can be contacted in an emergency, any specific requests the person wishes to make and any actions they wish to be taken. The card could easily be kept in a wallet, pocket, purse, etc. It is hoped that if a person is unable to speak for themselves, mental health professionals (and others such as the police) will take notice of what it says and, most importantly, contact the nominee. The accompanying instruction sheet notes the card is not legally binding but suggests that it may carry some weight. It stresses that the nominee should give their consent and suggests a second person should also be nominated in case the first person cannot be contacted.

People who at times are unable to speak for themselves may find this card reassuring and so may their families and friends. It is a way health professionals can be informed of a person's wishes. This assists communication between patients and health professionals. Some people may need help with completing it as they may not be clear about what they can and cannot request.

Crosstalk at work: cross-cultural communication in the workplace

FORMAT: 2 videos, 28 mins and 20 mins; with 94-page training notes and 7-page briefing notes

LANGUAGE: English

TARGET AUDIENCE: Trainers

PRICE: £202.00 + VAT

PRODUCER: BBC Training Videos, 1991

DISTRIBUTOR: BBC for Business

This training resource is for staff in industry and public sector services who are concerned with a wide range of human resource functions and/or the implementation of equal opportunities in recruitment and promotion. It aims to raise awareness of how different ways of communicating can lead to discrimination and seeks to enable trainees to devise ways of ensuring this is minimised. It was produced as part of the BBC's Continuing Education Mosaic Project which addresses issues of cross-cultural communication.

The first video, *Performance appraisal across cultures*, was filmed in the USA and features real interactions between white and East Asian people in a management setting. The second video, *Recruitment and training across cultures*, was filmed in the UK and features genuine interviews for jobs with London Transport, a recreated interview for a librarian post and an Asian interview panel interviewing three candidates (one white male, one African-Caribbean female and one Asian male) for a youthwork post. Both videos explore how people of varying cultural origins may communicate differently, with many 'hidden' assumptions operating. Both videos end with a recap of good practice points and have 'pause points' to enable discussion of each sequence.

The training notes have a comprehensive background section which identifies key issues operating in cross-cultural communication. There are sets of exercises to be used with each video. These are divided into essential and recommended exercises so that trainers can select according to time available and training objectives. Exercises relate directly to individual sequences from each video. The discussion-based exercises aim to raise awareness of the different assumptions which may operate in cross-cultural communication, to examine what is happening 'between the lines' in communication and to develop practical action guidelines.

Additional information for the trainer expands issues raised in the video and there are also comments about issues which may arise in the course of training. The notes are thorough but are not easy to use (e.g. several exercises on a page can make it difficult to follow). This is a training package which can be used by experienced trainers or those who are new to this area. There is enough material to examine issues in detail or select key issues for shorter training. Equality of opportunity is presented as not only fair, but also contributing to good business. The videos enable participants to approach the issue theoretically and practically and to gain a sense of what it feels like to be on the receiving end of 'crosstalk'.

A cry for change: an Asian perspective on developing quality mental health care

FORMAT: 106-page manual

LANGUAGE: English

TARGET AUDIENCE: Health professionals, primary healthcare teams, mental health teams, commissioners

PRICE: £7.50

PUBLISHER: Confederation of Indian Organisations, 1991

DISTRIBUTOR: Confederation of Indian Organisations

This manual is for anyone working in the field of mental health, whether as a practitioner or manager, and is relevant to both the statutory and voluntary sectors. Focusing specifically on the mental health of people from Asian communities, it aims to provide guidance and practical information on developing quality services to meet mental health needs, and suggests ways of ensuring good practice. It was funded by the Department of Health.

The manual draws on a survey of the mental health needs of Asian communities and interviews with mental health professionals within voluntary organisations. It also uses information from areas with sizeable Asian populations about issues and experiences of Asian communities and service provision. Of the nine chapters, four are described as 'core' and are recommended by the author to be read by all. Subsequent chapters are of relevance to particular professions (e.g. one chapter focuses on transcultural therapy). The core chapters highlight key issues and concepts, present research findings, examine the relevance of Western medical models and challenge stereotypes which can affect service delivery.

Reference sections are thorough with suggestions for further reading.

This manual presents a starting point from which mental health professionals and services can examine their practice and assess how well they are meeting the mental health needs of Asian communities. Trainers will find it a useful text particularly in challenging stereotypes and assumptions and bringing the debate about health care needs of different communities into the mainstream.

Curriculum audit tool for course administrators: to help promote equal opportunities in nursing for people from black and minority ethnic groups

FORMAT: 24-page manual

LANGUAGE: English

TARGET AUDIENCE: Health professionals, teachers, lecturers

PRICE: Free

PRODUCER: Royal College of Nursing, 1993

DISTRIBUTOR: Royal College of Nursing

This resource aims to promote equal opportunities in nursing education. It seeks to offer a means of auditing nursing courses and identifying good practice. It was developed by the Royal College of Nursing Education and Training Policy Committee working with the Race and Ethnicity Sub-committee. It is the first in a new RCN series Equal Opportunities in Action. The Commission for Racial Equality, Department of Health and the King's Fund contributed to the development of this resource.

Nine elements of courses are examined including selection and recruitment of course members, selecting and evaluating course teachers and course content. There is a standard setting statement for each element followed by suggested indicators of performance against which different aspects of courses can be measured. An action plan provides an opportunity to record good practices already achieved, practices which need to be reviewed and good practices which need to be initiated. A selected bibliography is included. This is a practical resource which will enable those involved in nurse training to examine their practice in a systematic way.

Cystic fibrosis: diagnosis and adolescence

FORMAT: Multimedia; with 2 cassettes, 3 transcripts

LANGUAGE: Cassettes in Gujarati and Urdu with English transcripts

TARGET AUDIENCE: Health professionals, social workers, parents

PRICE: Free

PRODUCER: Cystic Fibrosis Research Trust, 1993

DISTRIBUTOR: Cystic Fibrosis Research Trust

These audio cassettes are primarily for parents of children with cystic fibrosis but will also be of interest to other family members and carers. One cassette covers diagnosis and issues for babies and children, the other cassette covers adolescence and issues parents may face as their children approach adulthood. They were produced by the Cystic Fibrosis Trust with funding from BBC Children in Need and the Department of Health.

The cassettes consists of a discussion between

a doctor, facilitator and parents. The diagnosis cassette covers basic information about cystic fibrosis and answers common questions about life expectancy, range of severity, treatment, diet, immunisation, coping with school, support groups and financial help. The discussion tackles not only factual information but also suggestions for dealing with difficulties such as children refusing to eat. Emotions and feelings are also addressed such as relationships with siblings and fitting in at school.

The adolescence cassette seeks to cover the worries parents may have as their child grows up. Young people's non-compliance with treatment is discussed (diet, medication and physiotherapy), looking at it from the young person's point of view and encouraging parents to be honest and supportive with the young person. It stresses that many children with cystic fibrosis are now reaching adulthood and parents have at some point to step back so that the young person can take on the responsibility for his or her treatment.

These cassettes are very informative but also acknowledge the fears and worries parents have. They encourage parents to ask questions of professionals if they do not understand something or need more information. The value of support groups is mentioned and parents are encouraged to make contact. The tapes are based on interviews with parents of children with cystic fibrosis and doctors who work with families from Asian communities.

Day to remember: the wedding

FORMAT: Video, 15 mins; with 18-page tutors' booklet and 26-page student booklet

LANGUAGE: Hindustani dialogue with Bengali, English, Gujarati, Hindi, Punjabi or Urdu voice-over commentaries

TARGET AUDIENCE: General public, teachers, lecturers

PRICE: £21.95 inc.

PRODUCER: Birmingham City Engineers Road Safety Unit, 1988

DISTRIBUTOR: Birmingham Road Safety Unit

This video is for Asian communities and aims to raise awareness of road safety issues. The booklet is for students studying English as a second language and expands on the themes of the video. They are designed to be used together, but the video can be used alone. The booklets were produced with the help of an English as a second language tutor.

The video takes the form of drama following a family preparing to attend a wedding. The dialogue is in Hindustani with a voice-over. Scenes will be familiar to many families, last-minute preparations, children getting in the way and so on. The road safety issues tackled are safe maintenance of vehicles, drinking and driving, children running into the road, vehicle overcrowding, children in cars, distractions while driving and vulnerability of the elderly. The family reaches the wedding safely having met all of these hazards on the way. Cartoons reinforce safety messages throughout the video. It is suitable for group settings or viewing at home. However, if viewed with a road safety officer or community worker, safety advice could be expanded.

The accompanying booklets aim to highlight problems faced by users, develop students' vocabulary and understanding of road safety information, guide discussions and provide worksheets about road safety situations. The student booklet has 24 worksheets which can be used as a complete course or selected according to students' interest, time available, etc. The majority of the sheets are designed to be used in conjunction with the video. The tutor's booklet contains guidance for discussion with points to emphasise. It provides a course which almost everyone would find useful and practical. The video and booklets were produced in consultation with local Asian communities. The video was made by an Asian film production company.

Death with dignity: meeting the spiritual needs of patients in a multicultural society

PACK: Volume 1: 15-page booklet; volume 2: 18-page booklet

LANGUAGE: English

TARGET AUDIENCE: Health professionals, social workers, primary healthcare teams

PRICE: £9.95 inc.

PUBLISHER: Nursing Times, Macmillan Magazines, 1991

DISTRIBUTOR: Macmillan Magazines

These booklets explain briefly the main beliefs and practices of some religions and cultures, with reference to preferred practices concerning death and dying. The first booklet was originally produced as a series of articles in *Nursing Times*, which came to be written because a Jewish patient died unexpectedly with no family present, and staff were unsure what should be done. The second booklet addresses the diversity of religion within the Christian tradition. The author is a consultant in public health medicine. All of the major religions are described with main beliefs outlined and information about dietary preferences, care of the dying, post mortems and organ transplants, and procedures at death and funerals. Each chapter includes space for local information to be added such as phone numbers of local places of worship, preferred funeral directors, and burial grounds. The author stresses that within all religions there will be a wide spectrum of belief and observance, so staff must always consult the patient and family members if possible. The booklets are practical, well laid out and concise with a short bibliography at the end of each chapter. Information is also provided about arranging funerals abroad. The booklets will enable staff to deal more confidently and sensitively with patients and are useful as references for staff and support material for training.

Dental health video

FORMAT: Video, 15 mins; with 4-page transcript

LANGUAGE: Gujarati, Urdu

TARGET AUDIENCE: Parents

PRICE: £25.00

PRODUCER: Dewsbury Health Authority, 1988

DISTRIBUTOR: Dewsbury Health Authority

This video is for parents from Gujarati- and Urdu-speaking communities and aims to inform about dental health care for children. It was developed by linkworkers and produced by Yorkshire Arts Video for Dewsbury Community Dental Department and Dewsbury Community Health Council.

The video uses a dramatised sequence to demonstrate how to care for children's and babies' teeth. It follows a mother, her school-age child and baby through their daily routine. Advice is given about sugar-free foods, suitable drinks for babies, how to brush teeth correctly and helping children to do so, restricting sweets to once a day after meals. We also see them visit the dentist for a check-up (including the baby). At the end of the day grandmother visits with a gift of sweets which the parents thank her for and suggest the children may have after dinner. A traditional diet is reflected throughout. The main points are reiterated at the end. The video is suitable for viewing in group settings or for individual family viewing at home. It is short, practical and clear. Many families will find the video a helpful reminder of how to care for children's teeth.

Depression in ethnic minorities

FORMAT: Video, 17 mins; with leaflet

LANGUAGE: English

TARGET AUDIENCE: Health professionals, mental health teams, primary healthcare teams

PRICE: £35.50 inc.

PRODUCER: N Films for NAFSIYAT, 1991

DISTRIBUTOR: CFL Vision

This video aims to raise awareness among people from black and minority ethnic groups about depression and mental health services. It was made by NAFSIYAT (which means mind, body and soul), an intercultural therapy centre in London, and was funded by the Department of Health.

The video and accompanying leaflet describe the symptoms of depression. An Asian man, a Chinese man and a African-Carribean woman talk about how they have experienced depression (mainly as a reaction to life events such as bereavement). A panel of mental health professionals talk about how depression may affect people from ethnic minority communities. They identify social and economic factors and the effects of racism as contributory factors. A GP, community psychiatric nurse and psychotherapist briefly explain how they may be able to help. People are encouraged to talk about their problems with someone they trust and to see their GP if they need further help.

It is a short video and does not deal in detail with treatments and help available. It may be useful to talk about this further after the video, and to provide information about local counselling agencies and sources of help including if counsellors are available who speak the same language, are the same sex or have experience of counselling someone from a background other than their own. Viewed in a group setting this video could provide a starting point for discussion of how depression affects people and how to cope with it. It is of interest to health professionals as it touches upon how racism and disadvantage can contribute to depression and stresses the need to be aware of, and sensitive to, people's race, religion and culture.

Diet for the Asian diabetic

FORMAT: Video, 10 mins

LANGUAGE: English, Gujarati, Hindi

TARGET AUDIENCE: General public, primary healthcare teams, health professionals

PRICE: £25.00

PRODUCER: Leicestershire Health Authority, Health Education Video Unit, 1988

DISTRIBUTOR: Leicestershire HA Video Unit

This video is for people from Asian communities with diabetes. It aims to inform people about how to achieve a healthier diet which will contribute to more effective control of the illness. It was produced by Leicestershire Health Authority Health Education Video Unit.

The video uses a voice-over. Diabetes and the connection with diet are explained with the aid of animated graphics and general advice is given about diet for people with diabetes. People are recommended to avoid sugar and sugary foods, eat less fat, eat more foods with fibre and eat regular meals containing starch.

Suggested foods are clearly shown, including a selection of brand-named products. The need for a balanced diet is stressed and a traditional diet is reflected. The need for people who are using insulin to have small snacks between meals is noted.

The video is suitable for use with groups or individuals and would be most useful if viewed with a health professional so that questions could be answered and information expanded. The video is short but contains a lot of information. It may be helpful to pause it and view it in sections so that people have time to absorb the information and comment. The video recommends people to discuss diet further with their doctor and dietitian.

Don't know where to turn

FORMAT: Video, 20 mins; with leaflet

LANGUAGE: Bengali, Cantonese, English, Hindustani, Punjabi, Somali, Turkish, Vietnamese

TARGET AUDIENCE: Mental health teams, primary healthcare teams, general public

PRICE: £37.25 inc.

PRODUCER: N Films for Maudsley Hospital Outreach Support and Treatment Team, 1992

DISTRIBUTOR: N Films

This video aims to inform people about the kinds of help and treatment which are available for a range of mental health and emotional problems. It was funded by the Department of Health.

Dramatised scenes about common mental health and emotional problems are followed by a studio discussion by mental health professionals. They include community psychiatric nurses, a psychiatrist, GP, social worker and community worker. Each comments on the kind of help they could offer to each problem. A variety of situations are acted out including depression, obsessive behaviour, destructive behaviour, an interview between a psychiatrist and patient. Other sources of help in the community are demonstrated, including arranging for an interpreter or linkworker to talk to someone in their language. Although the studio discussion presents an ideal situation, it does explain the kind of help people can expect with mental health problems. Viewers will need to be informed about what help exists in their local area.

This video could be viewed in group settings or

by individuals/families at home. It may reassure those experiencing emotional problems that it is possible to get help. The video does not deal with more severe mental health problems or with provisions under the Mental Health Act. The accompanying leaflet reinforces the main points of the video.

Double discrimination: issues and services for people with learning difficulties from black and ethnic minority communities

FORMAT: 212-page manual

LANGUAGE: English

TARGET AUDIENCE: Service providers

PRICE: £11.95

PRODUCER: King's Fund Centre and Commission for Racial Equality, 1990

DISTRIBUTOR: Bournemouth English Book Centre

This manual aims to provide practical suggestions for improving services for people with learning difficulties from black and minority ethnic groups. It was funded by the King's Fund Centre and the Commission for Racial Equality and will be of interest to anyone involved in providing day-to-day care or developing policy in statutory or voluntary services. The manual brings together the limited work done so far in this field and reports on a national survey of services and an in-depth study of services in two areas of the country.

Well laid out, and using clear and direct language, it is accessible to parents and carers as well as managers of services. It systematically examines services provided to people with learning difficulties from birth through to older life. It also examines other issues which can cut across all services. These include the main principles and assumptions underlying service provision, the experiences of staff from black and minority ethnic groups and suggestions for developing anti-racist services. Examples of services which fail to meet needs are described through personal stories and interview extracts, mainly from parents and carers and some from service providers. 'Ideas in practice' consists of descriptions of services which are meeting the needs of people with learning difficulties from black and minority ethnic groups.

This book is a starting point for those providing services for people with learning difficulties from black and minority ethnic groups as it clearly identifies issues which need consideration. Each chapter contains an up-to-date reference section with suggestions for further reading, resources and organisations. Wry cartoons are also sprinkled throughout the book. The 'double discrimination' experienced by people with learning difficulties and their families and carers is clearly explained, leaving service providers in no doubt that change is necessary and possible. Those providing training for staff will find this a useful text.

Eating in pregnancy

FORMAT: Video, 25 mins

LANGUAGE: Bengali, English, Gujarati, Hindi/Urdu, Punjabi

TARGET AUDIENCE: Women, parents

PRICE: £29.00 inc.

PRODUCER: N Films for Asian Mother and Baby Campaign, 1986

DISTRIBUTOR: CFL Vision

This video for Asian communities aims to inform women and their families about the importance of a healthy diet during and after pregnancy. It was produced for the Department of Health and Save the Children as part of the Asian Mother and Baby Campaign.

Using a drama, the video follows a young couple through preconception care to after the birth of the baby. They are given advice by a number of health professionals including the family planning doctor, GP, dietitian in parentcraft classes, midwife and health visitor. The mother-in-law provides advice about nausea in early pregnancy. We see them shopping and eating together demonstrating a healthy diet. A traditional Asian diet is reflected throughout. The woman decides to breastfeed the baby and is supported in this by her husband and mother-in-law. The husband decides to give up smoking when the baby is born.

This is a useful video to trigger discussion about what is a healthy diet and will be of interest to women, their partners and family. In order to make most use of the information it would be helpful for people to see it in early pregnancy and presenters will need to ensure up-to-date information is provided about eggs and soft cheese as advice about this has changed since the video was made.

Eating well: feeling good

FORMAT: Video, 15 mins

LANGUAGE: Somali

TARGET AUDIENCE: General public, refugees, health professionals, community workers

PRICE: £30.00 inc.

PRODUCER: East London and the City Health Promotion Service, 1994

DISTRIBUTOR: East London & City HPS

This video for Somali communities aims to inform about healthy eating and enable people to make healthy, informed choices about their diet. It was produced by the Video Production Unit of East London and the City Health Promotion Service. The video was

made in conjunction with City and East London Family Health Services, the London Black Women's Health Action Project, and the Royal London Hospital Trust.

The video uses a voice-over and we are told a healthy diet can be enjoyable, inexpensive and contribute to overall health. Six steps to a healthy diet are identified – eat a variety of foods, eat more fibre, eat less fat, eat less sugar, drink plenty of fluid and eat less salt. The six steps are explored in more detail with foods clearly shown and food preparation methods demonstrated. A variety of common brand-named products are shown. It is stressed that a traditional Somali diet can be very healthy and this is reflected throughout. The main points are repeated at the end of the video.

The video has been designed for use in group settings with a facilitator or health professional who can expand the information and raise other issues as appropriate. It could also be used with individuals to trigger discussion about healthy eating. The video was produced with the involvement of Somali communities and health professionals in East London.

Eat well to protect your heart

FORMAT: 12-page booklet

LANGUAGE: English/Gujarati, English/Urdu

TARGET AUDIENCE: General public

PRICE: 90p

PRODUCER: Bolton Centre for Health Promotion, 1994

DISTRIBUTOR: Bolton Centre for Health Promotion

This booklet is for Gujarati-speaking communities and aims to inform about how a healthy diet can help to prevent heart disease. It was produced by the Bolton Centre for Health Promotion with the involvement of the Department of Nutrition and Dietetics of

Bolton NHS Trust and groups from the community.

The booklet has a colourful cover with photographs of food being prepared and eaten. Inside the information is provided bilingually in Gujarati and English with some line drawings. The booklet addresses heart disease and the contribution diet can make to its prevention – food groups to choose from for a balanced diet, foods to eat less of, ideas for meals in a day, tips about using oil, and eating more fibre, fruit and vegetables. It ends with three recipes to try, two of which are vegetarian. Throughout, a traditional diet is reflected and it is stressed that traditional foods can be very healthy.

The booklet is well laid out and the information is presented clearly. It is a resource which can stand alone and can easily be referred to at home. It could also be used in group settings, especially where there is an opportunity to try preparing and cooking meals and demonstrating the advice given. Groups from community organisations in Bradford contributed to the development of this resource.

Eczema ... how you can help your child

FORMAT: Video, 15 mins

LANGUAGE: Bengali with English subtitles

TARGET AUDIENCE: Parents, health professionals

PRICE: £15.00

PRODUCER: Tower Hamlets Health Promotion Service, 1988

DISTRIBUTOR: East London & City HPS

This video for Bengali communities aims to inform parents about eczema and how to deal with the condition. It was sponsored by the National Eczema Society.

The video begins with the introduction of a young boy, Saiful, who has eczema which we are told is a common condition in the UK and which most children grow out of. The video follows Saiful and his mother as she demonstrates how to care for him. Advice is given about bathing, oils/creams which may help, suitable clothing and bedding, appropriate detergents to use and reducing dust in the home. The video notes that some of these measures can be expensive and suggests contacting the Citizens Advice Bureau to ensure all applicable benefits are being received. Diet is mentioned as a possible contributory factor and consultation with the doctor advised about this.

This practical video may help to trigger discussion with parents about how to manage children's eczema. Suitable for home or group viewing, it would be enhanced by the presence of a health professional to answer questions and provide further information if necessary. Leaflets available from the National Eczema Society are shown and it may be helpful to have these to hand. This video was piloted by a group of Bengali families who found it useful.

Education is the key

FORMAT: Video, 26 mins; with 10-page booklet

LANGUAGE: English

TARGET AUDIENCE: Teachers, lecturers

PRICE: £40.78 inc.

PRODUCER: Berkshire Education Department Resources Unit, 1989

DISTRIBUTOR: Dramatic Distribution

This video is for teachers and educationists. It aims to inform about the aspirations, concerns and responses of black teachers and parents to the British educational system. The video focuses on a supplementary school for African-Caribbean children and young people in Slough. It was produced by the Education for Racial Equality Video Project of Berkshire Education Department Resources Unit.

The video documents in detail the work of the supplementary school. There is a description of how and why the school was founded and the school is seen in action. Teachers explain the aims of the school and stress that the students (of all ages) are being helped to improve their performance in mainstream schools. They challenge the view that supplementary schools are for slow-learners, pointing out high levels of achievement by students of all abilities. Parents voice their concerns about racism in mainstream education, high suspension rates, stereotyping and low academic expectations of students from their teachers. The video ends with comments from the students themselves.

The video can be used in group settings to trigger discussion on how teachers and the education system respond to African-Caribbean children and young people. The video and accompanying booklet raise many issues. For example – why are so many African-Caribbean students underachieving in mainstream schools and what is being done to combat racism in the school, amongst teachers and in the curriculum. The booklet also contains discussion points linked to the video. The resource will also be useful to those considering setting up a supplementary school.

Emergency multilingual phrasebook

FORMAT: 63-page pack

LANGUAGE: Contains list of essential questions in 28 languages with English translations – Amharic, Arabic, Bengali, Chinese, Czech, Farsi, French, German, Greek, Gujarati, Hindi, Hungarian, Italian, Japanese, Korean, Kurdish, Polish, Portuguese, Punjabi, Romanian, Russian, Somali, Spanish, Swahili, Tamil, Turkish, Urdu, Vietnamese.

TARGET AUDIENCE: Health professionals, primary healthcare teams

PRICE: £8.50 inc.

PRODUCER: British Red Cross, 1991

DISTRIBUTOR: British Red Cross

This phrase book is for use in medical emergencies and lists 43 essential questions and phrases (such as 'Have you any pain? Point where') in 28 languages. The aim is to enable basic communication between an English-speaking practitioner and non-English-speaking patient. The book is arranged so that the English and other language version of the question can be viewed simultaneously. Questions are phrased so that they can be answered by pointing or by a Yes and No type response.

The notes about how to use the book stress that the patient must be literate in the language chosen and advises that this may not always be immediately clear in an emergency situation. Practitioners are advised to use a trained and experienced interpreter if possible, but in an emergency the phrasebook may help until an interpreter can be found. A checklist is included which may help services to be prepared for finding an interpreter at short notice. Basic guidelines are also given about using an untrained interpreter (such as a relative). The book was prepared in collaboration with a large number of health professionals and has been piloted by staff at Tower Hamlets Health Authority.

Accident and emergency departments may find this book useful.

Entitled to be healthy: health visiting and school nursing in a multiracial society

FORMAT: 56-page pack, illustrations, black-and-white

LANGUAGE: English

TARGET AUDIENCE: Primary healthcare teams, health professionals

PRICE: £4.95 + 50p p&p non-members, £3.95 + 50p p&p members

PRODUCER: Health Visitors Association, 1989

DISTRIBUTOR: Health Visitors Association

This booklet aims to raise awareness among health visitors and school nurses of the needs of people from black and minority ethnic groups and makes recommendations for changes in practice. It was produced by the Health Visitors Association and is the report of the Racial Issues Working Party which was set up to look at racism in health visiting and school nursing.

The booklet covers a number of issues starting with a description of how racism can affect every aspect of a person's life. The chapter on the health needs of black people notes how little research exists about this and, after misguided approaches in the past, the need to work with communities is stressed. Other chapters examine: improving communication (covers linkworkers and interpreting), professional practice in a multiracial society, and education and training of health visitors and school nurses. Within each chapter points are made concisely, often illustrated with examples.

Recommendations are made at the end of each chapter and these are listed together at the end. Many of the recommendations target training of health professionals.

Although this booklet will be of interest to individual health professionals it will also be helpful to commissioners and purchasers of services. It is particularly relevant to those involved in training health visitors and school nurses.

An environment of dignity

FORMAT: Video, 32 mins

LANGUAGE: English

TARGET AUDIENCE: Primary healthcare teams, social workers, service providers, older people

PRICE: £30.00

PRODUCER: Retake Film and Video for Race Relations Committee, Camden Council, 1985

DISTRIBUTOR: Albany Video

This video aims to raise awareness of the needs of older people from black and minority ethnic groups. Although of most relevance to service providers it is also of interest to general audiences.

The needs of older people are identified through the medium of interviews with older people from a range of communities and with professionals from statutory and voluntary organisations. The isolation and loneliness people experience is starkly shown as is fear from racial harassment, poverty and lack of information about entitlements. The need for information (in community languages if necessary) and places to meet and socialise with other people from the same community is stressed. There are some examples of services which meet needs such as an African-Caribbean elders group and a mixed housing scheme which includes older Chinese people. The notion that black and minority ethnic groups have extended families who can always care for older people is challenged.

A political stance is taken about some of the issues as older people state their points of view. This video may be useful trigger material for service providers beginning to explore how to meet the needs of black and minority ethnic older people. It ends by stating that not to recognise cultural differences is to discriminate.

Equal chances: eliminating discrimination and ensuring equality in playgroups

FORMAT: 43-page manual

LANGUAGE: English

TARGET AUDIENCE: Community groups

PRICE: £7.75

PRODUCER: PPA National Centre, 1991

DISTRIBUTOR: Pre-School Playgroups Association

This manual, for those involved in pre-school playgroups, aims to assist groups to put equal opportunities policies into practice. It was written by a group of volunteers and staff from the Pre-School Playgroups Association which has endorsed equal opportunities policy statements on anti-racism, anti-sexism and attitudes to disability.

The manual begins with a concise definition of terms used and of settings where a 'playgroup' may be operating. Each of the five chapters addresses a different topic (the children, their families, playgroup environment, adults working together and strategies for dealing with change), and gives concrete examples of how equal opportunities could be put into practice. The chapter on dealing with change may be particularly helpful as it suggests a practical way of dealing with everyday issues to do with equal opportunities and may help staff and managers to recognise such issues. The book is written in an accessible manner and has a down-to-earth approach, stating briefly why something is important and then outlining what can be done. The appendices list useful books, resources and addresses. The book is stronger on anti-racism and anti-sexism than attitudes to disability.

Although targeted at playgroups this book will be useful to staff and managers of any service for young children. The practical nature of its suggestions will appeal to many. It is probably of most use in organisations where some thought has already been given to equal opportunities and first steps are being taken. It could also be used as part of training sessions on ways of ensuring equal opportunity.

Equal opportunities at work: race

FORMAT: Pack; with video, 30 mins, 24-page manual and 92-page handbook

LANGUAGE: English

TARGET AUDIENCE: Trainers

PRICE: £50 inc.

PRODUCER: BBC Education, 1992

DISTRIBUTOR: BBC Educational Developments

This training resource pack is for use with managers, human resource and equal opportunities staff in industry and public sector services. The pack seeks to examine and inform about what needs to be done to implement equal opportunities in the workplace. It was produced as part of the BBC's Continuing Education Mosaic project, which addresses issues of equality in a multicultural society. The pack was developed with assistance from the Local Government Management Board.

The video consists of nine clearly delineated sequences. Two relate to a multicultural society generally ('Here to stay' and 'Consumer power'). The others relate directly to equal opportunities in the workplace, e.g. advertising and recruitment, monitoring, setting targets, contract compliance. The video features well-known successful companies in the UK explaining aspects of their equal opportunities practice and stressing that this has contributed to the success of the company. The sequences are short triggers and are designed to be used in structured training sessions. The trainers' manual provides a series of discussion exercises linked to the video sequences. The purpose of the training is to enable participants to examine equal opportunities policy and practice in their workplace.

The *Equal opportunities handbook* addresses race equality in employment and is for anyone who is responsible for or concerned with equal opportunities practice. The first part discusses the range of interpretations of equal opportunities and the arguments for implementing race equality in the workplace. A detailed examination of the implementation of equal opportunities follows, with case studies and examples of good practice. These include how to foster the development of equal opportunities once the initial goal of establishing policy and practice has been achieved. The appendices of part one include flow charts, examples of training plans and quick reference questions and answers. Part two is an annotated bibliography, prepared with the assistance of the Runnymede Trust, of further reading and research relating to the issue.

This is a flexible resource pack which can be used for a variety of functions, for example to select a particular issue for debate and action planning, to examine organisational practice, or to establish/overhaul equal opportunities practice. The pack does not cover the reasons for equal opportunity. It assumes this has already been recognised and is about the next step – how to establish equality effectively with regard to race in the workplace. Although many of the examples in the video relate to industry, the issues are just as applicable to the public sector.

Essential skills for race equality trainers

FORMAT: 134-page manual

LANGUAGE: English

TARGET AUDIENCE: Trainers

PRICE: £75.00 inc.

PRODUCER: National Institute of Adult Continuing Education, 1992

DISTRIBUTOR: NIACE

This manual targets two groups – black people working within education settings who wish to develop race equality training skills; and trainers (black and white) who wish to develop their race equality training skills and who may be working with a wide range of public or private organisations. The manual aims to assist the development of essential training skills for race equality trainers. It was produced by the National Institute of Adult Continuing Education.

The manual has been designed for use by an experienced trainer with a group who wish to develop their training skills and is appropriate for courses such as trainer training. Eight units cover a wide range of topics relevant to providing race equality training such as self-assessment, learning processes, delivery of training and evaluation. Each unit includes aims and some information about the topic, plus practical tasks which enable groups to explore the topic in more depth. The manual also raises issues and concerns which black trainers may face when undertaking race equality work and considers some strategies for dealing with them. The manual was developed as a result of black trainer training courses run by Replan, a national programme to promote good practice in post-16 education and training for unemployed adults. The authors are experienced race equality trainers.

The ethnic health factfile: a guide for health professionals who care for people from ethnic backgrounds

FORMAT: Manual

LANGUAGE: English

TARGET AUDIENCE: Health professionals, primary healthcare teams

PRICE: £12.50

PRODUCER: The Health and Ethnicity Programme, North West/North East Thames Regional Health Authorities, 1992

DISTRIBUTOR: The Health and Ethnicity Programme

The factfile has been written for health professionals who 'care for people from ethnic backgrounds'. It is intended to be used as a quick reference guide to the major facts relevant to health care for each ethnic group.

The file consists of an A5 looseleaf ring binder. The first section deals with religious practices and covers Buddhism, Hinduism, Islam and Judaism. There follows an alphabetical listing of over 27 ethnic groups. Brief information is provided on languages, naming systems, religions, customs and practices, diet and issues of particular interest. A London-based address list of useful contacts is given for each group. A blank page for notes is included with each listing to enable users to add additional information. The file covers those groups known to be living in the North East and North West Thames Regions and thus does not cover all ethnic minority groups in the UK.

Some commentators have questioned the accuracy of the information relating to particular groups and the very limited choice of religions (i.e. Christianity is omitted as are some other religions). There are some inconsistencies as to how groups are listed. For example, Ghanaians and Nigerians are covered in the Africans section, while groups such as Somalis, Eritreans and Ethiopians are listed separately.

Everybody's hair

FORMAT: 25-page pack

LANGUAGE: English

TARGET AUDIENCE: Under-5s, Key Stage 1 (5–8), Key Stage 2 (8–12)

PRICE: £5.50

PUBLISHER: A. & C. Black, 1988

DISTRIBUTOR: A. & C. Black

Using a multiracial group of children, the pack explores the different kinds of hair people have. It starts with a group listening to the story of Rapunzel, then making puppets about the story. This is followed by visits from parents to demonstrate hair care such as a head wrap, hair beading and Sikh ceremonial jewellery. Colour photographs of the children accompany the text which would need to be read to younger children. The text describes the photographs and includes comments from the children.

This is an attractive and contemporary book. Children could look at this alone, but it would be enhanced by reading it with an adult. Within nurseries and schools it could be used in hairdressing areas/projects, curriculum work about myself and others, dressing-up areas and the book corner/library.

Facing the challenge

FORMAT: Video, 30 mins

LANGUAGE: English

TARGET AUDIENCE: Health professionals, primary healthcare workers, social workers, service providers, older people

PRICE: £42.62

PRODUCER: Haringey Social Services Department, 1992

DISTRIBUTOR: Ceddo Film/Video

This video focuses on the research findings of a study commissioned by the Department of Health into the low uptake of services by African-Caribbean older people and gaps in services for them. It aims to raise awareness among service providers at all levels of the needs of African-Caribbean older people.

The research findings are illustrated with examples of service provision which are meeting the needs of African-Caribbean older people. A range of community care services are seen in action: community support services assisting people in their homes, African-Caribbean meals on wheels and lunch clubs, a day centre, sheltered housing schemes and residential homes. Throughout, users comment on the kind of services they want and what they value about services. Professionals from voluntary and statutory sectors comment on changes as services strive to meet needs. Needs identified by the research were time and space for social gatherings and the importance of religious services, preference for care staff to be of the same ethnic group if possible.

This video can be used to encourage debate about how well services meet the needs of African-Caribbean older people. Service users as well as providers will find it of interest, with examples of good practice such as health check sessions incorporated into a day centre. The video presents a view of what is possible, but for many older people the reality is likely to be very different.

A fearful silence

FORMAT: Video, 52 mins

LANGUAGE: English

TARGET AUDIENCE: General public

PRICE: £50.00 inc.

PRODUCER: Azad Productions for Channel 4, 1985

DISTRIBUTOR: Albany Video

This video was made for a general audience and is about domestic violence against women from Asian communities. It examines the cases of three women and what happened to them as a result of violence in the home.

The stories of three women are told in a documentary format. One woman was believed to have committed suicide but her friends and others have since questioned the circumstances of her death. One woman did not appear personally because she had received threats and one woman has been left disabled as a result of attempted murder by her husband. Throughout, the stories are told by friends, barristers, counsellors and workers from women's refuges. Women from a support group for Asian women who have experienced violence talk about their lives and the lack of help they feel they received from their families and the community. The documentary highlights how the legal system treats men and women differently, how police fail to take domestic violence in Asian communities seriously, and how inadequate translation services lead to injustice.

This is a disturbing film as women describe what has happened to them and their friends. However there are more optimistic notes too. Groups such as Southall Black Sisters describe how they can help and support women. They also explain strategies they have used to raise the issues within Asian communities. This video could be used in group settings to trigger discussion about domestic violence, and inform women of sources of support. It is quite long and may need to be viewed in short sections. Although made some years ago the issues are still relevant today.

Female genital mutilation: a counselling guide for professionals

FORMAT: 9-page booklet

LANGUAGE: English

TARGET AUDIENCE: Health professionals, primary healthcare teams, social workers, teachers, lecturers

PRICE: £3.35 inc.

PRODUCER: Foundation for Women's Health (FORWARD), 1993

DISTRIBUTOR: Foundation for Women's Health

This booklet is for professionals (in health, social services or education settings) who may find themselves counselling women and families about the practice of female genital mutilation. It was produced by FORWARD which is funded by the Department of Health.

The booklet identifies accepted counselling skills which professionals will need to use in dealing with the issue. In addition, other skills such as keeping an open mind about traditions and beliefs different from one's own are noted. The booklet specifically covers how to raise the subject with families, mothers, fathers, young women and within group settings. The issue of racism (which families may face and professionals may be accused of when working on this topic) is raised. A case study explores what happens to a young girl and tries to identify the complex fears and emotions she may have as a result. Reference is also made to support workers' needs when working on such a difficult issue. There is a short reading list.

This booklet will be helpful to those who have a counselling role and who work with communities where female genital mutilation is practised. Many will find it supportive, as it acknowledges the complex emotions which exist around this issue and provides some practical advice on how to discuss it.

Firewatch

FORMAT: Video, 7 mins

LANGUAGE: Bengali, Cantonese, English, Gujarati, Hindi/Urdu, Punjabi, sign language and subtitles

TARGET AUDIENCE: General public

PRICE: £40.00 + VAT

PRODUCER: Greater Manchester County Fire Service, 1990

DISTRIBUTOR: Greater Manchester County Fire Service

This video is targeted at multiracial communities and aims to raise awareness of how fires start in the home and what to do to prevent them.

The video identifies five common hazards in the home based on research into fires. These are smoking materials (i.e. cigarettes), children playing with matches, overheating of oil during cooking, portable heaters, and electrical appliances. Each hazard is demonstrated in a home setting and we see a fire beginning. Prevention is also demonstrated (i.e. matches placed out of child's reach, sockets not overloaded, etc.). There is a very clear demonstration of how to deal with a fire in a pan of oil. The script is simple and specific with important points reinforced by a brief written message appearing on the screen. The video is short and to the point, information is presented clearly and is practical. The use of smoke alarms is advocated but there is no explanation of what they are. Similarly dialling 999 is not shown in full and presenters should ensure that people do know how to do this.

This is useful trigger material and could be used with any adult group to discuss fire prevention. It is also suitable for viewing in reception areas as the information stands alone and is likely to be of interest to all sections of the community.

The flame of the soul

FORMAT: Video, 30 mins

LANGUAGE: English

TARGET AUDIENCE: Primary healthcare teams, social workers, health professionals, general public

PRICE: £28.00

PRODUCER: Ceddo Film Video Workshop, 1990

DISTRIBUTOR: Ceddo Film/Video

This video is relevant to all sections of the community but will especially interest people who have sickle cell trait or anaemia, their family, friends and community around them. It aims to inform and raise awareness about the physical and emotional effects of the sickle cell blood disorder.

Sickle cell is explored through interviews with several young people from London who speak powerfully about how sickle cell has affected them, and how the attitudes, ignorance and racism of others heighten the difficulties they face. There is a clear explanation of what causes sickle cell anaemia and whom it may affect, including discussion of the painful 'crises' which may occur. Screening is mentioned and support groups for people with sickle cell are shown in action. The video emphasises how much the young people have achieved – despite the seriousness of the illness they encourage others to do as much as they can and not give up. Images of paintings by a young artist who has sickle cell anaemia are used as a focus throughout the video to place the illness within a social context and this makes the video striking and memorable.

This video could be used in any setting and with any group. Health professionals may find it thought-provoking as it sharply pinpoints the emotional impact the illness may have. It is a valuable resource for education about racism too as many issues are highlighted such as seeing sickle cell as a 'black' problem rather than as a 'health' problem.

Food routes

FORMAT: Pack

LANGUAGE: English

TARGET AUDIENCE: Key Stage 3 (12–14), Key Stage 4 (14–16)

PRICE: £18.50 + £4.50 p&p

PRODUCER: Education Department, Royal County of Berkshire, 1989

DISTRIBUTOR: Berkshire Design and Technology Centre

This pack of recipes from three areas of the world aims to support the teaching of home economics, design and technology. The pack is divided into three sections, providing recipes from the Caribbean, the Indian sub-continent and the Mediterranean. Each section has a brief introduction covering the traditional cooking of the region, historical and cultural influences on food, and religious observances related to food and diet. Each section also has a brief bibliography, usually of cookery books.

The tried and tested recipes can be completed in a double lesson. They are printed on one side of a looseleaf folder on durable card. Each recipe is illustrated with a colour photograph of the prepared dish. The producers suggest that the pack can support work which encourages students to share, and to learn from the cultural diversity of modern society. The pack was developed by a working party which met as a result of a home economics multicultural in-service course.

Four mothers

FORMAT: Video, 37 mins

LANGUAGE: English

TARGET AUDIENCE: Parents, general public
Price:£40.00 + p&p + VAT

PRODUCER: Islington Under Three's Group, 1985

DISTRIBUTOR: Concord Video and Film Council

This video for a general audience explores the realities of being a mother through interviews with four married women. It was produced by Islington Under Three's Group and the Islington Bus Company with support from Islington and Hackney Borough Councils, Camden and Islington Area Health Authority and the Commission for Racial Equality.

The multiracial group of women (one Asian, one African-Caribbean and two white), talk directly to the camera about their expectations of motherhood and the ups and downs of the reality. The women are filmed at home with their children and talk candidly about the impact that having a child has had on their lives. They comment on the difficulties they have experienced, changes in their relationships with their partners and how they have changed themselves.

The video is unusual in focusing on the demands of motherhood and how the women feel about being mothers. It is suitable for viewing at home or in group settings. It could be used in parents' and women's groups to trigger discussion about the effect having a baby has on a woman and to share experiences of adjusting to life as a mother. It is a good example of a multiracial resource, reflecting women from a range of cultural, racial and class backgrounds. Although it was made in 1985, the issues raised by the women are still relevant.

From chance to choice: a multi-ethnic approach to community genetics: the role of the primary healthcare team

FORMAT: Video, 23 mins; with 7-page booklet

LANGUAGE: English

TARGET AUDIENCE: Primary healthcare teams

PRICE: £30.00 inc.

PRODUCER: Institute of Child Health, 1993

DISTRIBUTOR: Institute of Child Health

This video for health professionals aims to inform about inherited genetic disorders, the availability of screening tests, genetic counselling and support from statutory and voluntary organisations. It was funded by the Department of Health.

The video focuses on four inherited disorders – cystic fibrosis, sickle cell, thalassaemia and Tay Sachs disease. Their prevalence in different ethnic groups is identified and the risks of inheriting each disorder explained. Screening tests are available for these disorders and the video shows services offered by the North Thames Regional Health Authority. Primary healthcare services are identified as suitable points for screening, preferably pre-natally, to enable people to make informed choices about having a child if there is a risk of an inherited disorder. A GP describes a research project designed to find effective ways of encouraging uptake of screening for cystic fibrosis.

The importance of offering counselling by someone trained in genetic counselling is stressed. This may be through one of the specialist centres or by a trained member of the primary healthcare team. Courses in genetic counselling are mentioned and details are included in the accompanying leaflet. The video also covers screening in pregnancy and the various tests available to check if the foetus is affected. The leaflet is densely packed with information which recaps the main points of the video. Useful contact addresses of voluntary and statutory services are included plus an up-to-date reading list.

This video will be of interest to all members of primary healthcare teams. It is not only informative but also demonstrates how screening can be made more widely available within a primary healthcare setting. It could be used in training health professionals at pre- and post-qualification levels. A large number of health professionals and voluntary groups concerned with genetic disorders contributed to the resource.

Great expectations

FORMAT: Video, 15 mins

LANGUAGE: English

TARGET AUDIENCE: Youth workers

PRICE: £10.00 maximum (prices vary according to purchaser)

PRODUCER: Asian Community Arts, 1992

DISTRIBUTOR: Asian Community Media

This video documents the views of Asian youth workers in Tameside about the lack of recognition and resources accorded to youth work with Asian young people. The video was produced by a group of youth workers, mainly women, on an Asian Community Arts Video Training Module.

Interviews with youth workers form the bulk of this short video. They point out that work with Asian young people, especially young women, is understaffed, limited by lack of space and facilities available and not understood by mainstream youth services or managers. They comment on how difficult it is for Asian young people to use predominantly white youth service facilities where little work is undertaken

on anti-racism and they note the need to gain parental support and confidence. This video may be useful in training sessions for youth workers and others involved with young people, including managers, to trigger discussions about how to meet the needs of all groups in the community.

Growing older, keeping well: Chinese elderly health care

FORMAT: Video, 25 mins

LANGUAGE: Cantonese, with or without English sub-titles

TARGET AUDIENCE: Older people, health professionals

PRICE: £25.00 inc.

PRODUCER: Orientations Ltd, 1991

DISTRIBUTOR: Camden and Islington Health Authority

This video, for older people from Chinese communities, aims to inform people about how to stay healthy in later life and make use of a range of NHS services. It was funded by the Department of Health in conjunction with the Health Education Authority. The message of the video is that older people can expect to enjoy life and that minor health problems associated with ageing can be treated via a range of health services. The video shows men and women making use of services – physiotherapy, chiropody, opticians, dentists, GPs and an audiology clinic. A health advocate assists some of the people with translations and information is given about how to contact a linkworker or advocate. Older people talk about healthy diet, keeping active and the importance of keeping in contact with family and friends. The gentle pace of the video enables information to be absorbed easily. It is suitable for viewing in groups wherever older people may meet and could also be viewed by individuals and families at home. It could be viewed in parts so that presenters can provide local information and encourage discussion of experiences of using health services.

The video was made after extensive consultation with members of Cantonese-speaking communities and with Chinese and English health professionals. It promotes a positive view of later life, encouraging people to make use of medical services if necessary and to look after themselves.

Growing up strong: starting your baby on solid foods

FORMAT: Video, 17 mins; with 38-page booklet

LANGUAGE: Bengali, Hindi or Urdu with English subtitles

TARGET AUDIENCE: Parents, primary healthcare teams

PRICE: £31.29 inc.

PRODUCER: Healthcare Productions Ltd, 1991

DISTRIBUTOR: Healthcare Productions

This video is for Asian families with small babies. It is specifically targeted at grandmothers and mothers. Made by the Royal College of Nursing and Heinz, it addresses the introduction of solid foods to infants' diets.

Using a flashback format two grandmothers remember the advice that they and their daughters/daughter-in-laws have been given about infant feeding. Interviews with professionals (health visitors, midwives and dietitians) are the main source of information. The main points regarding infant feeding are covered (e.g. hygiene, textured foods, avoidance of spices, sugar and salt) and preparation of first foods is clearly demonstrated using family foods. Baby clinics are shown to be friendly, interesting and welcoming to all family members. Home visits by a health visitor and linkworker are well handled with both mother and grandmother involved in the discussion and asking questions. Some of the advice given is not clear (e.g. mother is told that she will 'know' when her baby is ready to start solid food with no further suggestions about how she would know).

The accompanying glossy booklet features Heinz products and the video features them once briefly. The booklet reiterates the general advice given in the video and contains a daily feeding chart staged according to the age of the baby. The video is technically well made.

The mixture of grandmother's thoughts, home visits and professional interviews can be confusing, especially as two families are featured. It may be more useful to view the film in two parts as the babies are of different ages and therefore at different stages. This would allow time for discussion of the various points raised.

The video may be a useful starting point for discussion about infant feeding with groups of parents or individual families. Grandmothers may welcome an approach which recognises that they too are concerned and involved with children's wellbeing.

Guidelines for the evaluation and selection of toys and other resources for children

FORMAT: 26-page manual

LANGUAGE: English

TARGET AUDIENCE: Parents, teachers, lecturers

PRICE: £4.50

PRODUCER: Working Group against Racism in Children's Resources, 1990

DISTRIBUTOR: Working Group against Racism in Children's Resources

This manual aims to examine racism in children's resources and enable educationists, parents and carers to select resources which provide positive images of all children. The manual discusses how racism affects children from an early age – damaging black children and misleading white children. Criteria for evaluating children's toys are laid out and refer to toys which may be found in the home, such as dolls and jigsaws, plus other items which may be of interest to playgroups and nurseries, such as home corner equipment and musical instruments. Types of toys are discussed and guidance given about what to look for in checklist form (such as a range of skin colours, hair types and features in dolls). Well-known manufactured toys are mentioned and suggestions made about how to complain about racist toys or limited ranges and to lobby for improvements. A list of toy suppliers is included. This is a practical manual which will be of use to anyone concerned with childcare. It will also be of interest to parents. As well as guiding in the selection of toys, it can be used to trigger discussion about the effects of racism on young children and steps which can be taken to challenge stereotypes. The authors of the booklet have wide experience of childcare as well as experience of toy manufacturing and retailing.

Tài-liệu hướng dẫn cho những người ty-nạn từ Việt-Nam về cuộc sống tại Anh-Quốc

來自越南難民到英國居住的指南

A Guide to Living in Britain for Refugees from Vietnam

REFUGEE Action

Funded by: Home Office, Department of Education & Science, Department of Health, Training, Enterprise & Education Directorate & BARCLAYS

A guide to living in Britain for refugees from Vietnam

FORMAT: Pack, with 9 booklets

LANGUAGE: Cantonese, English, Vietnamese

TARGET AUDIENCE: Community workers, social workers, general public

PRICE: £5.00 inc.

PRODUCER: Refugee Action, 1991

DISTRIBUTOR: Refugee Action

This pack of information booklets is for refugees from Vietnam. The booklets aim to provide basic information about rights and general information about benefits, education, housing, health and employment. It was funded by the Home Office, Department of Education and Science, Department of Health, Training, Enterprise and Education Directorate and Barclays.

Each booklet provides brief information about the subject. For example, the health booklet covers registering with a GP, getting a medical card, dentists, prescriptions, chemists, hospitals, opticians, family planning, traditional medicine, accidents and emergencies, the elderly, the disabled, pregnant women and children's health. Each page has three translations, Vietnamese, Cantonese and English, and this can be difficult on the eye at times. People who are not confident with written language may find this confusing. Illustrations are also used, black-and-white photographs relating to services described in the text, line drawings of people with bubble-type messages and comic-strip pages. This breaks up the text and reinforces it by showing Vietnamese people using the services.

Each booklet provides addresses of organisations which may be helpful and this could be supplemented with local information. Ideally these booklets could support information from community workers who could explain in more detail, especially about interpreters and linkworkers. The pack is good value for money. Refugee Action consulted with Vietnamese people, community groups, refugee organisations and government departments about the development of the pack.

The gynaecological examination: what happens?

FORMAT: Video, 15 mins; with 14-page presenters' notes

LANGUAGE: Bengali, Cantonese, English, Greek, Hindi, Turkish. Version with subtitles and signing also available

TARGET AUDIENCE: Women

PRICE: £40.88

PRODUCER: Brook Advisory Centres, 1989

DISTRIBUTOR: Brook Advisory Centres

This video for women seeks to explain what a gynaecological examination is, why it may need to be done and to encourage women to attend for regular examinations and cervical screening.

The video consists of a number of women of different ages and from different communities talking about their feelings and experiences of having gynaecological examinations. The women comment that although they may feel apprehensive about them, they recognise they are part of maintaining good health. Two women are seen having an examination; both doctors are female, calm and reassuring. The

examination is shown in full, including the doctor's view – inserting a speculum and visualising the cervix. Women will need to be informed of this prior to viewing so that they are not embarrassed or shocked. Some women may find this difficult to watch and it may be preferable even to omit these sequences.

The video does explain exactly what is involved and what to expect. Many women will find this reassuring, especially if viewed with a health professional who can answer questions and provide any further information. It is probably best viewed in small groups or at home. The accompanying notes for presenters cover the points made in the video and make suggestions for further discussion after viewing.

The haircut

FORMAT: Video, 10 mins

LANGUAGE: English

TARGET AUDIENCE: Parents, community workers

PRICE: £60.00

PRODUCER: Central St Martin's College of Art and Design, 1992

DISTRIBUTOR: Cinenova

This short video records a young African-Caribbean boy having his hair cut while his parents have an argument. It was produced and directed by Veronica Martel, a student at Central St Martin's College of Art and Design as part of London Weekend Television's Adopt a Student Scheme.

This video is unusual in its subject matter – the relationship between parents who do not live together – and its style – close-up filming of the boy. The disagreement about the haircut leads on to other areas of discord. It is visually challenging as the father gently cares for his son, caresses him and plays with him. Fathers are rarely seen in these roles and the combination of this and the argument makes it very interesting. This video could be useful in parents' groups to spark discussion about mothers' and fathers' perceptions of parenting

This video aims to inform women about antenatal care. It is intended for women who are having their first baby (or their first baby in Britain).

The video follows a young couple having their first child. They visit a (male) GP for a pregnancy test and then the hospital for a booking appointment. As the woman speaks little English, her husband accompanies her to interpret. The video encourages women to bring someone to interpret if they do not speak English. The booking appointment and routine tests are fully explained. The ultrasound machine that is shown is dated and many hospitals now use more modern equipment. The woman has a chest X-ray which is not routine in many areas. Parentcraft classes for women with an interpreter and English classes for women are shown. This video is now dated, but parts of it may be useful such as the detailed explanation of the booking visit. It was made before linkworker and translation services were available and women will need to be given additional information about how to access these services locally.

and the realities of being a single parent for both mothers and fathers. It may also be interesting to use it with young people for discussion about becoming parents. Some people may find the use of four-letter words offensive. Most parents, whether living together or apart, will identify with some of the areas of disagreement.

Happy birthday

FORMAT: Video, 15 mins

LANGUAGE: English, Gujarati, Urdu

TARGET AUDIENCE: Parents, primary healthcare teams

PRICE: Free loan for two weeks

PRODUCER: Blackburn, Hyndburn & Ribble Health Promotion Unit, 1985

DISTRIBUTOR: Blackburn, Hyndburn & Ribble Valley HPU

Happy, smiling, healthy children

FORMAT: Video, 15 mins; with 48-page notes, 4 looseleaf sheets and 3 leaflets

LANGUAGE: Bengali, Punjabi or Urdu, with English subtitles

TARGET AUDIENCE: Parents, health professionals

PRICE: £16.00 + p&p + VAT

PRODUCER: Health Education Authority, 1989

DISTRIBUTOR: Concord Video and Film Council

This video is for parents from Asian communities and aims to inform about how to ensure their children have healthy teeth. The video was made by the Health Education Authority in consultation with Leeds Western Health Authority, the Dental Hospital, Leeds, and Leeds Eastern Health Authority.

The video uses a voice-over format and begins by noting that Asian children have high rates of dental caries. Three steps to healthy teeth are identified and explored in the video – avoidance of sugary foods and drinks, the importance of regular brushing and visiting the dentist. Lots of children (from babies to older children) and their families are seen in a variety of situations throughout the video. There are clear demonstrations of how to brush teeth correctly and parents are shown helping children to brush their teeth. A dentist explains the build-up of plaque on the teeth and the effect of acid attacks on the teeth after eating. A visit to the dentist and dental hygienist is also included.

Viewed in a group setting, it may be a helpful trigger in discussion with parents about children's oral health. It is also suitable for home viewing by families and can stand alone as the main points are clearly made and practical. Viewed with a health worker the guidance given could be expanded, for example in the section on sugar many points are touched upon such as the addition of sugar to manufactured foods. Also health workers may want to discuss how people can identify foods with more or less sugar and alternatives to sugary foods etc. This is an informative video for parents.

Hasina's story: a drama about HIV and AIDS

FORMAT: Video, 32 mins; with 16-page booklet

LANGUAGE: Bengali

TARGET AUDIENCE: General public, health professionals

PRICE: £20.00 inc.

PRODUCER: Tower Hamlets Health Promotion Service, 1991

DISTRIBUTOR: East London & City HPS

This video and accompanying booklet was developed for Asian (Bengali-speaking) communities to answer questions and provide information about HIV/AIDS. The video was produced by Newham Healthcare, the Royal London Trust and Tower Hamlets Health Authority and was funded by North East Thames Regional Health Authority.

Using a soap opera-type approach, the story unfolds of a married couple, Salim and Hasina. Salim is distressed to hear that an ex-lover is HIV positive and he is full of questions and worries about himself, his wife and family. The drama intensifies when Hasina is delighted to discover she is pregnant, but her husband does not seem pleased and starts to use condoms. Worried and confused she suspects him of being unfaithful. Both turn to friends in the community for advice and support. Salim visits a GUM clinic for a test and Hasina visits an Asian counsellor. Both learn more about HIV and AIDS, how it can and cannot be transmitted and how to protect against infection.

The video (and bilingual booklet) is very clear about how the HIV virus can be transmitted. Sexual transmission is dealt with openly and sensitively (the booklet mentions sexual activities explicitly). Use of condoms is suggested to protect against infection.

Presenters may wish to explain the correct use of condoms to support the information in the video. This needs to be carefully introduced to the audience and may be more appropriately discussed with individuals or single sex groups to avoid embarrassment. Local information about GUM clinics, linkworkers and Bengali-speaking counsellors may also be helpful.

The video is excellent trigger material as it leaves us with many questions – including is Salim's test positive or negative? The inevitable discussions will provide opportunities for information sharing and challenging myths about HIV and AIDS. This video has been made available to local video hire shops in Tower Hamlets for free loan and has been popular with video audiences. Members of Bengali-speaking communities were consulted throughout about the making of the video.

HB masters sickle

FORMAT: Video, 20 mins; with 16-page workbook and 2-page notes

LANGUAGE: English

TARGET AUDIENCE: Key Stage 2 (8–12), teachers

PRICE: £29.50 inc.

PRODUCER: Battersea Studios for Sickle Cell Society, 1990

DISTRIBUTOR: Sickle Cell Society

This video and workbook for children aims to inform about sickle cell anaemia, dispel myths and prejudices about the illness and give children with sickle cell the confidence to look after themselves. It was produced with financial assistance from the Department of Health and a number of companies.

A lively children's magazine-type programme is introduced by a well-known children's TV presenter, Floella Benjamin, accompanied by a red blood cell puppet called HB. The illness is explained simply with the aid of animated graphics, comments from a multicultural group of children and following one girl with sickle cell through an average day. Treatments, how to keep well and what happens during check-ups at the hospital (including blood tests and how a drip works) are covered. The video can be viewed in sections and is varied enough to hold interest. The workbook provides a range of activities and worksheets to support the video.

The video can be used in classroom settings to assist understanding of sickle cell and support children with sickle cell. Teachers and school support staff will also find it informative. It could be used to explain sickle cell to individual children with the illness and their siblings. The video takes a practical and positive approach, stressing that children with sickle cell can participate as fully at school as other children.

Health across cultures in Hertfordshire: a guide for practitioners

FORMAT: 15-page booklet

LANGUAGE: English

TARGET AUDIENCE: Health professionals, primary healthcare teams

PRICE: Free

PRODUCER: Hertford Family Health, 1992

DISTRIBUTOR: Herts Family Health

This booklet is for health professionals and aims to inform about the genetic, cultural, religious and dietary factors which may affect the health of members of black and minority ethnic groups. It was sponsored by a group of pharmaceutical companies in Hertfordshire.

The booklet contains an extremely brief summary of a range of communities, covering general points such as naming systems, birth, and body language. Some religious and cultural groups are briefly discussed, followed by notes on diseases and conditions that are more prevalent in specific ethnic groups. There is no guidance on further reading or sources of information. This booklet is only a starting point for health professionals seeking to learn more about communities with which they are unfamiliar and they will need further information. The print is small. The communities selected are those resident in the Hertfordshire area. Representatives of a range of communities helped with the preparation of this booklet.

Health and healthy living: a guide for older people

FORMAT: 46-page booklet

LANGUAGE: Bengali, Cantonese, English, Greek, Gujarati, Hindi, Punjabi, Turkish and Urdu

TARGET AUDIENCE: Older people

PRICE: Free

PRODUCER: Department of Health, 1992

DISTRIBUTOR: BAPS

This booklet for older people seeks to inform about how to maintain good health and make use of the National Health Service. It was prepared by the Department of Health.

The booklet deals with a wide range of topics such as what a person can do to improve their health (e.g. stop smoking or take regular exercise), how to cope with changes in the body in later life (e.g. eyesight or hearing), advice about taking medicine, common illnesses, mental health, carers, safety in the home, how to complain about services and other sources of help. A section entitled 'Ethnic minorities' briefly informs about linkworker schemes and interpreters, community support and health resources in community languages.

Each topic is presented concisely and clearly. Advice is practical and other sources of help and support are noted. There is a helpful personal record card at the front for details such as addresses and phone numbers of doctors, opticians and other services which can be used for handy reference. The booklet can stand alone and many people will find it informative. It could also be used to support advice and information from health professionals. People may need additional information such as how to contact their local linkworker scheme or translation service.

Health care in multiracial Britain

FORMAT: 250-page manual, tables, plates, black-and-white

LANGUAGE: English

PRICE: £49.95 inc.

PRODUCER: Health Education Council and National Extension College, 1985

DISTRIBUTOR: National Extension College

This handbook for health professionals and trainers aims to explore key issues in developing health services to meet the needs of a multiracial population. The handbook was one of the first comprehensive publications to draw together a range of issues and concerns about provision of health services and service delivery to Britain's black and minority ethnic groups. Much of the material in the handbook is still relevant even though it was published in 1985. It was produced by the Health Education Council and the National Extension College.

In four parts, it covers explanations of health inequalities, health needs and expectations of different communities, health service provision (including training of health professionals) and resources (which examines how to consult the local community about their health needs). The material can be used flexibly either for personal study or in group settings. Each chapter includes a short introduction, a full discussion of the issues, factual information illustrated with case studies and interview extracts, plus suggestions for action and discussion points.

This handbook will be useful to trainers as it provides a starting point from which to examine service provision and delivery in relation to black and minority ethnic groups and also challenges the student/reader to examine their own attitudes and beliefs.

Health in any language

FORMAT: 26-page manual

LANGUAGE: English

TARGET AUDIENCE: Health professionals, service providers

PRICE: £4.50

PRODUCER: North East Thames Regional Health Authority, 1990

DISTRIBUTOR: North East & North West Thames RHA

Note: At the time of going to press there were very few copies of this publication in stock. There are no current plans to reprint.

This short manual is for anyone who is considering producing educational or information material for non-English-speaking communities.

The manual gives practical advice on how to produce translated material which is relevant and culturally acceptable to people from black and minority ethnic groups. The case for translated material is made from an equal opportunities stance and the involvement of the target community is stressed as essential to 'getting the message right'. Processes used for translation and how to produce and distribute material are covered. The book is concise and well laid out, the key points are identified and emphasised. This is a useful text for anyone considering translating material. A wide group of people contributed to the book, all of whom had experience of translating material for use in a health setting.

Health information for women

FORMAT: 17-page booklet

LANGUAGE: English, Gujarati, Urdu

TARGET AUDIENCE: Women

PRICE: 90p

PRODUCER: Bolton Health Authority, 1992

DISTRIBUTOR: Bolton Centre for Health Promotion

This booklet is for women and aims to provide information about women's health. It was designed to supplement health care provided by health professionals or women's self-help groups. It was funded by the Department of Health in conjunction with the Health Education Authority.

The booklet has an eyecatching cover and is well laid out. Clear and direct language and the large print make it easy to read. Topics dealt with are pre-menstrual tension, menstruation, thrush, cystitis, breastcare, family planning and cervical smears, safer sex and HIV/AIDS. Emphasis is given to how women can help themselves, especially with self-help remedies. The sections on safer sex and HIV/AIDS give clear information and recommend condom use. Where to get condoms and help with family planning is mentioned.

Women will find the information in the booklet accessible and down-to-earth. It is the kind of booklet women will want to refer to when necessary. It was written by a range of health professionals and trialled with women and amended as a result before publication.

The Health of the Nation . . . and you

FORMAT: Booklet

LANGUAGE: Bengali, Cantonese, English, Greek, Gujarati, Hindi, Polish, Punjabi, Turkish, Urdu, Vietnamese

TARGET AUDIENCE: General public

PRICE: Free

PRODUCER: Department of Health, 1992

DISTRIBUTOR: BAPS

This booklet explains the Health of the Nation targets and identifies the key areas of coronary heart disease and stroke, cancers, mental illness, accidents and HIV/AIDS and sexual health. It also includes information and practical tips about healthier lifestyles.

The information provided is brief and to the point, emphasising what can be done to prevent ill health or detect illness at an early stage. One section entitled 'You and your health' outlines current advice about healthy eating, drinking sensibly, exercise, stopping smoking, HIV, and safety at home and on the roads. The booklet is illustrated throughout with photographs and colour drawings, many of which are multiracial. The plain cover does not make it clear what kind of information it contains but people who are interested in health will find it useful to read.

Health packs 1 and 2

FORMAT: Pack; with 2 sets of 20 looseleaf sheets, 7 leaflets

LANGUAGE: English, Gujarati, Hindi

TARGET AUDIENCE: Women, teachers, lecturers

PRICE: £1.00 inc.

PRODUCER: Language and Skills Unit, Bolton Community Education Service, 1991

DISTRIBUTOR: Language and Skills Unit, Bolton

These packs aim to support the teaching of English to speakers of other languages. They deal with common health-related issues.

Both packs consist of photocopiable worksheets for classroom use. *Health pack 1* tackles the basic vocabulary for common illnesses and treatments such as colds, sore throats, and for parts of the body. *Health pack 2* covers filling in health-related forms, such as prescription forms and following instructions about dosage and use of medicines. This pack also includes a selection of leaflets about vaccinations and use of medicines. Some of these are out-of-date and would need to be replaced with updated versions. Both packs have worksheets illustrated with multiracial line drawings. These offer a variety of tasks which can be carried out individually or in groups. This is a flexible and practical resource which many students will find useful and interesting.

Healthy eating

FORMAT: Video, 23 mins

LANGUAGE: Bengali with English subtitles, English

TARGET AUDIENCE: General public, health professionals

PRICE: £15.00

PRODUCER: Tower Hamlets Health Promotion Service, 1989

DISTRIBUTOR: East London & City HPS

This video for Bengali communities aims to inform about current advice on healthy eating.

The introduction by a man and a woman is somewhat stilted but the video then moves on to explore why people need to consider a healthier diet. Simple animated sequences explain some illnesses and diseases (CHD, diabetes, anaemia, tooth decay, constipation, rickets, obesity), which may be prevented or controlled by a healthy diet. It is stressed that eating well can help people to feel well and stay healthy. Four food groups are described (cereals, proteins, fruit and vegetables, dairy produce) and several varieties are clearly shown including common brand names. People are advised to eat some of each of these groups each day. Foods to avoid and eat less of are also shown (fat, sugar and salt).

Part of the video focuses on a traditional Bangladeshi diet and stresses that this can be very healthy.

Examples are given of typical meals throughout the day and the food groups identified. Mention is made of vitamin D and how to ensure an adequate intake. The video concludes with a brief summary of the main points.

This video does provide up-to-date information about healthy eating and emphasises that a healthy diet can also be an enjoyable one. It uses a voice-over format and has shots of families eating together and shopping for food. Where brand-named products are shown there are always several. It is probably most useful in a group setting, viewed in short sections with time for discussion and questions. The section on illness and healthy eating could be a valuable trigger and the presence of a health professional or community worker would enable more information to be provided. There is enough material for several sessions on the topic of healthy eating. The video was made in consultation with members of Bengali communities in Tower Hamlets and health professionals.

Healthy eating for Asian families

FORMAT: Pack; with A3 poster and 6-page leaflet

LANGUAGE: English/Gujarati

TARGET AUDIENCE: General public, health professionals

PRICE: £32.00 (32 leaflets and 1 poster)

PRODUCER: West Lambeth Community Care (NHS) Trust, 1993

DISTRIBUTOR: West Lambeth Community Care

The text of this poster and accompanying leaflet for Gujarati-speaking families appears bilingually in Gujarati and English. The resource was written by a senior dietitian and a health visitor and produced by St George's Health Care as part of the Look After Your Heart campaign.

The poster is mainly text, highlighting key points for a healthy diet. One side is written in English and the other in Gujarati. A triangle in the middle uses traffic light colours (red, amber and green) to indicate which foods to eat less of, which to eat some of and which to eat more of. The poster could easily be displayed in the kitchen or in public places such as clinics and community centres for easy reference and as a reminder.

The leaflet explains what a healthy diet consists of in more detail. Advice is given about foods to eat and those to cut down on and why. Sensible limits for alcohol are noted. Also included are tips and hints on food preparation and choosing foods. The traffic light triangle of foods from the poster is repeated. Both the poster and the leaflet reflect a traditional diet and stress this can be very healthy. This resource can stand alone or be used to support discussion and advice from health professionals.

Healthy eating for people with diabetes

FORMAT: Video, 8 mins; with 3-page notes

LANGUAGE: Sylheti, with or without subtitles

TARGET AUDIENCE: General public, health professionals, primary healthcare teams

PRICE: £15.00 inc.

PRODUCER: Tower Hamlets Health Promotion Service, 1992

DISTRIBUTOR: East London & City HPS

This video is for people with diabetes from Bengali (Sylheti-speaking) communities. It aims to inform people, especially the newly diagnosed, and their families/carers about the importance of diet in the treatment of diabetes. It is one of a planned series for the Bengali community on various aspects of diabetes care. It was produced by the Video Production Unit of Tower Hamlets Health Promotion Service in conjunction with clinical nurse and linkworker specialists in diabetes and nutrition and the Royal London Hospital Trust.

The video uses a voice-over format and gives general advice about diet for people with diabetes. We see food being prepared, eaten and enjoyed by all the family. It is stressed that the diet suggested for people with diabetes is a healthy way of eating for everyone. The aims of the diet are – avoiding sugary foods, eating more food containing fibre, eating less fat, avoiding being overweight and eating regular meals. Why these are important is explained and advice given about how to achieve a healthier diet. Suggested foods are clearly shown including a selection of common brand names. The foods suggested reflect a traditional diet and alternative items (e.g. oil instead of ghee) are shown. The video notes that specialist diabetic foods are expensive and unnecessary. Key points are reinforced at the end.

The video has been designed for use by health professionals with groups or individuals as an aid to teaching, to trigger discussion and encourage basic understanding of diabetes and simple guidelines for healthy eating. The video provides general advice and the notes state that people must receive more specific advice from a dietitian. The video was made in response to the needs of the local community.

Healthy eating the Moroccan way

FORMAT: 7-page booklet

LANGUAGE: Arabic with English subtitles

TARGET AUDIENCE: General public, health professionals

PRICE: Enquire for details

PRODUCER: Parkside Community Dietetic Department, 1993

DISTRIBUTOR: Central and North West London HPU

This booklet for Moroccan communities aims to inform people about healthy eating using traditional foods. It was made by Parkside Community Dietetic Department, Parkside Health Promotion Unit, Al Hasaniya Moroccan Women's Centre and the Look After Your Heart Community Project Scheme.

The colourful booklet uses clear photographs of traditional foods, with short sentences in Arabic and English promoting healthy eating, such as eat more fibre, and eat less sugar and fat. Advice is given about what kinds of food to eat more of, how often to eat certain foods and food preparation. It is attractive, clearly laid out and provides information about current thinking on healthy diet. The eating patterns suggested are achievable and reflect traditional foods. The booklet can stand alone or be used with a health worker to discuss and illustrate healthy eating. Members of Moroccan communities were involved in the production of this booklet.

Healthy eating with Afro-Caribbean foods

FORMAT: Pack; leaflet, A5, illustrations; poster, A2, colour

LANGUAGE: English

TARGET AUDIENCE: General public, health professionals

PRICE: £1.50 inc.

PRODUCER: Parkside Health Promotion Centre, 1987

DISTRIBUTOR: Central and North West London HPU

This full-colour poster and accompanying leaflet provide advice about, and encourage healthy eating with, African-Caribbean foods. They were produced by Parkside Health Authority Dietetic Department and the London Food Commission.

The poster features photographs of three groups of food (fruit and vegetables; cereals, peas and beans; and fish, meat, dairy foods and oils). A short text advises what to eat more of and what to limit. The leaflet relates directly to the poster with line drawings of the photographs. The foods are named individually and the text provides information about the nutritional content of the food and tips for food preparation (such as trimming fat off meat). Both items can stand alone but are enhanced if used together. They are helpful in reinforcing the idea that a traditional African-Caribbean diet is healthy and may be useful to health professionals and others who are not familiar with an African-Caribbean diet.

Healthy pregnancy, safe birth

FORMAT: Video, 35 mins

LANGUAGE: Bengali, Cantonese, English, Gujarati, Punjabi, Urdu, Vietnamese

TARGET AUDIENCE: Parents, women, primary healthcare teams

PRICE: £49.99

PRODUCER: Maternity Links and Community Video Unit, 1987

DISTRIBUTOR: Maternity Links

This video is for women from Asian and Chinese communities and aims to inform them about the maternity services and linkworker schemes. It was produced by Bristol and Weston Health Authority in conjunction with the Community Video Unit. It was filmed in community clinics and the Bristol Maternity Hospital.

The video follows a woman from the point of visiting her GP for a pregnancy test and meeting a maternity linkworker. The woman, assisted by the linkworker, goes through the booking-in procedure and routine antenatal checks in the course of her antenatal visits. This includes attending parentcraft classes and a visit to the labour ward where pain relief options are explained. Another woman is seen in labour with a glimpse of the birth followed by postnatal care on the ward. Throughout, the viewer is introduced to routine procedures and familiarised with hospital settings. The linkworker is seen as developing a relationship with the woman and assisting communication between the patient and health professionals.

The video could be used with women at various stages of their pregnancy to explain what will happen and to trigger discussion about choices available and preferences for care. Presenters will need to ensure that local information is provided as the video refers to services in Bristol. The video may be particularly useful in familiarising women with hospital equipment and procedures which may otherwise be alarming. The video was made in close cooperation with Bristol Maternity Linkworkers.

A healthy start

FORMAT: Video, 20 mins

LANGUAGE: Bengali, English, Gujarati, Hindi, Punjabi, Urdu

TARGET AUDIENCE: Parents

PRICE: £26.50 inc.

PRODUCER: Medicus Productions Ltd for Asian Mother and Baby Campaign, 1984

DISTRIBUTOR: Healthcare Productions

This video is for mothers from Asian communities and aims to inform them about weaning and the importance of a healthy diet for infants and the rest of the family. Heinz sponsored the video and some Heinz products are shown.

Throughout the video, foods for a healthy diet are displayed and these reflect traditional diets. Mothers explain confidently how they weaned their children, giving examples of the kinds of food given at different ages, preparation of the food, difficulties they encountered and worries they had about feeding their children. Breastfeeding is mentioned positively. The importance of meals as a social occasion is also noted with shots of families, including babies, enjoying meals together. Manufactured baby foods are mentioned and shown briefly. The mothers demonstrate how they prepare family food for the baby, leaving out chilli and salt. Parents are seen shopping and advice is given about foods to buy (i.e. fresh fruit and vegetables). Presenters should note eggs are recommended and advice about this has now changed.

The video is useful trigger material, the mothers discussing their experiences of weaning are likely to be of the most interest. It is suitable for viewing in group settings or at home and many parents and carers will find it a practical and interesting video.

Hepatitis B and HIV: information for African communities

FORMAT: Video, 22 mins; 19-page notes

LANGUAGE: English

TARGET AUDIENCE: General public, health professionals

PRICE: £37.00 + £2.00 p&p

PRODUCER: South East London Health Authority, 1993

DISTRIBUTOR: Health First

This video aims to inform people from African communities about hepatitis B and HIV and how to protect themselves and others from infection. It was produced by South London Health Promotion Service in conjunction with Stockwell Health Project and was funded by the South East London Commissioning Agency.

The video follows a training group who have come together to find out about hepatitis B and HIV and AIDS. Still shots of the training group, graphics and colour drawings are accompanied by the commentary, some of which uses a question-and-answer format. The first part of the video deals with hepatitis and the second part with HIV. Both viruses are fully explained covering transmission, symptoms if any, testing, vaccination (against hepatitis B), treatments available, and precautions to take against infection (safer sex and safer drug use) plus good hygiene practices. Condom use is advocated and a demonstration of correct condom use is included. Information is presented clearly, emphasising what can be done to prevent infection. Sources of help and support for people who have hepatitis B or are HIV positive are noted.

The accompanying booklet reinforces the information from the video with additional brief notes for healthcare workers who may be concerned they are at risk from patients. It also lists names and addresses of organisations (local and national) which can provide further help. The video is suitable for viewing in group settings to trigger discussion. It would be helpful to view it with a health professional or community worker so that questions can be answered and information expanded if required. It could also be viewed individually at home. Members of African and Vietnamese communities and health professionals contributed to the development of this resource and volunteered to act in the video.

Hepatitis B and HIV: prevention for Chinese and Vietnamese communities

FORMAT: Video, 40 mins; 19-page notes Vietnamese, 15-page notes Cantonese

LANGUAGE: Cantonese, Vietnamese

TARGET AUDIENCE: General public, health professionals

PRICE: £37.00 + £2.00 p&p

PRODUCER: South East London Health Authority, 1993

DISTRIBUTOR: Health First

This video aims to inform people from Vietnamese and Chinese communities about hepatitis B and HIV and how to protect themselves and others from infection. It was produced by South London Health Promotion Service in conjunction with Stockwell Health Project and was funded by the South East London Commissioning Agency. The video follows a training group who have come together to find out about hepatitis B and HIV and AIDS. Still shots of the training group, graphics and colour drawings are accompanied

by the commentary, some of which uses a question-and-answer format. The first part of the video deals with hepatitis and the second part with HIV. Both viruses are fully explained covering transmission, symptoms if any, testing, vaccination (against hepatitis B), treatments available, and precautions to take against infection (safer sex and safer drug use) plus good hygiene practices. Condom use is advocated and a demonstration of correct condom use is included. Information is presented clearly, emphasising what can be done to prevent infection. Sources of help and support for people who have hepatitis B or are HIV positive are noted.

The accompanying booklet reinforces the information from the video with additional brief notes for healthcare workers who may be concerned they are at risk from patients. It also lists names and addresses of organisations (local and national) which can provide further help. The video is suitable for viewing in group settings to trigger discussion. It would be helpful to view it with a health professional or community worker so that questions can be answered and information expanded if required. It could also be viewed individually at home. Members of African and Vietnamese communities and health professionals contributed to the development of this resource and volunteered to act in the video.

HIV/AIDS: a guide for carers of young children

FORMAT: Pack; with 50-page booklet and 38 × 30 cms poster

LANGUAGE: English

TARGET AUDIENCE: Community workers, primary healthcare teams, carers

PRICE: £3.60 inc.

PRODUCER: Lambeth Women and Children's Health Project, 1992

DISTRIBUTOR: Lambeth Women and Children's Health Project

This booklet and poster aim to provide comprehensive information and guidance on HIV/AIDS and related issues for those working and caring for young children. The guide was funded by the South East London Commissioning Agency.

The guide presents information about what HIV/AIDS is, how it is transmitted, the antibody test and good hygiene practices. It addresses childcare issues directly, such as responsibilities under the Children Act and information about illness and immunisation. Suggestions for talking to children and support available for parents and carers are also covered. The discussion of confidentiality encourages the reader to think about who might need to know of someone's HIV status and why. The poster lists good hygiene practice in checklist form and could be helpful in reminding staff of procedures that need to be followed. It stresses that good hygiene procedures reduce the risk of passing on all infections. The booklet is illustrated with multiracial drawings and is a good example of a multiracial resource.

The booklet can be used flexibly as a stand-alone resource to inform, or as a basis for training. It may be a particularly helpful starting point for voluntary and statutory sector groups seeking to develop policy/guidelines on HIV/AIDS and the care of young children. The guidelines in the book have been adopted as the approved standard for the London Borough of Lambeth and South East London Health Promotion Service. A steering group of local representatives from statutory and voluntary childcare settings wrote the guide, and a wider group were consulted about the draft version.

HIV/AIDS: the choice is yours

FORMAT: Video, 15 mins; with notes

LANGUAGE: Cantonese with English subtitles

TARGET AUDIENCE: Community workers, general public, health professionals

PRICE: £20.00 inc.

PRODUCER: Tower Hamlets Health Promotion Service, 1990

DISTRIBUTOR: East London & City HPS

This video is for adults and young people from Chinese-speaking communities and aims to inform about HIV/AIDS and to support education programmes within Chinese communities about HIV/AIDS. It was jointly funded by Tower Hamlets Health Authority and the London Borough of Tower Hamlets.

The video is introduced by a doctor and addresses what HIV/AIDS is, how it is transmitted, how it cannot be transmitted, how people can protect themselves and where to get further information/advice. The video is clear and specific about transmission. Injecting drug use is dealt with openly and advice is given about how drug users can protect themselves. The correct use of a condom is demonstrated with a condom model. Some viewers may find this embarrassing or shocking and presenters will need to be sensitive to this, perhaps informing people in advance of the content. It also stresses that people who are HIV positive need the support of the community. The video refers to the National AIDS Helpline.

The video has been designed to stand alone but can also be used by community workers and health professionals with groups to trigger discussion and share information. The accompanying notes provide additional information for facilitators especially with regard to safer sex and different sexualities. The notes include information about sources of support nationally and locally. The video was produced in consultation with community groups, health professionals, the London Chinese Health Resource Centre and Tower Hamlets Chinese Association.

HIV and AIDS

FORMAT: Cassette, 12 mins

LANGUAGE: Sylheti

TARGET AUDIENCE: Women, health professionals, community workers, primary healthcare teams

PRICE: £1.50 inc.

PRODUCER: Culture Waves for Bloomsbury and Islington Health Authority, 1992

DISTRIBUTOR: Camden and Islington Health Authority

This audio cassette is one of a series of three for women from Bengali (Sylheti-speaking) communities. It aims to inform about HIV and AIDS, explain what HIV is, methods of transmission and how to protect against infection. The cassette is the third in a series of three community health information tapes for women from the Bengali community.

The cassette adopts a radio drama approach and we hear two women, Sufia and Aisha, discussing a relative whose husband has other sexual partners. The women are concerned about disease and the discussion leads to HIV and AIDS. The women realise they do not know much about the topic and they decide to ask the Bengali health worker for more information. She explains the difference between HIV and AIDS and how it can and cannot be transmitted. The women have an emotional discussion about how to talk to their husbands and how to protect against infection. One woman says that if her husband has other partners she would consider her relationship with him finished. The other woman thinks using condoms would be best as she says 'but who knows what will happen, people make mistakes'. The drama ends with the women disagreeing but more informed.

This short cassette touches upon worries women may have about their partners and a variety of viewpoints is expressed. This is a useful way of gaining the listeners' involvement. Information is provided about where to get condoms locally in Camden and Islington.

As this information is also printed on the cassette sleeve it could easily be replaced with relevant local information. The National AIDS Helpline is mentioned including when Bengali counsellors are available. The cassette is designed to be available, free of charge, in lending libraries, GP surgeries, clinics and community centres, etc. It may be a useful trigger for discussion in women's groups, although some women may prefer to listen to it in the privacy of their own homes. It is good value for money. The cassette was produced in close consultation with local Bengali communities.

HIV and AIDS information for seafarers

FORMAT: Video, 15 mins; with 31-page booklet, also available separately

LANGUAGE: English, Polish, Spanish, Tagalog

TARGET AUDIENCE: Seafarers

PRICE: £15.00 + £2.50 p&p. Booklet only, £1.00 + 80p p&p

PRODUCER: Health Education Authority and British Red Cross, 1993

DISTRIBUTOR: Health Education Authority

This video and accompanying booklet aim to give seafarers factual information about HIV and AIDS and how to protect against infection.

The video uses animated sequences of two characters – a captain and a helmsman – to explain what HIV is and how it is transmitted, how to practise safer sex, other precautions to be taken against HIV and good first-aid procedures. This is intercut with contemporary documentary footage of the seafaring industry and its workers. The animated characters are amusing and the information is presented clearly. The accompanying booklet reinforces the video and explains in more detail how to practise safe sex and how injecting drug users can ensure equipment is sterile and minimise the risk of HIV transmission. The booklet uses clear, unambiguous language and explicit colour drawings accompany the text. Both the video and booklet comment on the risks from blood transfusions, surgery and dentistry outside the UK.

This video and booklet are accessible to a wide audience and although most seafarers are men which the video reflects, women will also find it of interest. The video is suitable for both individual and group viewing and has been made to stand alone. The video won the Gold Award in the 1992 International Visual Communication Association Festival and the Craft Award for Best Graphics in the same festival. The resource was produced in response to questions asked by seafarers about HIV.

HIV infection and the black communities

FORMAT: 28-page pamphlet

LANGUAGE: English

TARGET AUDIENCE: Service providers

PRICE: £5.00 inc. (first copy free to health authorities)

PRODUCER: London Association of Metropolitan Authorities, 1990

DISTRIBUTOR: Local Government Management Board

This report is about local authorities' responses to the needs of black communities for information and services in relation to HIV. Although primarily targeted at policy officers and managers within local authorities it is also of interest to those involved in health services in the statutory and voluntary sectors. It was produced by the Local Authority Associations' Officer Working Group on AIDS.

A national seminar on the needs of black people in relation to information, services and support over HIV provided much of the information for the report. The report summarises key issues for black communities in relation to HIV, such as the need for women to have a safe space to meet with other women to discuss issues to do with HIV infection, and a common belief that black people do not inject drugs. Also noted are practice issues relevant to service provision (such as access to services, appropriate delivery of services), translation services and training of staff. Policy issues are also identified in terms of consultation with communities and users, and resource implications of developing this work. The report is summarised in checklist form at the end which may help to inform planning and evaluation of services and service development.

HIV, homelessness and local authority housing

FORMAT: 16-page booklet

LANGUAGE: English, Hindi, Portuguese

TARGET AUDIENCE: General public, social workers, community workers

PRICE: Single copies free, £2.50 inc. for multiples of 10

PRODUCER: Threshold Housing Advice, 1993

DISTRIBUTOR: Threshold Housing Advice

This booklet aims to provide information about local authority housing for people who are living with HIV and are homeless or threatened with homelessness. It was produced by Threshold HIV Project.

It contains a clear description of the law relating to homelessness and the practice followed by most local authorities in England and Wales. The process of applying to a local authority for housing is explained and applicants are advised to consult a housing advice agency first if possible. There is a discussion about whether or not to reveal your HIV status and how this may help speed up the process in some authorities. This is a practical guide which will be of use to anyone seeking local authority housing as it concisely outlines the process of applying for housing under the 1985 Housing Act (Housing the homeless).

Home birth: your choice

FORMAT: Video, 30 mins; with 7-page notes

LANGUAGE: English

TARGET AUDIENCE: Primary healthcare teams, women, community workers

PRICE: £15.00 individual, £25.00 funded organisations, + £2.00 p&p

PRODUCER: NCT Outreach, 1992

DISTRIBUTOR: Outreach

The video aims to inform women about home birth and addresses concerns women and health professionals may have about safety. It was made by a group of women who were members of ante- and postnatal groups in South London. The video is a good example of a multicultural resource as it features a wide range of women and families of different races, social backgrounds and home situations. It is presented through interviews with mothers (and some fathers and siblings). Women explain in their own words why they chose a home birth, including a lesbian mother, a Vietnamese woman who does not speak English, an 'older' mother and so on. Some women recount experiences of being transferred to hospital and point out that hospital delivery may be necessary if problems occur.

This video is excellent trigger material and will be of interest to women who are considering home birth. It is reassuring about safety issues but stresses the need for regular checks throughout pregnancy to identify any potential problems. Several shots of different homes are included to reinforce the point that an ordinary home is suitable for a home birth. Health professionals may also find this useful and challenging material as it clearly identifies women's reasons for wanting home birth and emphasises the importance of a partnership between health professionals and women. The women who made the video were involved in all the stages of its production. The video challenges the notion that only white, middle-class women choose to have home births.

The home medicine box

FORMAT: Video, 12 mins; with 3-page notes

LANGUAGE: Sylheti

TARGET AUDIENCE: General public

PRICE: £15.00 inc.

PRODUCER: Tower Hamlets Health Promotion Service, 1992

DISTRIBUTOR: East London & City HPS

This video is for Bengali- (Sylheti-) speaking communities. It aims to inform about medicines and home treatments for common, non-serious illness and injuries. The video was made as a result of research among GPs who identified a need for information about easily available treatments for minor illnesses and injuries.

The introduction deals with safe storage and dosage of medicines. The first half of the video examines eight common 'over-the-counter' items, and when and how they might be used. The second half is about the contents of a first-aid box and treatment of minor injuries. A home setting is used throughout with clear descriptions and demonstrations. Treatment of children is also covered. The importance of reading labels on medicines and following instructions is stressed. The video features brand-named products because GPs found people were more familiar with, and likely to recognise, a brand name than a generic pharmaceutical name. However several products are always shown rather than just one. Avoiding 'over-the-counter' medicines if pregnant or taking other medication is not mentioned. However it is stressed that more serious or persistent illness must be referred to a doctor.

The video is designed to stand alone and not require additional material or support. This is a useful resource for waiting areas and could also be viewed at home. Used in a group setting it could promote discussion of how people can treat minor illnesses themselves.

Housing for the ethnic elderly

FORMAT: Video, 30 mins

LANGUAGE: Bengali, Cantonese, English, Greek, Gujarati, Hindi, Punjabi, Turkish

TARGET AUDIENCE: Older people, service providers, community workers

PRICE: £22.50

PRODUCER: SCEMSC (Standing Conference of Ethnic Minority Senior Citizens), 1990

DISTRIBUTOR: SCEMSC

This video was made as a follow-up to a report produced in 1984 and aims to inform and advise local community organisations and older people about housing. It was produced by the Housing Associations Charitable Trust and the Standing Conference of Ethnic Minority Senior Citizens. Funding was provided by Help the Aged and Leicester City Council.

The video aims to explain what sorts of housing may be available around the country to older people. A number of housing schemes are seen in operation and are described by residents and managers. These are local authority 'Care and repair – stay put schemes', peripatetic wardens, mixed age housing developments, sheltered housing (one for Caribbean people and one for Asian people). It ends with advice abut how to get information about local provision. Where provision does not exist local communities are encouraged to consider supporting the development of schemes.

The video may be helpful in explaining to older people and their families the range of provision which may be available. It could also be used to trigger interest from community groups, local authorities and housing associations in developing appropriate housing for older people from black and minority ethnic groups.

Hysterectomy

FORMAT: Video, 23 mins; with leaflet

LANGUAGE: Video in Bengali, English, Gujarati, Hindi/Urdu, Punjabi. Leaflet in Bengali, English, Gujarati, Hindi/Urdu, Punjabi.

TARGET AUDIENCE: Women, health professionals

PRICE: £37.50 inc.

PRODUCER: N Films, 1991

DISTRIBUTOR: N Films

This video is for Asian women who may have had or are about to have a hysterectomy. It provides basic information about the operation and examines some of the common worries and emotional responses women may have. The video was made for the UK Asian Women's Conference and was funded by the Department of Health. The first part is dramatised. A woman returns home from hospital and her husband and daughters are sympathetic and supportive. The second part is a studio discussion between a group of Asian women – a consultant obstetrician, a linkworker, a woman who has had a hysterectomy and a counsellor. The video focuses more on how women feel and on dispelling myths than on details about the operation and what to expect. It is a useful introduction to hysterectomy and touches upon many of the concerns women may have (such as weight gain afterwards, sadness if they have not had a male child, and fears about loss of femininity).

It could be viewed by women's groups or individual women at home. If seen pre-operatively it may enable fuller discussion between women, their families and health professionals and if viewed with a health professional questions could be answered immediately.

It is also of relevance to women who have recently had a hysterectomy as information is given about diet and post-operative care. It therefore may be helpful for women to see during their stay in hospital. Presenters need to be aware that not all women have supportive partners and families. The accompanying booklet reiterates the information given in the video and has useful national addresses. Presenters may wish to add local information (about counselling, linkworkers and support groups, etc.).

Immunisation in the first years of life

FORMAT: Video, 8 mins

LANGUAGE: Bengali with and without English sub-titles

TARGET AUDIENCE: Parents, primary healthcare teams

PRICE: £15.00 inc.

PRODUCER: East London and The City Health Promotion Service, 1989

DISTRIBUTOR: East London & City HPS

This video for parents from Bengali communities aims to inform about serious childhood diseases which may affect babies and young children and can be prevented by immunisation. It was produced by the Video Production Unit of East London and City Health Promotion Service.

A family doctor at a child health clinic is seen talking with mothers and immunising babies. He explains to the viewer the importance of immunisation in preventing diphtheria, tetanus, polio, whooping cough, measles, rubella and mumps. The immunisation schedule for the first two years of life is covered. The importance of attending appointments so that all doses are given is emphasised. The doctor talks about tuberculosis, explaining it is still common in Bangladesh and anyone visiting or receiving visitors from there will need to consider immunisation against this and should discuss it with their doctor. There is brief mention of parental concerns about possible side effects of immunisation but the doctor stresses that some of the diseases are very dangerous and babies are more at risk from these than immunisation.

The video was made before the Hib vaccine was available so parents will need additional information about this and about the booster injection. It will interest parents and viewed with a health professional could be a useful way of triggering discussion and information sharing about immunisation. Suitable for home viewing it is short enough to be watched during a home visit. The video was made in consultation with local Bengali communities and health professionals in East London.

Important appointments

FORMAT: Video, 20 mins

LANGUAGE: Cantonese, English, Urdu

TARGET AUDIENCE: Parents, primary healthcare teams, health professionals

PRICE: £30 + p&p

PRODUCER: Central Birmingham Health Authority and Sparkhill Health Project, 1990

DISTRIBUTOR: Steven Bywater

This video for parents aims to raise awareness about the importance of immunisation and inform about the seriousness of childhood diseases.

The video features a multiracial group of parents and children. One mother describes her experiences of having polio as a child and its effect on her life. Two other mothers describe how their children had whooping cough and measles. Both state strongly that they wished their child had been immunised. The risks of the whooping cough vaccine are discussed and immunisation is recommended. Diphtheria, tetanus, mumps and rubella are covered briefly. A simple explanation is given about how immunisation works. The kinds of question asked before a child is immunised are covered including family history. This may mean a child should not be immunised. Reactions to immunisation are mentioned but no advice is given about how to deal with this other than to consult the GP when severe reactions occur.

The immunisation schedule has changed since the video was made and presenters would need to update this and include information about other developments such as the Hib vaccine. It is suitable for viewing in group settings or the home but some input from a health professional is needed to provide up-to-date information. Sequences of the video could be used (for example the mother describing her child ill with whooping cough) to trigger discussion about childhood illnesses and parents' concerns about immunisation.

In their own words

FORMAT: Video, 59 mins; 10-page booklet

LANGUAGE: English

TARGET AUDIENCE: Teachers, lecturers, women

PRICE: £40.78 inc.

PRODUCER: Berkshire Education Department Resources Unit, 1989

DISTRIBUTOR: Dramatic Distribution

This video aims to present the diversity of Asian women's lives in Britain today. It consists of a series of interviews with women from different communities and cultures. They vary in age and background and are all professionals.

The women talk about their lives directly to the camera. The video is divided into sections entitled: 'Describing ourselves', 'Overcoming struggles', 'Influences', 'Histories', 'Frustrations', 'Happiness and aspirations'. An accompanying booklet contains selected quotes from each section with suggestions for discussion points which encourage the viewer to think about their own experiences. There is enough material for several sessions, with the makers recommending it be viewed in sequence. Many issues are highlighted and could be pursued. These include attitudes to women's education, challenging stereotypes of Asian women and the difficulties of balancing career and family. Perhaps most powerfully this video presents role models for younger women and although the arts are represented more than other spheres, this in itself challenges stereotypical views of which professions Asian women choose.

Information pack for parents

FORMAT: Pack; with 15-page booklet

LANGUAGE: Arabic, Bengali, Cantonese, English, Gujarati, Punjabi, Spanish, Urdu

TARGET AUDIENCE: Parents

PRICE: Free

PRODUCER: Down's Syndrome Association, 1992

DISTRIBUTOR: Down's Syndrome Association

This information pack is for parents who have just had a Down's syndrome baby. It consists of a booklet, further information about the association and a literature list.

The booklet has been written by parents and is

entitled *Perhaps we can help*. It explains clearly what Down's syndrome is, with sources of help, hints for babycare and suggested activities to stimulate the baby. Comments from parents, grandparents, brothers and sisters are the main component of the booklet and a mother describes how she created a stimulating environment for her baby. It is illustrated with multiracial line drawings and photographs of babies. Although the booklet has an optimistic tone it acknowledges how difficult it may be for parents when their baby is diagnosed. Readers are encouraged to contact the association and meet other parents. The booklet may help parents to identify issues they want more information about and may be useful for other family members such as grandparents.

Inside out

FORMAT: Video, 18 mins; with 9-page notes

LANGUAGE: English, Urdu

TARGET AUDIENCE: Parents, health professionals

PRICE: £25.00 each, £40.00 set of Urdu and English

PRODUCER: Cambridgeshire County Council and Peterborough City Council, 1993

DISTRIBUTOR: Cambridgeshire Road Safety

This video is for parents from Asian communities and aims to highlight ways of preventing accidents to children in the home and on the road. The video was produced in conjunction with Peterborough Arts Centre and members of the local community. North West Anglia Health Authority assisted with funding for the project. The video highlights some of the main hazards facing young children at home and on the roads and demonstrates ways in which accidents can be prevented. Divided into sections, the video examines children making journeys on the road by themselves, children left alone at home, children wandering out of their homes or gardens into the road, safe places for children to play, children unsupervised in the kitchen,

children in cars and hazards in the bathroom and on the stairs. A presenter narrates throughout the video, asking questions and reinforcing how to prevent accidents. The approach used is of showing a hazard (e.g. a hot iron within reach of a toddler) and then returning to the scene with the hazard made safe (the iron safely out of reach). It is stressed that parents are responsible for ensuring the safety of their children.

The accompanying notes suggest discussion points and provide factual information about each section, including information about the law where relevant. The video is quite dramatic and will be a useful trigger for discussion. Children almost have accidents, there are slow-motion sequences of what happens to children in car accidents, etc. It is suitable for viewing in group settings and each section provides enough material for one session. Presenters will need to preview the video carefully to ensure they pause it at the correct points as it has quite a swift pace. Safety equipment is mentioned and it may be useful to have at hand details of any loan schemes operating locally. It may also be helpful to talk with parents about what to do if a child has an accident.

Interpreters in public services

FORMAT: 141-page manual

LANGUAGE: English

TARGET AUDIENCE: Health professionals, service providers, social workers, commissioners

PRICE: £9.45

PRODUCER: Department of Health, Further Education Unit, 1991

DISTRIBUTOR: Venture Press

This manual is for managers and service providers in a wide range of statutory services such as health and education which need to employ interpreters. It may also be relevant to voluntary and community organisations and to those providing professional training (either for professionals who may need to work with interpreters or training interpreters).

The manual contains a detailed analysis of the different models of interpreting services based on a survey of practice in 51 local authorities. The need for interpreting services is discussed and supported by recent research. Guidance is provided about the legal aspects of interpreting with relevant legislation identified. All aspects of providing an interpreting service are covered in some depth, for example: planning, starting and managing a service, codes of practice, training for interpreters and for professionals working with interpreters.

This is a practical and thorough book which outlines the need for professional interpreting services, highlights key issues in the development of services and provides comprehensive guidance for delivery of interpreting services.

An introduction to diabetes

FORMAT: Video, 6 mins; with 3-page notes

LANGUAGE: Sylheti with or without English subtitles

TARGET AUDIENCE: Primary healthcare teams, general public

PRICE: £15.00 inc.

PRODUCER: Tower Hamlets Health Promotion Service, 1992

DISTRIBUTOR: East London & City HPS

This video aims to inform people with diabetes and their families/carers about diabetes and how it may be treated. The video is the first in a planned series for Bengali communities on various aspects of diabetes care. It was produced in conjunction with clinical nurse and linkworker specialists in diabetes and nutrition at the Royal London Hospital NHS Trust.

The video uses a voice-over format as we see people with diabetes living with the condition and controlling it. A simple explanation of diabetes is given with the aid of graphics. The symptoms and treatments (including insulin) of diabetes are described. It is stressed that diabetes is a life-long condition and dietary control is the most vital part of the treatment. The doctor and dietitian are identified as sources of further information about this. The video has been designed for use by health professionals with groups or individuals to trigger discussion and encourage basic understanding of diabetes. The makers recommend that presenters have a good understanding of diabetes themselves before showing it. The video was made in response to the needs of the local community.

It's hard being a woman

FORMAT: Video, 25 mins

LANGUAGE: English

TARGET AUDIENCE: Women, general public

PRICE: £25.85 inc.

PRODUCER: Central Television, 1990

DISTRIBUTOR: Central Television

This video, for a general audience, explores the role of women in some Muslim communities and challenges stereotypical views of Muslim women.

The video has a documentary style and is introduced by Shahwar Sadeque, a scientist, a Commissioner for Racial Equality and a BBC governor. She describes herself as a 'British, Muslim, Bengali', and stresses the importance of faith in her life. Ms Sadeque visits a group of young Bengali women attending further education classes. She talks to them about their lives which are very different from hers.

The young women must deal with traditional expectations from their families and elders and, at the same time, adapt to life in a

Western society. A group of Muslim women, working with community organisations, comment on the role of women in Islam and question the view that women should be submissive to men. They also suggest that issues such as alcohol abuse, divorce, sexual abuse, homosexuality and lesbianism need to be discussed and acknowledged within Muslim communities.

This is a thoughtful video and gives women an opportunity to voice their diverse views of women's roles within some Muslim communities. It may be of interest to a wide audience (e.g. Muslim communities, students and professionals) to trigger discussion about Islam and the role of women.

I've got gonorrhoea?

See *Counselling and sexuality*

Kamla's story: a drama about HIV and AIDS

FORMAT: Video, 34 mins; with 16-page booklet

LANGUAGE: Gujarati. Booklet in English/Gujarati

TARGET AUDIENCE: General public, health professionals

PRICE: £20.00 inc.

PRODUCER: Tower Hamlets Health Education Service, 1991

DISTRIBUTOR: East London & City HPS

This video and accompanying booklet were developed to answer questions and provide information about HIV/AIDS. The video was produced by Newham Healthcare, the Royal London Hospital NHS Trust and Tower Hamlets Health Authority and was funded by North East Thames Regional Health Authority.

Using a soap opera-type approach the story unfolds of a married couple, Deepak and Kamla. Deepak is distressed to hear that an ex-lover is HIV positive and he is full of questions and worries about himself, his wife and family. The drama intensifies when Kamla is delighted to discover she is pregnant but her husband does not seem pleased and starts to use condoms. Worried and confused she suspects him of being unfaithful. Both turn to friends in the community for advice and support. Deepak visits a GUM clinic for a test and Kamla visits an Asian counsellor. Both learn more about HIV and AIDS, how it can and cannot be transmitted and how to protect against infection.

The video (and bilingual booklet) are very clear about how HIV can be transmitted. Sexual transmission is dealt with openly and sensitively (the booklet mentions sexual activities explicitly), and use of condoms is suggested to protect against infection. Presenters may wish to explain the correct use of condoms to support the information in the video. This needs to be carefully introduced to the audience and may be more appropriately discussed with individuals or single-sex groups to avoid embarrassment. Local information about GUM clinics, linkworkers and Gujarati-speaking counsellors may also be helpful.

The video is excellent trigger material as it leaves us with many questions, including: is Deepak's test positive or negative? The inevitable discussions will provide opportunities for information sharing and challenging myths about HIV and AIDS. This video has been made available to local video hire shops in Tower Hamlets for free loan and has been popular with video audiences. Members of Gujarati-speaking communities were consulted throughout about the making of the video.

Keep active, keep healthy

FORMAT: Video, 15 mins; with 4-page leaflet

LANGUAGE: Bengali, English, Gujarati, Hindi/Urdu, Punjabi

TARGET AUDIENCE: Women

PRICE: £37.25 inc.

PRODUCER: N Films and UK Asian Women's Conference

DISTRIBUTOR: N Films

This video for women from Asian communities promotes physical activity as a way of contributing to good health. It notes increased rates of heart disease within Asian communities compared with the rest of the population and promotes regular physical activity to help prevent heart disease. The video was made by the UK Asian Women's Conference and was funded by the Department of Health.

Throughout the video women of all ages are seen participating in and enjoying a range of physical activities. Some are organised classes such as keep fit and aerobics, others are activities which can be incorporated into everyday life, such as using the stairs rather than the lift, walking more, and stretching exercises which can be done at home. Traditional activities such as dance and yoga are included and involving the whole family in a more active lifestyle is encouraged. Women-only classes and sessions at swimming pools are noted and information is provided about what to wear for women who prefer to keep their legs covered. A section on healthy eating advises less fat, salt and sugar in the diet. Foods to eat less of and those to eat more of are clearly shown. This includes traditional and convenience foods.

This is a stand-alone resource suitable for viewing individually or with the family at home. It is also suitable for use in group settings. It may be helpful in providing women with an overview of the kinds of physical activities they can do and reinforcing the importance of physical activity in promoting health.

The accompanying leaflet highlights the main points from the video with some useful addresses. A number of health professionals and organisations concerned with health were involved in advising the producers.

Keep it clean: commercial kitchen hygiene

FORMAT: Video, 13 mins

LANGUAGE: Bengali, Cantonese, English, Gujarati, Urdu

TARGET AUDIENCE: General public, environmental health officers

PRICE: £15.00

PRODUCER: Gatehouse Television for Bolton Metropolitan Borough Environmental Health Services, 1992

DISTRIBUTOR: Bolton Environmental Health Services

This video is targeted at owners and managers of take-away food establishments and restaurants. It aims to inform about commercial kitchen hygiene and was designed to support courses and talks on kitchen and food hygiene.

The video visits a commercial kitchen which is unhygienic and dangerous, the narrator introduces the viewer to the biggest hazard in the kitchen – Kamal, who is the chef! The hazards in the kitchen are highlighted including those Kamal contributes to, such as smoking, sneezing and uncovered cuts. The consequences of poor kitchen hygiene are noted (possible closure, loss of customers and reputation and fines). Basic information is provided about food poisoning and the conditions in which bacteria thrive. Kamal learns how to run a hygienic kitchen and demonstrates this, including training other members of staff. Throughout, the video stresses legal requirements and that these are the responsibility of the owner or manager. Good kitchen hygiene is shown as contributing to a successful and profitable business.

The video could be used in a variety of ways to support training and information about kitchen hygiene – as a trigger for discussion or in a more structured way to examine practices in a commercial kitchen. The video was made with the involvement of environmental health officers.

Keep warm, keep well

FORMAT: 20-page booklet

LANGUAGE: Bengali, Cantonese, English, Greek, Gujarati, Hindi, Polish, Punjabi, Turkish, Urdu, Welsh

TARGET AUDIENCE: Older people

PRICE: Free

PRODUCER: Central Office of Information, updated annually

DISTRIBUTOR: Keep Warm, Keep Well

This booklet is for older people and aims to provide information and advice about how to keep warm in winter and cope with cold weather generally. It was produced as a result of a joint venture between Help the Aged, Age Concern, Neighbourhood Energy Action, Departments of Health and Social Security and the Welsh Office.

The booklet covers foods to eat, appropriate clothing and heating, paying fuel bills, welfare benefits and grants, emergencies and sources of further help and advice. The information is clear and practical, line drawings illustrate the text and there is a list of useful phone numbers at the end for people to fill in themselves. Most people will find the information helpful and relevant. Community workers may find it a support for sessions with groups of older people on coping with cold weather.

Lancashire Family Health Services Authority: working for patients

FORMAT: Video, 23 mins; with 35-page booklet

LANGUAGE: Bengali, English, Gujarati, Hindi, Punjabi, Urdu

TARGET AUDIENCE: General public

PRICE: £25.00 inc.

PRODUCER: Lancashire Family Health Services Authority, 1991

DISTRIBUTOR: Lancashire FHSA

Made for Asian communities to explain the role of the FHSA, it looks in detail at four of the services provided (GPs, dentists, pharmacists and opticians). It was made by Lancashire FHSA and funded by the Department of Health in conjunction with the Health Education Authority. The video stresses that FHSAs are 'working for patients'. The four services are thoroughly described and a young Asian woman is seen using each of them.

Basic information is given about what to expect from each service and practical advice about how to use it (such as how to make an appointment, and how to find a late-opening pharmacist). General advice about health-related issues is also given such as not sharing prescribed treatment with others, and having regular dental checks.

The video mentions that patients may wish to see a woman doctor but does not show one. The only female health professionals shown are a nurse and a pharmacist. The use of interpreters and linkworkers is not explained and it may be helpful to have such information available when viewing the video.

Similarly, information such as the address of the local FHSA and leaflets about prescription charges would also be useful to have to hand. The accompanying booklet has the script of the video translated into each language (but it is in very small print). This informative video could be viewed by any group interested in health. It is also suitable for viewing in a 'waiting area'. It is broken up into sections dealing with each service and recaps the main points.

Languages in Berkshire

FORMAT: Video, 20 mins; with 10-page notes

LANGUAGE: English

TARGET AUDIENCE: Parents, teachers

PRICE: £40.78 inc.

PRODUCER: Berkshire Education Department Resources Unit, 1987

DISTRIBUTOR: Dramatic Distribution

This video aims to raise awareness of the importance of the language children speak at home and its influence on their general educational development. It is of interest to teachers, educationists and parents. The video charts the historical background to teaching English to children who speak other languages. Educationists explain that the maintenance and development of the child's mother tongue is beneficial to the child's all-round educational achievement. Examples of good practice in schools in Berkshire are demonstrated, with children reading books in their mother tongue, students developing drama in their mother tongue, etc. Dialect languages such as Creole are discussed and the role they play in the cultural heritage. Teachers state how important they believe it is for children to speak their mother tongue well and how this may enhance their ability to learn English and other languages.

The video could be used in group settings to raise awareness of multilingualism and promote discussion about language development. Parents and teachers may find it

useful to view the video together. The accompanying notes include questions for discussion. The video was filmed in schools in Berkshire.

Let's go back a little

See *Counselling and sexuality*

Let's talk sickle

FORMAT: Video, 20 mins; with 11 leaflets and 3 looseleaf sheets

LANGUAGE: English

TARGET AUDIENCE: Primary healthcare teams, social workers, general public, health professionals

PRICE: £19.99 inc.

PRODUCER: Sickle Cell Society, 1990

DISTRIBUTOR: Sickle Cell Society

This video aims to inform about sickle cell anaemia and explain and promote the work of the Sickle Cell Society. It is targeted at people and families who may be affected by sickle cell disease and is also of interest to general audiences.

The work of the Sickle Cell Society is explained through a series of interviews with workers from the society and families affected by sickle cell disease. Mothers describe how the disease has affected their children and family life. They explain how the Sickle Cell Society has supported them, through counselling, support groups, provision of information, etc. The potential seriousness of the disease is emphasised as we hear of a child who has died and a child who has brain damage as a result of strokes following 'crises'. Counselling is explained and demonstrated. Mothers talk about how it has helped them cope with problems and realise they are not alone. Support groups are seen in action and workers from the society talk about the kind of help the society can give.

A brief animated section at the beginning explains simply what sickle cell disease is and could be explained in more detail to some audiences if appropriate. The video is well made and has a comfortable pace. It is suitable for viewing by groups or families at home. Those who are newly diagnosed or new to the society will find it informative. It is of interest to health professionals in outlining the kind of support available and the kind of support people find helpful. It could also be used to raise awareness about sickle cell disease and its potentially serious effects.

Listen my sister . . . putting AIDS into context

FORMAT: 27-page booklet

LANGUAGE: English

TARGET AUDIENCE: Women

PRICE: £1.00 inc.

PRODUCER: King's Healthcare, 1992

DISTRIBUTOR: King's Healthcare

This booklet covers topics raised by women during HIV/AIDS awareness courses and aims to put that information together with information about women's health and race. The authors state that this booklet 'has been produced, researched and written by and for women of colour'.

The booklet covers eight topics – Black and in Britain, Double standards, Taking care, Putting AIDS into context, Protection and prevention, Negotiating safer sex, Giving and receiving blood, Pregnancy and after. It is frank and realistic about sexual relationships acknowledging that they may be heterosexual, lesbian or bisexual. Clear information is provided about safer sex practices and it is stressed that this is also relevant to women who have lesbian relationships. The section on negotiating safer sex suggests some strategies which may help women persuade partners to use condoms or barriers. The booklet is illustrated with colour drawings of women with bubble messages, some serious and some funny. This breaks up the text and is striking as so rarely are all the illustrations of women from black and minority ethnic groups.

This is an unusual booklet as it tackles the subject matter openly and clearly. Some women may want to have further information as it is fairly brief, but they would be able to pursue it from the references in the booklet. Each section has a list of further reading and useful (national) addresses. Sources of help are also listed but are mainly for women living in London. This is probably the kind of booklet women will read alone but later discuss with a friend. Women's groups may find it a useful starting point for discussions, particularly of more difficult topics such as negotiating safer sex.

Looking after your health … where to go for help

FORMAT: Video, 20 mins; with notes

LANGUAGE: English

TARGET AUDIENCE: Older people, primary healthcare teams

PRICE: £15.00

PRODUCER: Standing Conference on Ethnic Minority Senior Citizens, 1991

DISTRIBUTOR: SCEMSC

This video aims to encourage older people from black and minority ethnic groups to use primary healthcare services. It seeks to inform people about the range of services available and stresses the importance of registering with a local GP. Throughout the video, older people from various communities are seen using a range of services (for example, visiting the chiropodist, district nurse, and dentist). The video also follows an Asian woman as she registers with a new GP – she chooses a woman doctor and meets her before registering. The range of services a GP may offer is described and it is stressed that these are free. How to complain about a service is also covered.

Notes accompany the video with suggestions for how to use it in a group. The video is broken up into small sections which can be viewed separately and the notes suggest discussion points for these. Information about local services would be useful so that people can contact them if they wish. This video would be of interest to groups of older people and would certainly trigger discussion of experiences and expectations of primary healthcare services.

Looking after your teeth: tutors' pack

FORMAT: 9-page pack

LANGUAGE: English/Urdu

TARGET AUDIENCE: Teachers, lecturers

PRICE: £10.00 inc.

PRODUCER: South Buckinghamshire NHS Trust, Dental Health Department, 1993

DISTRIBUTOR: South Buckinghamshire NHS Trust

This pack was developed for teaching English to speakers of other languages. It aims to provide information about dental health in a form that can be used in English classes.

The pack has bilingual information in English and Urdu, accompanied by colour illustrations. Regular brushing of teeth is recommended and a suitable toothbrush and amount of fluoride toothpaste is shown. Foods and drinks which are good for teeth and those which are bad for teeth are clearly illustrated. These include traditional foods and confectionery such as sweets and chocolate. There are bilingual question sheets which relate to the information and activities to match words and sentences with appropriate illustrations. The pack is short, but does provide an introduction to the topic of oral health and will also equip students with a basic vocabulary.

It is suitable for use with individual students or with groups. The pack does provide opportunities for demonstration of correct brushing techniques (perhaps from a visiting health professional) and discussion of how to care for teeth. It has been used with groups of women learning English who found it interesting and helpful.

Managing your asthma

FORMAT: Video, 15 mins; with factsheet

LANGUAGE: Bengali, Gujarati, Hindi, Punjabi, Urdu

TARGET AUDIENCE: General public, primary healthcare teams, health professionals, community workers

PRICE: £5.00 inc.

PRODUCER: National Asthma Campaign, 1992

DISTRIBUTOR: National Asthma Campaign

This video aims to help people with asthma in Asian communities by increasing understanding of the disease, its signs and symptoms, available treatments and their appropriate use. The video strongly promotes the message that most people with asthma may expect the best from life with regular preventive treatment. It was funded by the Department of Health.

The video uses a documentary style with a voice-over. We see a range of people with asthma (from children to the elderly) in a variety of settings. What happens to the lungs during an asthma attack is explained with the aid of graphics. Various treatments are clearly demonstrated and also the use of peak flow meters for monitoring. The video does not have any interviews with people who have asthma. A fact sheet of basic information accompanies the video (i.e. a separate fact sheet for each language).

Asian researchers and actors were used in the production of this video. It is excellent value and could be used in a variety of settings, e.g. asthma clinics. Health professionals may find it a useful aid to communication with patients. However it will be of most interest to people with asthma and their families.

Maternity care

FORMAT: Video, 20 mins

LANGUAGE: Cantonese, with or without English subtitles

TARGET AUDIENCE: Parents, primary healthcare teams

PRICE: £69.00 inc.

PRODUCER: Orientations, 1991

DISTRIBUTOR: Camden and Islington Health Authority

This video aims to explain antenatal care and encourage women to use antenatal services. It was made by Bloomsbury and Islington Health Promotion Department and funded by the Department of Health in conjunction with the Health Education Authority.

A group of pregnant women meeting with a Chinese midwife ask her about different aspects of maternity care. Her answers are reinforced by sequences of two of the women attending for antenatal care. Diagnostic tests such as ultrasound scanning, routine blood tests, and blood pressure checks, are shown as are parentcraft classes featuring breathing exercises and explanations of the birth process. Information is also given on healthy diet in pregnancy and how to find out about maternity benefits.

Shown in early pregnancy, women and their partners will find the video informative and interesting. Antenatal care is presented as supportive and women are encouraged to register early in pregnancy. All of the midwives shown speak Cantonese. This will not be the experience of many Chinese women so presenters will need to discuss with women how to arrange for linkworkers or translators if needed. The video was made after consultation with members of Cantonese-speaking communities and with Chinese- and English-speaking professionals.

Maternity pack

FORMAT: Pack, with 124-page and 33-page booklets

LANGUAGE: Japanese/English

TARGET AUDIENCE: Parents

PRICE: £20.00 inc

PRODUCER: Japanese Friendship Group, 1993

DISTRIBUTOR: Nakayoshi Kai

This pack aims to explain the British healthcare system in relation to pregnancy, birth and care of infants. The pack has been written bilingually in order to enable communication between health professionals and parents. It was produced by Nakayoshi Kai – the Japanese Friendship Group – a voluntary group supporting Japanese mothers. Assistance in production was provided by the Maternity Alliance, the Royal College of Midwives, various charities and commercial companies.

The pack consists of two booklets which are written bilingually (one page in English and the facing page in Japanese). One booklet covers everything you need to know if you are having a baby and have recently arrived in the UK. The stages from registering with a GP to developmental checks during the infant's early years are explained. Information is provided about sources of support and advice specifically for Japanese communities although these are mostly London based. Communication with health professionals is tackled directly with common terms and phrases relevant to pregnancy and labour included.

The other booklet is the well-known Persil Birthplan *Your baby, your choice* which covers choices available to woman in labour and birth. This can be used by the woman herself to write a birth plan or as a framework for antenatal classes dealing with birth. The booklet does contain a reference to Persil washing powder.

The booklets are clear and well written. They do not focus on the changes which occur during pregnancy but cover more practical information about antenatal care, choices in childbirth and administrative details such as registering the birth in the UK and Japan. The booklets have been well received by Japanese communities and have also been used by English-speaking women in Japan.

Maternity services for Asian women

FORMAT: 23-page booklet

LANGUAGE: English

TARGET AUDIENCE: Healthcare professionals, primary healthcare teams, commissioners

PRICE: Free

PRODUCER: NHS Management Executive, 1993

DISTRIBUTOR: BAPS

This booklet for purchasers of maternity services may also be of interest to providers and users of services. It particularly addresses maternity services for women from the Indian sub-continent. It is part of a series produced by the NHS Management Executive which aims to present users' views about current services and what a quality service would consist of. The Department of Health and the Share project at the King's Fund cooperated closely in the production of this booklet. The booklet concisely outlines current concerns about maternity services. This covers some issues specific to women from the Indian sub-continent and others relating to maternal and child health and effective use of maternity services. A longer section examines what can be done to improve services and make them more responsive to users. It includes examples of good practice from around the country and pinpoints particular issues such as promoting advocacy and making information more accessible. Throughout, quotes from women highlight the issues raised and this gives the booklet a human touch and firmly roots it in women's experience of services. There is a checklist at the end to assist purchasers to examine how maternity services are meeting the needs of all sections of the community.

This booklet is short enough to be read by everyone involved in purchasing or providing maternity services. It provides a useful basis for discussion about services and refreshingly examines services from the users' point of view.

Meeting Hindu families

FORMAT: Multimedia: video, 10 mins; 3 discs for IBM computer

LANGUAGE: English

TARGET AUDIENCE: Healthcare professionals, primary healthcare teams, trainers

PRICE: £350.00

PRODUCER: Southern Derbyshire Health Authority, 1992

DISTRIBUTOR: Southern Derbyshire NHS Trust

This is an interactive video designed for use by health professionals. It aims to inform about how to approach a Hindu family and communicate without causing offence or confusion. It was produced by Community Health Services which is part of Southern Derbyshire Health Authority.

It consists of a video and software which is installed on the computer, and the format and content are similar to the companion video, *Meeting Muslim families*, described below. It takes 40 to 50 minutes to work through the package.

Meeting Muslim families

FORMAT: Multimedia: video, 10 mins; disc for IBM computer

LANGUAGE: English

TARGET AUDIENCE: Healthcare professionals, primary healthcare teams, trainers

PRICE: £350.00

PRODUCER: Southern Derbyshire Health Authority, 1992

DISTRIBUTOR: Southern Derbyshire NHS Trust

This is an interactive video designed for use by health professionals. It aims to inform about how to approach a Muslim family and communicate without causing offence or confusion. It was produced by Community Health Services which is part of Southern Derbyshire Health Authority.

It consists of a video and software which is installed on the computer. The video and computer need to be side by side but not linked. The user is given instructions by the computer about when to play the video and the video prompts when to return to the computer. The package is based on the visit by a health visitor to a Muslim family. It covers working with an interpreter, introductions, appropriate dress for visitors, styles of dress, use of names and symbols in Muslim culture, identifying the head of the household and appropriate etiquette during the visit.

An easy-to-use and practical guide to the keyboard makes it accessible to those who have never used a computer before. The user watches a sequence from the video and then answers questions on it using the computer. The program also contains information sections which are available at any time and cover aspects of the video in more detail, such as family structure, and Muslim religion. It is a flexible package and can be worked through at the user's own pace and sections can be returned to easily. It is suitable for individual study or may be used by a group to discuss experiences and share learning. By basing the package on a common situation – a home visit – many aspects which can cause embarrassment are examined. The package does not cover ending the visit and users might want more information about this. It takes 40 to 50 minutes to work through the package.

Meeting Sikh families

FORMAT: Multimedia: video, 10 mins; disc for IBM computer

LANGUAGE: English

TARGET AUDIENCE: Healthcare professionals, primary healthcare teams, trainers

PRICE: £350.00

PRODUCER: Southern Derbyshire Health Authority, 1992

DISTRIBUTOR: Southern Derbyshire NHS Trust

This is an interactive video designed for use by health professionals. It aims to inform about how to approach a Sikh family and communicate without causing offence or confusion. It was produced by Community Health Services which is part of Southern Derbyshire Health Authority. It consists of a video and software which is installed on the computer, and the format and content are similar to the companion video, *Meeting Muslim families*, described above. It takes 40 to 50 minutes to work through the package.

Memory pictures

FORMAT: Video, 24 mins

LANGUAGE: English

TARGET AUDIENCE: General public

PRICE: £27.00

PRODUCER: Pratibha Parmar, 1989

DISTRIBUTOR: Out on a Limb

This video explores the history and experiences of members of a family who migrated from India to Canada and the UK. It was produced by an independent film company and funded by the Arts Council.

The video uses a variety of media – poetry, still photography, family photographs, readings from family letters – which give it an intimate and poignant quality. A black gay man explores his family's experiences by simply recounting how things happened and describing his current life. It is illustrated with his photographic work including a photo text exhibition about his family. This video could be used in group settings (schools, colleges, community groups) to explore family history, social history, experiences of migration and racism.

The menopause

FORMAT: Video, 18 mins; 5-page leaflet

LANGUAGE: Video: Bengali, Cantonese, English, Gujarati, Hindi/Urdu, Punjabi, Somali, Turkish and Vietnamese; Leaflets: Bengali, English, Gujarati, Hindi, Punjabi and Urdu

TARGET AUDIENCE: Women, health professionals

PRICE: £37.25 inc.

PRODUCER: UK Asian Women's Conference, 1992

DISTRIBUTOR: N Films

This video for women from Asian communities aims to inform women about the menopause. It covers how to deal with some of the discomforts they may experience and the help a GP can offer at this time. It was made for the UK Asian Women's Conference and funded by the Department of Health.

The video uses a dramatised sequence following a woman experiencing the menopause – she visits her GP and a consultant gynaeocologist who both explain more about the menopause and treatment which can help. A women's group talk of their experiences of the menopause. It is explained as a natural change in the body and the symptoms are clearly identified. Both doctors briefly describe treatment such as vaginal pessaries and hormone replacement therapy. The gynaeocologist explains that the woman will have a thorough examination thus giving women a good idea of what to expect from referral to hospital. Information is provided about osteoporosis which we are told is prevalent in Asian communities. Advice is given about a diet rich in calcium and vitamin D. Women are advised not to smoke and to take more exercise, with examples of kinds of exercise to consider.

The video is accompanied by a leaflet containing key information from the video. It is suitable for use in a group setting or for women to view at home. It could be used to support advice from a health professional or to trigger discussion. Women will need more information about hormone replacement therapy (e.g. it is not suitable for everyone and risks versus benefits). Many women will find this a useful and informative video.

Menopause: a time to look forward

FORMAT: 12-page booklet

LANGUAGE: English, Gujarati, Urdu

TARGET AUDIENCE: Women

PRICE: 68p

PRODUCER: Bolton Centre for Health Promotion, 1992

DISTRIBUTOR: Bolton Centre for Health Promotion

This booklet is for women approaching or experiencing the menopause. It aims to explain the signs of the menopause, treatments and self-help remedies available. It was funded by the Department of Health in conjunction with the Health Education Authority.

The booklet is well laid out although the print is small. The language used is clear and direct.

Menopause is presented as a stage of life rather than an illness. How women can help themselves overcome any discomfort experienced during the menopause is emphasised. Medical treatments such as hormone replacement therapy are also discussed. Women who want clear and practical information about the menopause will welcome this booklet. Reading it may give women enough confidence to be able to initiate a discussion with their doctor. Women's groups may find it a useful starting point for discussion about how the menopause affects women's lives. Other women will prefer to read it privately perhaps as a support to advice and information from a health professional. The booklet was trialled with women's groups in the Bolton area.

The menopause: coping with mid-life change

FORMAT: 8-page pack, illustrations

LANGUAGE: Bengali, English, Gujarati, Hindi, Punjabi, Urdu

TARGET AUDIENCE: Women

PRICE: Free

PRODUCER: Organon Laboratories

DISTRIBUTOR: Organon

These booklets are for women who are going through or approaching the menopause. They aim to provide some information about the menopause and about hormone replacement therapy (HRT). The booklets are produced by Organon Laboratories who market HRT.

The booklet refers to the menopause as a mid-life change and presents it as a normal and healthy part of a woman's life. Discomforts of the menopause are briefly described and advice is given about self-help such as relaxation and pelvic floor exercises. The advice given is general with no detail (for example, pelvic floor exercises are recommended but not described). Approximately one-third of the booklet refers to HRT, describing generally its benefits, how it may be taken and checks a doctor should make before prescribing it. Possible side effects are briefly mentioned.

Women may find this a useful booklet and it is a way of informing women about the existence of HRT and of raising the sensitive issue of discomfort women may experience going through the menopause. However it does indirectly promote HRT which some may find unacceptable. Others may feel that with additional information from a health professional it is helpful.

Mental health and Britain's black communities

FORMAT: 28-page booklet

LANGUAGE: English

TARGET AUDIENCE:

PRICE: £7.00 inc.

PRODUCER: King's Fund Centre, 1993

DISTRIBUTOR: Bournemouth English Book Centre

This short report aims to generate discussion and debate on the provision of effective and sensitive mental health services for black and minority ethnic groups. It is of interest to purchasers and providers of services at all levels. It was produced by the King's Fund Centre, the NHS Management Executive Mental Health Task Force and the Prince of Wales Advisory Group on Disability.

The report concisely comments on mental health concerns for African-Caribbean, Asian, Chinese, refugee and Vietnamese communities. The most prevalent diagnosis and responses/treatments are noted with information from relevant research findings and reports, plus comments from users of mental health services. Common issues for all communities are noted such as the effects of racism on mental health and misdiagnosis. Good practice is identified and a list of services which aim to meet the mental health needs of black and minority ethnic groups is included. There is a checklist for service provision and a series of suggestions for purchasers and providers at all levels to consider. These are intended to provide a focus for implementing ideas or identifying areas of further work.

Mistaken for mad

FORMAT: Video, 40 mins

LANGUAGE: English

TARGET AUDIENCE: Healthcare professionals, mental health teams, primary healthcare teams, general public

PRICE: £28.99 inc.

PRODUCER: Twenty Twenty Television for Channel Four, 1990

DISTRIBUTOR: Healthcare Productions

This video is a documentary which examines some controversial issues about the diagnosis and treatment of mental health problems within African-Caribbean communities and Asian communities.

The first half explores mental health services in relation to African-Caribbean communities. A number of worrying statistics and trends are identified such as the disproportionately large numbers of young black men detained under the Mental Health Act and seemingly higher dosages of drugs given to black patients. The issues are discussed in interviews with psychiatrists, community organisations and users of mental health services. A series of questions is asked about how fair and appropriate mental health services are for members of African-Caribbean communities and a need for further research is identified.

The second half explores mental health services in relation to Asian communities. The very low take-up of services is examined and the different ways mental distress may be expressed by members of Asian communities is discussed. An innovative group for Asian people in hospital is shown and a community support group for women. It is noted that psychotherapy ('talking treatments') are less likely to be offered to African-Caribbean and Asian people although the community initiatives shown appear to use this with some success.

This video is useful trigger material as it highlights a series of controversial issues in mental health services. Medical staff and service providers may find it a useful starting point for training and discussion about the impact of race and culture on mental health – including definitions of and responses to mental health problems.

Moving on: a photopack of travellers in Britain

FORMAT: Pack; with 32-page workbook and 24 A4 photocards

LANGUAGE: English

TARGET AUDIENCE: Key Stage 1 (5–8), Key Stage 2 (8–12), Key Stage 3 (12–14), Key Stage 4 (14–16), teachers

PRICE: £3.00

PRODUCER: Minority Rights Group Education Project, 1987

DISTRIBUTOR: Minority Rights Group

This pack consists of a photopack and booklet of classroom activities for teachers to use with pupils of Key Stages 1 to 4. It seeks to challenge misconceptions and racist views about traveller communities and inform about the history, culture and life today of those communities. The pack was produced by the Minority Rights Group Education Project and funded by a group of statutory authorities and charitable organisations.

The booklet contains activities which can be used across the curriculum to learn about traveller communities. These are mostly discussion based and some involve children carrying out their own investigations (e.g. talking to older family members about travellers, examining place names for links with travellers in the past). The A4 photographs are black-and-white and record different aspects of life in traveller communities. They are designed to be used with the activities in the pack. The activities encourage children and young people to examine the nature of prejudice. The producers advise that the pack should be used as part of a wider anti-racist approach within the whole school and not only when traveller children attend the school.

The pack was developed by a wide group of educationists, many of whom are travellers themselves and who work with traveller communities. It took over three years' work in mainstream schools and travellers participated in trialling the materials in schools.

Mrs Khan goes for breast-screening

FORMAT: Video, 25 mins; with 22-page notes

LANGUAGE: Bengali, English, Gujarati, Hindi/ Urdu, Punjabi

TARGET AUDIENCE: Women, primary healthcare teams, health professionals

PRICE: £35.00

PRODUCER: South Birmingham Health Authority, 1992

DISTRIBUTOR: South Birmingham Health Authority

This video aims to explain to women in, or approaching the 50–64 age group, the purpose and procedure of breast-screening as realistically as possible. The video follows Mrs Khan from the point of receiving a letter inviting her to attend for breast-screening through the complete process including recall for further tests. Mrs Khan reflects the worries women may have about breast cancer but rarely voice. Different kinds of interpreting are shown and the teaching notes suggest this is discussed after the video, so that women can comment on which kind of interpreting they prefer. Throughout, breast-screening is presented as a sensible health choice – a means of ensuring breast cancer is treated early or of ensuring all is well. The teaching notes give a synopsis of the video, guidance for planning sessions around the video, information about

breast-screening and answers to common questions. The video is designed for use in women's groups but could also be viewed by individuals in the privacy of their own home. The makers suggest it could also be used with groups of men especially if they are reluctant for wives to attend for breast-screening. It is an excellent trigger for discussion.

The video shows the screening process in full with Mrs Khan undressed to the waist. The makers acknowledge that some may find this embarrassing but they and the actress felt strongly that women should know exactly what is involved. The notes stress that presenters must prepare people for this before showing the video. The video has been pre-tested with groups of women and the notes identify a few areas of confusion which may occur in one language.

Mrs Lal's arthritis

FORMAT: Video, 18 mins; with 5-page booklet

LANGUAGE: Bengali, English, Gujarati, Hindi/ Urdu, Punjabi

TARGET AUDIENCE: General public, health professionals, primary healthcare teams

PRICE: £45.82 inc. (statutory/commercial organisations), £14.67 inc. (community organisations)

PRODUCER: N Films for Arthritis Care, 1992

DISTRIBUTOR: N Films (free loan from Arthritis Care)

This video aims to raise awareness about arthritis, its symptoms, treatment and management. It was funded by the Department of Health.

The video takes the form of a dramatised sequence about Mrs Lal, a mother of two school-age children who develops arthritis. The viewer follows Mrs Lal as she visits her GP who diagnoses arthritis and refers her to hospital to see a specialist. She also discovers that Arthritis Care has a local support group which she attends. The consultation with the specialist includes the kinds of examination likely to be done and questions asked. Mrs Lal visits the physiotherapist for exercises and treatment. Equipment and adaptions in the home are also shown. Mrs Lal visits her GP with her husband who interprets for her and later at the hospital a linkworker assists. The accompanying booklet explains what arthritis is in more detail and how to contact Arthritis Care.

The video is suitable for viewing in group settings or in the home. It may be of most interest to people newly diagnosed with arthritis and their families. The explanations of treatment and tests are very clear and reassuring. It may be helpful for people to have access to a health professional to answer questions and provide information about how to arrange linkworkers, find out more about using adaptations, etc.

Multilingual AIDS: HIV information for black and minority ethnic communities

FORMAT: 98-page booklet

LANGUAGE: English

TARGET AUDIENCE: Health professionals, service providers

PRICE: £4.99 + 88p p&p

PRODUCER: Health Education Authority, 1992

DISTRIBUTOR: Health Education Authority

This booklet aims to evaluate HIV health education materials which are targeted directly at black and minority ethnic groups.

The booklet comments on resources (leaflets, posters, videos) which were produced in community languages or English between 1984 and 1990. Requests to statutory and voluntary organisations produced 150 examples of health education resources or

initiatives. These were then evaluated on a quantitative and qualitative basis. The qualitative analysis covered accuracy of information provided, production quality and the appropriateness of the language/tone used. A summary of each resource provides a brief description and notes any problematic areas such as inaccurate information, complicated use of language, etc. Also included are brief outlines of 41 resources which were produced after 1990 and so were not evaluated as part of the study.

The book includes a discussion of issues involved in informing black and minority ethnic groups about HIV which also has relevance for other health promotion messages, for example issues involved in language and translation. The comments about individual resources are a mixture of specific points (such as size of print, levels of literacy required to read it) and more general comments (such as 'insensitive'). Anyone involved in the production of health promotion resources for black and minority ethnic groups will find this book interesting.

My mum thinks she's funny!

FORMAT: Video, 20 mins; with 15-page booklet

LANGUAGE: English

TARGET AUDIENCE: Community groups, parents, women

PRICE: £40.00 (VOLCUF members), £50.00 (non-members)

PRODUCER: Voluntary Organisations Liaison Council for Under Fives, 1991

DISTRIBUTOR: VOLCUF

This video and accompanying booklet aim to make parents from black and minority ethnic groups aware of a range of voluntary organisations which provide services for families with young children. The organisations described are a befriending project, National Childminding Association,

Working Mothers Association, National Association for the Welfare of Children in Hospital, community health workers, playbuses, playgroups and toy libraries. The film was funded by the Department of Health and made by the voluntary organisations featured.

The film has an unusual format and begins with a comedienne recounting her experiences of being a mother. The information sections about the various organisations are interspersed with comments by the comedienne. Some people may not appreciate the humour and there is a reference to smoking which some may object to. However the information sections are interesting, with each organisation describing their service, followed by a sequence of the service in action. It is stressed that cultural issues are important and need to be taken into account when providing services for young families.

The film would be most useful if supported by information about local provision. The booklet provides national addresses and has the introduction only translated into five Asian languages. It is probably best viewed by groups of parents and will provide information about some services they may already know of and some which may be new to them. It could be used as a trigger for discussion about the kinds of services parents want and for information swapping about local provision. Some groups may prefer to view the information sections only. It is an expensive film so it may be worth finding out if it can be borrowed locally or alternatively hire it for a week.

Myself

FORMAT: Pack; with 34-page manual, 4 booklets, and set of cards

LANGUAGE: English

TARGET AUDIENCE: Key Stage 1 (5–8), Key Stage 2 (8–12), teachers

PRICE: £22.50 inc.

PRODUCER: Afro-Caribbean Education Resource Centre, 1987

DISTRIBUTOR: Acer Centre

A teaching pack for use with Key Stages 1 and 2 children in early years education and in schools. It was produced by ACER – the Afro-Caribbean Education Resource Centre – which aims to design learning materials that recognise the existence of racial and cultural diversity. The pack was developed and trialled with teachers and children in a large number of schools.

The four booklets can be used as stand-alone material for children to look at and read themselves, or with pupils or parents. They have bright and interesting contemporary photographs of a multiracial group of children accompanied by simple text which encourages the reader to consider how they look and feel. Each booklet has brief notes at the end which give some guidance to the parent/carer/teacher about how to read with the child. It is suggested that it is helpful for the child to notice differences between him/herself and others and that this helps foster respect for other people.

The accompanying teaching manual contains a series of activities which can be used in a classroom setting. These focus on the topics raised by the four booklets: me, my body, my senses, my feelings. There are suggestions for building good relationships with parents. The manual stresses the importance of every child valuing him/herself and of being valued. Ideas for building this into the curriculum are included. There is an extensive resource list but this would need some updating now.

National Sickle Cell Programme pack

FORMAT: Pack, with 5 booklets and 50 × 38 cms poster

LANGUAGE: English

TARGET AUDIENCE: General public, health professionals

PRICE: Enquire for details

PUBLISHER: National Sickle Cell Programme, 1986–89

DISTRIBUTOR: National Sickle Cell Programme

This pack aims to inform about sickle cell anaemia and sickle cell trait. It is for people who may be affected by sickle cell themselves or have a family member or friend affected by it. The pack was produced by the National Sickle Cell Programme which seeks to promote wider understanding of sickle cell for patients, families and professionals.

The pack consists of booklets, leaflets, a poster and record books. The leaflets inform about sickle cell in general. One gives a fairly technical description of six haemoglobin conditions. The poster has mostly closely typed text describing sickle cell with a large drawing of a normal blood cell and one of a sickle cell. People can fill in the personal record books to monitor their condition and include details such as hospital appointments, records of crises, etc. There is also a leaflet about sickle cell trait illustrated with smiley face drawings and minimal text which may be useful for people who are not confident readers.

The pack is useful for raising awareness about sickle cell among health professionals and could be helpful in training. People with sickle cell anaemia may find the record book useful and some will be interested in the more detailed booklet.

New faces, new places: learning about people on the move

FORMAT: Pack, with 21-page handbook and 6 booklets

LANGUAGE: English

TARGET AUDIENCE: Key Stage 1 (5–8), teachers

PRICE: £9.00 inc.

PRODUCER: Save the Children, 1992

DISTRIBUTOR: Save the Children

This pack, for use with Key Stage 1 children in the classroom, focuses on themes of leaving home, journeys, life in a new home and welcoming newcomers. The pack aims to increase children's understanding of why people leave their homes and to develop a positive attitude towards cultural diversity.

The pack contains four units, each of which tells the stories of children from different parts of the world – Africa (Mozambique and Sudan), Vietnam, Palestine and Kurdistan. Each unit contains background information notes for teachers plus booklets of children's stories with drawings and photographs. The children describe their experiences and situations in everyday language which many children will be able to read themselves. The teachers' handbook contains a series of classroom-based activities on the four themes of the pack. It is suitable for large and small group work. Relevant National Curriculum attainment targets are identified for geography, history, science and English.

This is a useful classroom resource presenting a variety of activities for approaching learning about refugees. Although targeted at Key Stage 1 it may also be appropriate for Key Stage 2. It is unusual in seeking to present such issues to this age group and does so in a concrete and accessible manner. A number of organisations working with refugee communities contributed to the pack.

A nurse to meet your needs

FORMAT: Video, 15 mins

LANGUAGE: Bengali, Cantonese, Gujarati, Hindi, Punjabi, Urdu – with English subtitles

TARGET AUDIENCE: Older people, healthcare professionals, community workers

PRICE: £27.46 inc. (RCN members), £31.29 (non-members)

PRODUCER: Healthcare Productions, 1990

DISTRIBUTOR: Healthcare Productions

This video aims to explain the District Nursing Service to older people from Asian and Chinese communities. Made by the Royal College of Nursing and Department of Health, it presents the service mainly from a provider's point of view with nursing professionals describing the role of the district nurse. The film stresses how linkworkers and interpreters can assist the district nurse to communicate with people whose first language is not English.

The video shows the district nurse visiting people at home and seeing people in health centres and GP surgeries. Some of the people shown are from Asian and Chinese communities as are some of the nurses. Linkworkers and interpreters explain their roles clearly and they are seen working with district nurses in health centres.

There are no interviews with service users describing their experiences of the District Nursing Service. The service is explained generally rather than specifically so people may need further information about the kind of treatment or care a district nurse provides. Local information will also need to be provided about the availability of linkworkers, interpreters and male nurses. The video could be viewed at home by potential or new users of the District Nursing Service to inform and reassure them. The video could also be used with groups of older people to explain the service and share experiences of using it.

Nursing for all: career opportunities for the Asian communities

FORMAT: Video, 15 mins

LANGUAGE: Bengali, English, Gujarati, Hindi, Punjabi, Urdu

TARGET AUDIENCE: General public

PRICE: £26.50 inc.

PRODUCER: Royal Society of Medicine, 1988

DISTRIBUTOR: Healthcare Productions

This video aims to encourage more people from Asian communities to consider nursing as a career choice. It was produced by the Royal Society of Medicine and funded by Tower Hamlets Health Authority, the Department of Health, Home Office and various Task Forces in England.

The video uses a mixture of interviews with nurses from Asian communities and those involved in training nurses to explain the role of a nurse and the career opportunities available. The entrance requirements are outlined and the training is briefly explained. An access student describes her course and her expectations on starting training. Nurses are seen in many roles in hospitals and in the community working in partnership with other health professionals. The video notes that nurses are needed from all communities and that this can help to offer a more responsive health service to patients. Women are interviewed throughout although a male nurse is shown in the opening shots.

This video may be of interest to young people, perhaps as part of careers education, and to those considering a change of career or returning to work after a break. The video does not provide information about pay scales, length and type of training, etc. but if shown in a group setting this could form part of the discussion.

Nutrition in minority ethnic groups: Asians and Afro-Caribbeans in the United Kingdom – a briefing paper prepared for health professionals

FORMAT: 28-page booklet

LANGUAGE: English

TARGET AUDIENCE: Health professionals

PRICE: £2.99 + 80p p&p

PRODUCER: Health Education Authority, 1991

DISTRIBUTOR: Health Education Authority

The booklet is for health professionals and brings together all the available information about nutrition in Asian and African-Caribbean communities. It aims to inform about the cultural food beliefs and eating patterns of these communities. It was produced by the Health Education Authority.

This booklet briefly outlines the dietary practices of the various communities including patterns of change and infant feeding practices. The nutritional implications of diets for groups within communities (such as pregnant women) are explained based on current research findings. Controversial and non-conclusive research is also mentioned. The booklet concludes with some recommendations about nutrition education and suggestions for further research areas. There is a comprehensive reference section. This concise booklet will be of interest to health professionals concerned with nutrition.

One way history

FORMAT: Video, 15 mins

LANGUAGE: English

TARGET AUDIENCE: People with learning difficulties, community workers

PRICE: £24.50 inc.

PRODUCER: 20th Century Vixen, 1990

DISTRIBUTOR: 20th Century Vixen

In this short video, made with a racially mixed group, four young women with learning difficulties discuss their experiences and understanding of racism and disability. The video was originally made for a staff training workshop on race, disability and gender but tutors decided staff could best learn from the women's group, black women's group and self advocacy group and so women were asked to participate in a discussion for the video.

The video records the discussion among the women as it unfolded. Some may find the pace of the discussion slow as the women find the words to express their thoughts and views. However, people with learning difficulties may find the pace just about right for them. The women talk about how they are aware of racism and this is challenging as it is rare to hear people with learning difficulties commenting on such issues. Not only could it be used to illustrate what a discussion group is like for people with learning difficulties, but as a trigger to discuss issues of race and disability. Used with staff groups, it could raise expectations of what it is possible for people with learning difficulties to achieve and to reinforce how important it is to challenge racism and to provide services which do not discriminate.

At times the group tutors prompt the women, but overall the women speak spontaneously and with great feeling, as they find their own words to express their thoughts and views. The women have worked together for some time on a range of issues and this may be inspiring for many viewers. Advocacy groups may be particularly interested in this video. It is unusual to see people with learning difficulties stating their opinions and even more unusual for those people to be black women.

. . . only a call away . . .

FORMAT: Video, 30 mins; with 3-page notes

LANGUAGE: English, Hindi

TARGET AUDIENCE: General public, trainers

PRICE: £26.50 inc. (HVA members), £28.50 inc. (non-members)

PRODUCER: Royal Society of Medicine, 1986

DISTRIBUTOR: Healthcare Productions

This video is for general and professional audiences. It aims to explain the role of the health visitor and to give some examples of the diversity of work health visitors undertake. It was produced by the Film and TV Unit of the Royal Society of Medicine and the Health Visitors Association with support from the National Dairy Council.

The video uses a documentary style and health visitors describe their work through interviews. Parents talk about the support they have received from health visitors and how they felt about this. It is filmed throughout the country in inner cities and rural settings. Health visitors are followed as they work in health centres and in the community visiting families. Some parents describe the help health visitors gave them during difficult situations such as cot death, breakdown of a relationship, violent partners, etc. Brief mention is made of working with families where the health visitor does not share a common language and the assistance of a linkworker is needed.

The accompanying notes give some general advice about showing the video in group sessions. The video would be useful in illustrating the varied role of health visitors to other professionals such as teachers and social workers, perhaps as part of a training programme. It is quite lengthy and detailed for a general audience but selected clips tailored to the topic or target audience may be appropriate.

Our people: HIV/AIDS and the black communities

FORMAT: Video, 30 mins

LANGUAGE: Bengali, Cantonese, English, Gujarati, Hindi, Punjabi, Swahili, Urdu

TARGET AUDIENCE: General public, community workers

PRICE: £20 each language

PRODUCER: Picture Talk Films for Black HIV/AIDS Network, 1990

DISTRIBUTOR: Picture Talk Films

DISTRIBUTOR: Black HIV/AIDS Network

This video is for people from African, Asian and African-Caribbean communities in the UK. It aims to explain what HIV and AIDS are, how HIV is transmitted, how to protect against HIV. Support and advice is offered for those living with HIV. It was funded by the Department of Health, the London Borough of Southwark, Brent HIV Centre, the London Borough of Camden AIDS Unit and the London Borough of Islington HIV Unit.

The video is presented by three well-known actors from black communities who explain why they think HIV and AIDS are important issues for their communities. An interesting format is used in which the actors tell the stories of people who have been affected by HIV and AIDS. Care has been taken to select a range of situations and lifestyles, for example a married woman with children, the sister of a gay man who is HIV positive, an ex-drug user and so on. This puts the factual information about transmission, protection and support networks in a human context. An animated graphics sequence clearly explains what HIV and AIDS are and how HIV is transmitted.

The buddy system is explained and a woman tells us why she chose to become a buddy.

The video identifies some complex issues such as women negotiating use of condoms with partners and the implications this may have for their relationships. This kind of issue could be explored further in discussion. The video is informative and mentions support networks and further sources of help – it may be useful to have local information available (in the relevant community language if necessary) to support this. The video could be used in a group setting to spark discussion about a range of issues to do with HIV and AIDS and provide opportunities for information sharing as well as discussion of feelings and attitudes.

Partnership 2000

FORMAT: Video, 15 mins; with 55-page report

LANGUAGE: English

TARGET AUDIENCE: Service providers

PRICE: Write for details

PRODUCER: Save the Children, 1991

DISTRIBUTOR: Partnership Project

This video examines the experiences and principles leading to the development of an inter-agency project which shared responsibility for delivering quality services to traveller communities. The project partners are Save the Children, West Midlands Education Service for Travelling Children, Walsall Health Authority and the National Gypsy Council.

This short documentary uses photographic stills, cartoons and animated graphics. It examines traveller communities' access to services and how service structures discriminate against travellers. The work of the project is described and we hear of health and education services which are working with traveller communities rather than for them. In terms of health provision the project has resulted in increased uptake of childhood immunisations, use of family planning services, cervical screening, access to mainstream medical services and patient-held medical records. The project advocates cooperation between agencies and the involvement of travellers themselves, both locally and nationally.

This video may be of interest to those providing services to traveller communities and to those considering adopting an inter-agency approach. The video is accompanied by a report of a conference held in 1991 to raise awareness of the needs of Traveller communities.

Patient's charter standard: respect for religious and cultural beliefs

FORMAT: 41-page manual

LANGUAGE: English

TARGET AUDIENCE: Service providers, commissioners

PRICE: £12.50

PRODUCER: Mount Vernon Hospital NHS Trust, 1992

DISTRIBUTOR: Mount Vernon Hospital NHS Trust

This manual aims to enable professional carers (e.g. health professionals) to meet the cultural and religious needs of clients/ patients. It was produced with assistance from a large number of individuals and organisations of different religious and cultural groups.

The manual consists of an A4-size booklet and two laminated inserts. Issues covered in the manual include brief details of a large number of religions with preferences regarding diet, care of the dying, post mortems, organ donation, fasting, prayer, etc. noted. Issues to do with death and dying such as procedure for registration of death, burial abroad, guidelines for viewing the body with regard to different religious observances are included. The inserts give phone numbers of helplines and voluntary organisations and guidelines for hospital staff in the use of interpreters. The manual contains an audit form to assist managers assessing standards relating to respect for religious and cultural beliefs. Suggestions of books and leaflets for resource packs which should be available in clinical and non-clinical areas are included plus suggestions for books in patient areas. This is a useful resource which can be used everyday for reference in institutional settings and as part of general training. Although written with hospitals in mind it may also be of interest to GPs and others involved in primary care.

People are people

FORMAT: Video, 20 mins; with 40-page teaching notes

LANGUAGE: English

TARGET AUDIENCE: Health professionals, primary healthcare teams, trainers

PRICE: £33.21 inc.

PRODUCER: Royal Society of Medicine, 1986

DISTRIBUTOR: Healthcare Productions

This video and accompanying teaching notes have been designed as training materials to enable health professionals to explore prejudice and stereotypes. They were produced as part of the Asian Mother and Baby Campaign. The package was funded by the Department of Health and supported by the Health Visitors Association and the Royal College of Midwives.

The video uses six dramatised scenes to present common forms of stereotyping, prejudice and racism. Five scenes are set in a maternity ward and one is set in the community based around a health visitor. The bulk of the video is about the attitudes and behaviour of staff to clients/patients but it also

deals with staff facing the racist views of clients. The difficult issue of prejudice and racism within staff teams is also identified, particularly in hierarchical situations. The teaching notes recognise how threatening this subject may be for participants and facilitators. The notes recommend the training is only undertaken by facilitators who have had some training in group processes and who have done some work on racism themselves. The notes contain a series of exercises, discussion topics and information to be used with the video and further reading.

This is a useful video which sharply identifies many aspects of prejudice and stereotyping. The format of short scenes enables discussion to be focused and enough material is provided for several sessions on this topic. The material has been presented in a manner which enables the viewer to consider how stereotyping and racism could be challenged and to identify ways of ensuring prejudice does not occur in service delivery.

Phototalk books

FORMAT: Pack; with 9 photo books and 2 leaflets

LANGUAGE: No text

TARGET AUDIENCE: Under 5s, Key Stage 1 (5–8), parents, teachers

PRICE: £37.50 (complete set), £4.50 (each)

PRODUCER: ILEA Learning Resources Branch, 1984

DISTRIBUTOR: AMS Educational

These books for children under 5 are about everyday activities, and seek to help children make sense of their own world and understand more about other people's.

In the clear, colour photographs, children of different races and cultures are involved in activities all children will identify with. Many of the activities are broadly health related. The books have no text so children can talk about the pictures and create their own stories. As the books can be 'read' in any language they are extremely accessible to families who are speakers of other languages, enabling child and adult to share the book in their mother tongue. Accompanying leaflets (one with the set and one with each book) aimed at parents and carers note the kinds of issues the books may prompt children to raise and suggest ways of using them.

These books will be a valuable addition to any setting for young children. They present attractive and interesting images of children from multiracial communities, thus counteracting the predominantly white imagery of many books for children. Produced on thick card and spiral bound, they are durable and easy for young children to handle.

Physical and mental handicap in the Asian community: can my child be helped?

FORMAT: Video, 22 mins; with 24-page notes

LANGUAGE: Bengali, English, Gujarati, Hindi/Urdu, Punjabi

TARGET AUDIENCE: Parents

PRICE: £29.90 inc.

PRODUCER: N Films and National Children's Bureau for Department of Health, 1989

DISTRIBUTOR: CFL Vision

This video is for parents from Asian communities who have a child with a disability and aims to inform them of services and sources of help. It stresses the important role parents and family play in the child's development and achievement of full potential. The video encourages parents to be more confident about their ability to help their child.

Throughout, families are seen in a range of situations with their children, playing at home and in the park, at self-help groups,

participating in physiotherapy sessions and discussing their child with health professionals. The voice-over encourages parents to question professionals and to persist if they are not satisfied with the response. Different ways of interpreting are shown – using a partner, relative or linkworker – and this may be a useful trigger for discussion with parents about what kind of interpreting they prefer. Benefits are mentioned and presenters will need to ensure they have up-to-date information available about these.

The accompanying notes identify the main themes of the video. They also give some basic information about Asian families and advice on providing appropriate and effective help. Guidelines for services for families with children with special needs and a list of useful organisations are included. The video mentions some conditions but does not examine any disabilities in detail. Parents will want more information about their child's condition. The list of organisations may be helpful, but most of them do not produce material in languages other than English.

The video is of most use to parents of newly diagnosed children. They will be interested to hear what other parents have to say, the scenes of parents and children together are optimistic but also acknowledge the difficulties parents may face. It is suitable for viewing in small groups but many families may prefer to view it at home. The presence of a health professional or community worker may be useful to provide support and answer questions. The video was produced with advice and support from the Working Party on Physical and Mental Handicap in the Asian Community.

To plan a family

FORMAT: Video, 25 mins

LANGUAGE: Bengali, English, Hindi

TARGET AUDIENCE: Primary healthcare teams, health professionals

PRICE: £26.50 inc.

PRODUCER: Royal Society of Medicine, 1986

DISTRIBUTOR: Healthcare Productions

This video for health professionals aims to explore the social and cultural context of family planning within Asian communities. It was produced by the National Health Service Training Authority as part of the Asian Mother and Baby Campaign and is endorsed by the Health Visitors Association and Royal College of Midwives.

Through a series of interviews health professionals (family planning doctors, nurse, linkworker and health visitor) explain their services and roles and discuss how they work with Asian communities. A mullah discusses spacing a family and religious views on family planning. A series of husbands and wives give their views on whether or not to use family planning – all of the women express interest in family planning but have anxieties about it, the men present more mixed views. The video is not about family planning methods but is much more about how family planning may be regarded by Asian communities and difficulties such as language barriers which may be experienced in accessing services.

The video will be of interest to health professionals who may find the discussion about how to raise the issue of family planning helpful. It could also be used within the community to enable discussion of different views about family planning and to share information.

Play

FORMAT: Video, 11 mins (Bengali version); 13 mins (Cantonese version); 9 mins (English version); with 3-page English script

LANGUAGE: Bengali, Cantonese, English

TARGET AUDIENCE: Parents

PRICE: £15 inc.

PRODUCER: Tower Hamlets Health Promotion Service, 1987

DISTRIBUTOR: East London & City HPS

This video aims to inform parents about the importance of play in the development of children. It demonstrates suitable materials and activities for children of different age groups. It was produced by Tower Hamlets Health Promotion Unit in conjunction with the Occupational Therapy Department of Tower Hamlets Health Authority Community and Priority Services.

The video features several families (white and African-Caribbean), with both parents and children involved in play activities at home. Home-made toys and activities are demonstrated (such as household equipment and 'scrap' toys). It is stressed that children enjoy and learn from a range of activities and that parental involvement and approval are important to children. A range of toys suitable for children at different ages are shown. One sequence focuses on safety and ensuring that toys are safe to use. Toy libraries are mentioned and parents may benefit from local information about these services. Information about local play facilities such as parent and toddler sessions and playgroups may also be useful.

The video is suitable for viewing with groups of parents at home. It can be used to start discussion about the importance of play and to inform about opportunities for play in the community.

Play with confidence: a training pack for those wishing to introduce children to multiracial Britain

FORMAT: Pack

LANGUAGE: English

TARGET AUDIENCE: Teachers, lecturers

PRICE: £55.00

PRODUCER: Southampton Council of Community Services, 1991

DISTRIBUTOR: Southampton Council of Community Services

This pack seeks to 'provide carers of under-fives with the tools and skills necessary to ensure all children receive care that will allow them to develop a positive self-identity and non-racist attitudes'. It was developed by a group of professionals working with under-fives convened by Southampton Council for Under Fives. It was produced by Southampton Council of Community Services.

The pack contains seven sections held in an A5 ring binder. The main section covers exercises and topics for discussion. The exercises vary from information giving (with photocopiable handouts), awareness raising, examining current practice and resources, through to practising challenging racism and tackling attitudes among parents and children. There are suggestions for structuring training with sample programmes. The pack includes some information from other sources relevant to anti-racist practice in under-fives' settings and suggests users of the pack add to this. The section on multi-cultural play equipment is limited with no information about sources of items listed. Parts of this pack will be useful to those working in under-fives' settings, especially those working in predominantly white settings. Many of the exercises provide starting points for exploring anti-racist ways of working and will trigger discussion about why and how this should be done. The pack has been piloted with a range of under-fives' workers and was received positively.

Positive action: a report of the programme to implement race equality throughout NACRO projects and guidance on good practice

FORMAT: 20-page report

LANGUAGE: English

TARGET AUDIENCE: Service providers

PRICE: £2.00 + 50p p&p

PRODUCER: National Association for the Care and Resettlement of Offenders, 1990

DISTRIBUTOR: NACRO

This report outlines NACRO's Positive Action Programme which was designed to ensure that all NACRO's services demonstrated a commitment to tackle racism and provide services equally.

The report explains the background to the development of the programme and how it was implemented in two parts. Strategies for achieving positive action cover: dealing with racist language and behaviour, changing the culture and ethos, providing relevant services, public relations, referral sources and systems, work placements and links with black communities. Examples of good practice and progress from NACRO projects around the country are included. These range from projects which are beginning to examine racism to those which have developed systems for ensuring racial equality is considered at all stages. Organisations implementing similar programmes may find this report interesting, particularly its unequivocal stand on racist language and behaviour.

Positive images

FORMAT: Video, 15 mins × 3; with 1-page leaflet

LANGUAGE: English or Urdu voice-over

TARGET AUDIENCE: Key Stage 4 (14–16), young people (16-plus), parents, teachers

PRICE: £50.00

PRODUCER: Hammerhead Productions, 1992

DISTRIBUTOR: City of Bradford Metropolitan Council

These videos are for parents and young people from Asian communities. They aim to show the variety of further education, training and work options that are available. They were produced as a result of a joint project between QED Bradford, City of Bradford Metropolitan Council and Hammerhead Productions and were financed by a group of private companies and public authorities.

There is a video for young people, available in English only, and one for parents, available in English and Urdu versions. Each video features local men and women from Asian communities in Bradford talking about their careers. A number of different occupations are described – a medical technician, environmental health officer, headteacher, financial adviser, managing director of a computer training company, TV editor and a project manager in industry. Each person discusses their education and career history. For some this was via university while others gained qualifications while on the job. All stress the importance of experience and determination. Salary ranges and future prospects are mentioned.

The video aimed at parents includes comments about parental support and encouragement. Parents are encouraged to consider a wider range of occupations, discuss career options with their son or daughter and talk to career officers. They are also encouraged to consider university and college training for young women, with the assurance that women-only accommodation is available if required.

The videos are designed to trigger discussion about career options which are available and to challenge the notion that only traditional professions such as the law or medicine are 'successful'. They can be used in a variety of settings at school or college with young people, at parents' or governors' meetings with parents. The parents' video can also be viewed at home.

Postnatal depression

FORMAT: Video, 30 mins

LANGUAGE: Bengali, English, Hindi

TARGET AUDIENCE: Parents, primary healthcare teams, health professionals

PRICE: £26.50 inc.

PRODUCER: Royal Society of Medicine for Mother and Baby Campaign, 1986

DISTRIBUTOR: Healthcare Productions

This video for Asian communities aims to raise awareness and explain about postnatal depression.

Through a series of interviews with health professionals such as a health visitor, GP, psychiatrist, the different forms of postnatal depression are described and explained. There are also interviews with mothers who describe how they felt when they were postnatally depressed. Husbands and a mother-in-law also give their accounts of the illness.

The GP suggests the most common form of treatment is reassurance and a listening ear. However, he notes that in Asian languages there is no synonymous word for depression, and that mental illness can be viewed as a stigma. Other treatments (anti-depressants) for more serious illness are discussed. The video stresses that the most important thing is to ask for help.

This video may be useful in raising awareness generally about postnatal depression and the need for support and understanding for mothers in the postnatal period. The video could also be used in training health professionals as it does touch upon the importance of an awareness of people's culture in diagnosing and treating depression.

Prevention of coronary heart disease

FORMAT: Video, 40 mins; with 21-page notes *(Action on coronary heart disease in Asians)*

LANGUAGE: Bengali/English, Gujarati/English, Hindi/Urdu/English, Punjabi/English

TARGET AUDIENCE: General public

PRICE: £29.00 + p&p + VAT

PRODUCER: Health Education Authority, 1990

DISTRIBUTOR: Concord Film and Video Council

This video for Asian communities shows how coronary heart disease can be prevented by simple measures. It was produced as part of the Look After Your Heart campaign and funded by the Department of Health and the Health Education Authority.

After a middle-aged man, Ajit, has a mild heart attack, he is given advice in the hospital coronary care unit about how to make changes to his lifestyle and diet. Ajit and his family (wife and two adult children) put the advice into practice. This includes a healthier diet, regular exercise, giving up smoking, limiting alcohol, keeping weight under control and learning to cope with stress. A dietitian explains the importance of a low fat diet and stresses that a traditional Asian diet is healthy and can easily be adapted to include current dietary advice. The doctor gives Ajit some tips about giving up smoking and Ajit is seen putting this into practice.

This video is suitable for viewing in group

settings or individually at home, with or without health professionals, to trigger discussion about healthier lifestyles and awareness of coronary heart disease. People who have experienced heart disease may find it particularly informative and discussion within whole families may encourage and support changes in lifestyles. An accompanying booklet for health professionals explores risk factors and provides an action plan for health promotion. The video and booklet were produced with the help of a multidisciplinary group which included representatives from Asian communities.

Profile on prejudice

FORMAT: Pack; with 28-page handbook, 8-page profiles × 3 and 178 × 21 cms poster

LANGUAGE: English

TARGET AUDIENCE: Key Stage 2 (8–12), Key Stage 3 (12–14), teachers

PRICE: £6.95

PRODUCER: Minority Rights Group Education Project, 1985

DISTRIBUTOR: Minority Rights Group

This resource pack for teachers is for use with Key Stages 2 and 3 students. It aims to provide material and ideas for teaching about prejudice (as defined by the authors) and about minority groups. It was produced with funding from Oxfam and the European Economic Community.

The pack consists of a handbook for teachers and three 8-page profiles about travellers, Palestinians and native Americans. The handbook provides a series of classroom-based activities which can be used to examine and challenge the nature of prejudice. They all use active learning methods and include work for small groups. The profiles encourage students to apply what they have learned about prejudice in relation to how these groups are treated and represented. Information would need updating to include recent developments. The profiles use people's own words as far as possible. Designed to encourage debate and questioning of stereotypical views, the handbook was produced with the assistance of teachers and the pack was trialled in a number of schools.

RaceTracks: a resource pack for tackling racism with young people

FORMAT: Pack, various extents, illustrations, tables

LANGUAGE: English

TARGET AUDIENCE: Youth workers, social workers, teachers, lecturers, trainers

PRICE: £45.00 inc. (cheque with order: London Borough of Greenwich)

PRODUCER: Greenwich Anti-Racist Curriculum Project (GARCP)

DISTRIBUTOR: Greenwich Education Services

This pack is for youth workers and anyone who works with young people in a range of settings. It is also relevant to trainers, managers and providers of services who wish to develop anti-racist approaches.

The pack seeks to enable those working with young people to find practical and effective ways of challenging racism in their work. It was produced by the London Borough of Greenwich as a result of consultation, research and resource development undertaken by the Greenwich Anti-Racist Curriculum Project – set up in direct response to growing concern about racism and its effects on young people in the borough.

The pack consists of six units, all of which are well laid out, easy to follow and contain a follow-up list of further resources, reading and useful contacts. Unit 1 is 'Groundwork' and aims to introduce and clarify ideas about anti-racism. Unit 2 'Ethos' examines what happens in youth groups in terms of promoting anti-racism. Unit 3 aims to inform about the links between slavery, colonialism and racism; this includes information about historical and contemporary events. Unit 4 'Responses' tackles ways of dealing with racist behaviour (of colleagues and young people). Unit 5 'Blackness' explores working with black young people. Unit 6 'Facts and figures' provides statistical data to use to counter racist arguments (mostly referring to Greenwich).

Each unit presents a variety of photocopiable materials – background information, checklists, activities to use with young people, examples of good practice in youth settings, exercises teams can use in training or planning. The pack is illustrated with photographs, drawings and cartoons. The pack can be used in formal or informal training with groups and can be worked through unit by unit or used more flexibly and selectively to work on specific issues. The pack is also relevant to individuals.

This comprehensive and thorough pack seeks to make anti-racist youth work a reality rather than a statement of intent. It provides practical ideas and suggestions for challenging racism and attempts to equip youth workers with confidence, knowledge and strategies for developing anti-racist practice. It will be helpful to anyone working with young people. A large number of youth workers contributed to the development of this pack.

Racism: what's it got to do with me?

FORMAT: Pack, 8 looseleaf sheets

LANGUAGE: English

TARGET AUDIENCE: Teachers, lecturers, youth workers

PRICE: £6 inc.

PRODUCER: British Youth Council and Joint Committee Against Racialism, 1991

DISTRIBUTOR: British Youth Council

This pack has been designed for use by youth workers and teachers to tackle racism.

The pack consists of a folder containing a number of A4-size sheets. Each sheet addresses a different topic – anti-racist groups, education, employment, immigration, the law and the police, racist groups, youth service/facilities. The sheets consist of densely packed text with a few black-and-white photocopied photographs. The text provides some historical information and generally explains anti-racist approaches to the topic. Some suggestions are made for action (e.g. challenging racist remarks) and questions for discussion are included. The pack is probably most useful in providing background information for those working with young people. There is no guidance about how to introduce discussion of racism or how to tackle it effectively in a youth setting.

Recognising racial discrimination at work

FORMAT: Video, 30 mins; trainers' manual

LANGUAGE: English

TARGET AUDIENCE: Trainers

PRICE: £50 inc.

PRODUCER: BBC Education, 1992

DISTRIBUTOR: BBC Educational Developments

This training resource pack is for those working in advice agencies and industrial tribunals. It will also be of interest to trade unions and race equality councils. It aims to enable staff to recognise possible racial discrimination cases and refer on or to prepare cares up to a hearing. It was produced as part of the BBC's Continuing Education Mosaic project and was developed with assistance from the Commission for Racial Equality.

The pack consists of a video and a trainers' manual. The video has five sequences. The first is an introductory discussion from the chief executive of the Commission for Racial

Equality, followed by four role plays. The first two relate to a case of possible discrimination and are seen twice; first with an advice worker who does not acknowledge the possibility of racial discrimination and secondly with an advice worker who does pursue this. The third role play is a discussion between two employees about a recent failed promotion attempt. The fourth is a first interview between an advice worker and a person (a senior nurse) who has not been shortlisted for an interview and suspects racial discrimination. The video is designed to be used as a trigger for structured training.

The trainers' manual contains exercises which examine and clarify direct and indirect discrimination, and unlawful victimisation in promotion or dismissal. Good and bad practice in initial interview situations is also explored. The manual includes handouts for participants with samples of documents relating to preparing a case for an industrial tribunal. The training exercises relate directly to the video but reference is also made to another complementary Mosaic video and manual, *Equal before the law*. In order to offer a thorough training session, both resources would be needed.

This is a practical training resource which enables participants to systematically examine their knowledge of racial discrimination and the law and develop skills in advising competently. The manual was written by a solicitor and is based on experience of conducting racial discrimination cases.

Refugees in today's Europe: new hopes, new fears

FORMAT: Video, 25 mins; with 39-page teachers' notes

LANGUAGE: English

TARGET AUDIENCE: Key Stage 4 (14–16), young people (16-plus), teachers

PRICE: £29.38 inc.

PRODUCER: International Broadcasting Trust and Yorkshire Television, 1991

DISTRIBUTOR: Academy Television

This pack for use with Key Stage 4 students aims to encourage learning about refugees, what leads to people becoming refugees and what life is like for them. The video in the pack is based on extracts from four programmes made by Yorkshire Television and shown on Channel 4 in 1991. The pack was produced by the International Broadcasting Trust with financial support from a large number of charitable organisations.

The pack consists of a video and a manual of teachers' notes plus students' activities. The video has nine clearly delineated sequences exploring issues such as 'how does it feel to leave your country?' and 'how do we receive refugees?' The video is a mixture of refugees, (mostly but not exclusively young people) talking about their experiences and perceptions, interviews with people and organisations which work with refugee communities and sequences of refugee people around the world. Students' activities are directly linked to each sequence in the video. Most are discussion based and suitable for small group work but some individual work is included. It has been designed to support the National Curriculum and can be used across the curriculum. The pack seeks to inform students about refugees and encourage thought about concepts such as human rights and justice.

The pack is well designed, clearly laid out and contemporary. Additional information may be needed to update sections to reflect changing world situations such as where refugees come from. Teachers (and youth workers and adult education staff) will find this pack a practical way to introduce complex concepts to students. Although relevant to all, schools and colleges with refugees students may be particularly interested in this resource. Health professionals in contact with refugee communities (and those training health professionals) may find some of the activities

and parts of the video useful in raising awareness about refugee communities and their needs.

Religion, ethnicity and sex education: exploring the issues

FORMAT: 124-page pack

LANGUAGE: English

TARGET AUDIENCE: Teachers, lecturers, parents, trainers

PRICE: £10.50 (Bureau members), £15.50 (non-members)

PRODUCER: National Children's Bureau, 1993

DISTRIBUTOR: National Children's Bureau

This resource is for teachers and others working with young people. It aims to enable them to grasp the range of religious and moral perspectives on sexuality and personal relationships, so that they are able to respond to the needs and identities of the young people they work with. It was produced by the National Children's Bureau for the Sex Education Forum – an umbrella group of 30 religious and secular organisations concerned with provision and support of sex education for young people.

The resource is the result of a project on religion and ethnicity undertaken by the Sex Education Forum. A questionnaire was sent to representatives of seven religions. The responses form the bulk of the resource and cover the broader philosophy and rationale behind specific religious prescriptions, plus views on sexuality and sex education. The wide diversity of opinion and belief within each religion is stressed and each response should not be considered an authoritative religious perspective. Responses cover Anglican, Hindu, Islamic, Jewish, Methodist, Roman Catholic and Sikh perspectives plus a secular perspective. A personal story about a young Asian Muslim man who is gay is also included. There is a section on equal opportunities and sex education with a checklist for teachers.

This resource will be of interest to all teachers concerned with sex education and should enable them to plan such work more effectively and consult with parents and communities more confidently. It includes some activities which could be used in inset training or parents' and staff meetings to open up discussion about this sensitive subject. They are quite challenging and probably need an experienced facilitator. The relevant requirements of the National Curriculum are noted and there is a reading list of other helpful resources. A wide group of people from a range of communities and experienced in personal and health education contributed to the development of the resource.

Remedies and recipes: Caribbean reflections on health and diet

FORMAT: 27-page booklet

LANGUAGE: English

TARGET AUDIENCE: Older people, health professionals, community workers

PRICE: £4.95

PRODUCER: Age Exchange, 1991

PRODUCER: Age Exchange

This booklet is for a general audience but will be of particular interest to people who grew up in the Caribbean. It is a collection of contributions from older Caribbean people about remedies and treatments for illnesses, diet and attitudes to health. It was produced by Age Exchange, a reminiscence centre in London, with financial support from the Commission for Racial Equality.

The booklet takes the form of transcribed interviews with older people who describe herbal treatments and home remedies for minor illnesses. Some are remembered from their childhood in the Caribbean and others are treatments people use today. There are also contributions from a herbalist and sections on traditional Caribbean diets. The booklet is illustrated with photographs of the contributors and of life in the Caribbean. It is written in an informal, conversational manner which brings the book to life. Many people will enjoy reading this book alone but it can also be used in group settings to spark discussion about approaches to health and diet. Although it is particularly interesting to older people it is also accessible to other age groups and health professionals will find it informative.

Report and reflections on the challenging racism course for white community workers

FORMAT: 33-page pack

LANGUAGE: English

TARGET AUDIENCE: Community workers, youth workers, trainers

PRICE: £4.00

PRODUCER: Greater Manchester Community Work Training Group, 1989

DISTRIBUTOR: Greater Manchester Community Work Training Group

This report is a description and plan of anti-racist training courses which were developed for white youth and community workers. It was written by two youth workers (a black and white team) who developed and facilitated the courses.

The report begins with thoughts and reflections from the facilitators including why they chose to take on the work. Information about the course programme follows and covers organisation of the course, examples of exercises used and comments from participants. The course is designed to enable participants to identify and challenge racism. Suggested role plays are set in youth and community settings dealing with young people's attitudes, as well as those of the staff and management committees. The report is written in an informal manner which makes it accessible to all. The authors identify resources which form part of the course (e.g. videos).

This is a practical report describing a tried and tested course which is firmly rooted in youth and community work practice. The authors stress that they aim to enable people to challenge racism rather than simply be aware of it and feel guilty about it.

Reporting a racist incident

See *Visit to the X-ray department*

The right to be understood: a training video on working with community interpreters

FORMAT: Video, 30 mins; with 66-page manual

LANGUAGE: English

TARGET AUDIENCE: Health professionals, primary healthcare teams, trainers

PRICE: For hire only, £10 + p&p + VAT

PRODUCER: National Extension College, 1987

DISTRIBUTOR: Concord Video and Film Council

This video training package for professionals who work with interpreters and for those on professional qualifying courses (such as

nursing, social work, and teaching) aims to increase awareness of the need for good communication, develop practice skills in working with interpreters and raise policy issues about the provision of interpreting services. It was funded by a range of statutory and charitable organisations.

The video dramatises three situations in each of which a different approach to interpreting is used. The situations and people involved reflect a wide range of issues for consideration (such as age and gender, training of interpreters, briefing and planning, confidentiality, family members as interpreters, and interpreting emotional distress). The accompanying notes outline the main themes from the video and suggest sample training courses (ranging from 2 hours to 5 days). The script for the video is included with suggestions for trigger questions and exercises for each scene. A checklist is included to assist structuring interviews using an interpreter.

This package can be used flexibly to provide a range of training experiences in a variety of settings. It could easily be incorporated into existing courses especially those for the caring professions. It could be used for in-service training to assist the development of interpreting services and will be of interest to quality assurance and equal opportunity officers.

Although produced by a mainly white group there was extensive consultation with people from many minority communities about the development of the package.

Rights and choices in maternity care

FORMAT: Video, 20 mins

LANGUAGE: Bengali, Cantonese, Gujarati, Hindi, Punjabi, Urdu – with English subtitles

TARGET AUDIENCE: Parents, women, primary healthcare teams

PRICE: £30.65 inc.

PRODUCER: Healthcare Productions, 1990

DISTRIBUTOR: Healthcare Productions

This video, for women from Asian and Chinese communities, explains the various rights and choices they can expect from the maternity services. It was made by the Royal College of Midwives and the Department of Health. Three women are followed through their pregnancies. We see them talking with midwives, either in their own language or through a linkworker. The women all need different care – Sun Lam is an older woman having her first baby; Sufia has recently settled in Britain, her mother-in-law accompanies her and she uses a linkworker; Sunita has a Caesarean delivery. The women discuss with their midwives the tests available in pregnancy, preferences and concerns about labour and delivery, diet, what to bring into hospital, breastfeeding and family planning. The film stresses the importance of antenatal care and the central role of the midwife in maternity care.

Risks associated with tests such as amniocentesis and chorion villus sampling are not mentioned, so presenters need to ensure this information is available to women. Supplementary information about local services would also be helpful, such as how to contact linkworkers and whether or not female doctors will be able to attend women if required. The film could be viewed by women in their own homes to inform them about the maternity services and possibly with their partners – one sequence shows a home visit by a midwife discussing with the new parents the mother's recovery and family planning. The film is a good trigger for discussion and women's groups may find it a starting point for sharing experiences and expectations of maternity care. It may also be of use to antenatal or parentcraft classes, but only if shown early in pregnancy.

This is a pleasant video presenting pregnancy and birth as normal life events, stressing that women have the right to make choices about maternity care.

The role of the linkworker

FORMAT: Video, 12 mins

LANGUAGE: English

TARGET AUDIENCE: Health professionals, primary healthcare teams, social workers, service providers

PRICE: £26.50 inc.

PRODUCER: Save the Children Fund, 1984

DISTRIBUTOR: Healthcare Productions

This video is for health professionals and managers of health services at all levels. It examines the need for linkworkers and explains the vital role they can play in the provision of health care. It is one of a series of videos made as part of the Asian Mother and Baby Campaign and funded by the Department of Health.

In a series of interviews health professionals (nurses, midwives, health visitors, a GP and a consultant obstetrician) describe the difficulties they experience with patients who speak little or no English. The frustration of being unable to communicate, difficulties of finding someone to interpret competently and concerns about using family or children as interpreters are commented on. A mother describes her difficulties in communicating and we see a linkworker in action with a woman attending for antenatal care. The linkworkers are recruited from the community and bring to the job understanding and awareness of people's background and culture as well as language. This enables both patient and health professional to communicate more effectively.

Although made some years ago, the video is still relevant and pertinent to today's health service. It could be used to promote discussion among health professionals about the complexities of communicating with someone with whom you do not share a common language and to demonstrate the role of the linkworker.

Rommaneskohna: traditional gypsy attitudes towards health, hygiene and healing

FORMAT: 16-page booklet

LANGUAGE: English

TARGET AUDIENCE: Health professionals, primary healthcare teams, social workers

PRICE: Free

PRODUCER: Dorset Health Commission, 1993

DISTRIBUTOR: Dorset Health Commission

This booklet is for health professionals who may be working with traditional gypsies and travellers. It aims to inform about health-related attitudes and beliefs of traditional gypsy and traveller communities. The booklet was written by a health visitor.

The booklet contains nine short sections covering a range of issues to do with attitudes towards health, healing, birth and death. Guidance for hospital staff and primary healthcare teams and pitfalls for professionals to avoid are included. It provides a brief insight into traditional gypsy and traveller culture and way of life which may be useful to professionals and others providing services to these communities. The booklet refers to traditional gypsy beliefs and was written with advice from the British Rommani Union. Some commentators have noted that the wide variation of tradition and culture within gypsy and traveller communities is not reflected in this booklet.

Rubella

FORMAT: Video, 17 mins

LANGUAGE: Bengali or Hindi with English subtitles

TARGET AUDIENCE: Parents

PRICE: £10.00 inc.

PRODUCER: National Rubella Council, 1989

DISTRIBUTOR: Child 2000

This video aims to inform Asian women about rubella and the MMR vaccine for children. It was produced by the National Rubella Council with support from a range of organisations and the Department of Health.

The video consists of a variety of interviews presented by Geetha Bala. It begins with a family doctor explaining the symptoms of rubella. It moves on to a mother who tells us of her son's deafness, which was the result of rubella she had while pregnant. A mixture of interviews follows explaining the importance of vaccination, recommending blood tests to check immunity, and stressing conception must not occur for three months after the vaccination. The final section deals with the MMR vaccine for pre-school children. Guidance about immunisation schedules has now changed and viewers will need to have up-to-date information available about this. This section does not have subtitles.

This video is useful trigger material for women and their families who may not be aware of the dangers of rubella and the availability of a vaccination. Parents of girls and young women may also find it of interest as the importance of the vaccination for young women is stressed. Suitable for home or group viewing, it would benefit from the presence of a health professional or community worker, especially to explain recent changes in immunisation.

Sabiha's story: a drama about HIV and AIDS

FORMAT: Video, 30 mins; 15-page booklet; 13-page script

LANGUAGE: Urdu; booklet in Urdu and English; script in English

TARGET AUDIENCE: General public, health professionals

PRICE: £20.00 inc.

PRODUCER: Tower Hamlets Health Promotion Service, 1991

DISTRIBUTOR: East London & City HPS

This video, and accompanying booklet, was developed for Asian (Urdu-speaking) communities to answer questions and provide information about HIV/AIDS. The video was produced by Newham Healthcare, the Royal London Hospital NHS Trust and Tower Hamlets Health Authority Video Production Unit. It was funded by North East Thames Regional Health Authority.

Using a soap opera-type approach the story unfolds of a married couple, Kamal and Sabiha. Kamal is distressed to hear that an ex-lover is HIV positive and he is full of questions and worries about himself, his wife and family. The drama intensifies when Sabiha is delighted to discover she is pregnant but her husband does not seem pleased and starts to use condoms. Worried and confused she suspects him of being unfaithful. Both turn to friends in the community for advice and support. Kamal visits a GUM clinic for a test and Sabiha visits an Asian counsellor. Both learn more about HIV and AIDS, how it can and cannot be transmitted and how to protect against infection.

The video (and bilingual booklet) is very clear about how HIV can be transmitted. Sexual transmission is dealt with openly and sensitively (the booklet mentions sexual activities explicitly). Use of condoms is suggested to protect against infection. Presenters may wish to explain the correct use of condoms to support the information in the video. This needs to be carefully introduced to the audience and may be more appropriately discussed with individuals or single-sex groups to avoid embarrassment. Local information about GUM clinics, linkworkers and Urdu-speaking counsellors may also be helpful.

The video is excellent trigger material as it leaves us with many questions including: is Kamal's test positive or negative? The inevitable discussions will provide opportunities for information sharing and challenging myths about HIV and AIDS. This video has been made available to local video hire shops in Tower Hamlets for free loan and has been popular with video audiences. Members of Urdu-speaking communities were consulted throughout about the making of the video.

Safer play – safer sex: an audio-visual package aimed at young people from the South Asian communities

FORMAT: Multimedia: with video, 4 mins; 6 × cassettes, 6 mins each; 4-page users' guide, leaflet and 25 condoms

LANGUAGE: Video in English, cassettes in Bengali/English, Gujarati/English, Hindi/English, Punjabi/English, Turkish/English, Urdu/English

TARGET AUDIENCE: Youth workers, young people (16-plus)

PRICE: £80.00 inc.

PRODUCER: Naz Project, 1992

DISTRIBUTOR: Naz Project

This audio-visual pack is for young Asian people from South Asian communities and aims to promote discussion about sexual behaviour, sexuality, HIV/AIDS and safer sex. It was produced by the Naz Project (an HIV/AIDS service for South Asian and Muslim communities) and funded by Brent HIV Centre, Ealing Health Promotion and Hounslow HIV Strategy.

The short pop video uses a song about condoms accompanied by images of people engaged in sensuous activities (such as close-ups of kissing and stroking). The images reflect heterosexual, lesbian and gay relationships. The fast pace, with glossy colourful images is a style many young people will be familiar with. The audio cassette contains two songs about condom use, one in English and one in the featured community language; the songs are different in each language version. Posters and leaflets support the message of the video and audio cassettes and promote condom use. Condoms are supplied in the package (in a pack which depicts an Asian heterosexual couple).

The brief users' guide suggests a broad outline for discussion in sessions using the package. The guide does not suggest explaining correct condom use (nor does the video) or how to obtain condoms.

Teachers/presenters will need to ensure this topic is covered. The video gives helpline numbers for advice in community languages and it may be helpful to repeat this information. The guide does not suggest how to structure the session.

The package could be used as trigger material in informal settings such as youth clubs or colleges. It is challenging as some sexual activities are shown explicitly and some may find the video erotic. The package is unusual in its direct approach to sexuality and Asian communities. Teachers/presenters may find a place for this package within sex education programmes. Young people were involved in the development of this resource.

Sapna jal giaa [The dream that went up in flames]

FORMAT: Video, 30 mins; with 7-page booklet and A4 poster

LANGUAGE: Video in English or Hindi. Poster and booklet in English/Hindi

TARGET AUDIENCE: General public

PRICE: £60.00

PRODUCER: West Midlands Fire Service, 1992

DISTRIBUTOR: West Midlands Fire Service

This fire prevention video for Hindi-speaking communities aims to encourage awareness of fire hazards and provide basic information about fire safety in the home.

The Bright Colours of Danger

A booklet supporting the Video
The Dream That Went Up In Flames

A folk-type story is used to warn of the danger of fire and the foolishness of not taking safety precautions. An old man tells the story of how his only daughter nearly lost her child and home by not taking care. Music, special video effects and dreamlike sequences make the video unusual. It ends with guidance about fire safety in the home presented by a female firefighter. Hazards are shown in a home setting and precautions explained, there is a clear demonstration of how to call emergency services which includes appropriate verbal responses.

An accompanying booklet reinforces the main points about fire prevention and action to take in the event of fire. The booklet is colourfully illustrated with the text in Hindi and English. Some fire services have made the video available on free loan and have given copies to video shops for free loan. It is an adaptable resource suitable for group and home viewing. In a group setting people could discuss further what they can do to prevent accidental fires and what to do in an emergency. The video was made in consultation with the local Hindi-speaking community.

Satwant's story: a drama about HIV and AIDS

FORMAT: Video, 28 mins; 16-page booklet; 14-page script

LANGUAGE: Video in Punjabi; booklet in Punjabi and English; script in English

TARGET AUDIENCE: General public, health professionals

PRICE: £20.00 inc.

PRODUCER: Tower Hamlets Health Promotion Service, 1991

DISTRIBUTOR: East London & City HPS

This video, and accompanying booklet, was developed for Asian (Punjabi-speaking) communities to answer questions and provide information about HIV and AIDS. The video was produced by Newham Healthcare, the Royal London Hospital NHS Trust and Tower Hamlets Health Authority Video Production Unit. It was funded by North East Thames Regional Health Authority.

Using a soap opera-type approach the story unfolds of a married couple, Kartar and Satwant. Kartar is distressed to hear that an ex-lover is HIV positive and he is full of questions and worries about himself, his wife and family. The drama intensifies when Satwant is delighted to discover she is pregnant but her husband does not seem pleased and starts to use condoms.

Worried and confused she suspects him of being unfaithful. Both turn to friends in the community for advice and support. Kartar visits a GUM clinic for a test and Satwant visits an Asian counsellor. Both learn more about HIV and AIDS, how it can and cannot be transmitted and how to protect against infection.

The video (and bilingual booklet) is very clear about how HIV can be transmitted. Sexual transmission is dealt with openly and sensitively (the booklet mentions sexual activities explicitly), and use of condoms is suggested to protect against infection. Presenters may wish to explain the correct use of condoms to support the information in the video – this needs to be carefully introduced to the audience and may be more appropriately discussed with individuals or single-sex groups to avoid embarrassment. Local information about GUM clinics, linkworkers and Punjabi-speaking counsellors may also be helpful.

The video is excellent trigger material as it leaves us with many questions including: is Kartar's test positive or negative? The inevitable discussions will provide opportunities for information sharing and challenging myths about HIV and AIDS. This video has been made available to local video hire shops in Tower Hamlets for free loan and has been popular with video audiences. Members of Punjabi-speaking communities were consulted throughout about the making of the video.

Sawitri's story: a drama about HIV and AIDS

FORMAT: Video, 32 mins; with 16-page booklet

LANGUAGE: Hindi

TARGET AUDIENCE: General public, health professionals

PRICE: £20.00 inc.

PRODUCER: Tower Hamlets Health Promotion Service, 1991

DISTRIBUTOR: East London & City HPS

This video, and accompanying booklet, was developed for Asian (Hindi-speaking) communities to answer questions and provide information about HIV/AIDS. The video was produced by Newham Healthcare, the Royal London Hospital NHS Trust and Tower Hamlets Health Authority and was funded by North East Thames Regional Health Authority.

Using a soap opera-type approach, the story unfolds of a married couple, Kanai and Sawitri. Kanai is distressed to hear that an ex-lover is HIV positive. He is full of questions and worries about himself, his wife and family. The drama intensifies when Sawitri is delighted to discover she is pregnant, but her husband does not seem pleased and starts to use condoms. Worried and confused she suspects him of being unfaithful. Both turn to friends in the community for advice and support. Kanai visits a GUM clinic for a test and Sawitri visits an Asian counsellor. Both learn more about HIV and AIDS, how it can and cannot be transmitted and how to protect against infection.

The video (and bilingual booklet) is very clear about how HIV can be transmitted. Sexual transmission is dealt with openly and sensitively (the booklet mentions sexual activities explicitly), and use of condoms is suggested to protect against infection.

Presenters may wish to explain the correct use of condoms to support the information in the video – this needs to be carefully introduced to the audience and may be more appropriately discussed with individuals or single-sex groups to avoid embarrassment. Local information about GUM clinics, linkworkers and Hindi-speaking counsellors may also be helpful.

The video is excellent trigger material as it leaves us with many questions including: is Kanai's test positive or negative? The inevitable discussions will provide opportunities for information sharing and challenging myths about HIV and AIDS. This video has been made available to local video hire shops in Tower Hamlets for free loan and has been popular with video audiences. Members of Hindi-speaking communities were consulted throughout about the making of the video.

Schizophrenia: notes for relatives and friends
Psychiatric diagnosis: notes for relatives and patients

FORMAT: Pack; with 8-page and 4-page booklets

LANGUAGE: Bengali, English, Punjabi, Urdu

TARGET AUDIENCE: Carers, mental health teams, primary healthcare teams, general public

PRICE: 50p

PRODUCER: National Schizophrenia Fellowship, 1994

DISTRIBUTOR: National Schizophrenia Fellowship Midlands

The main booklet in the pack is for relatives and friends of people who has been diagnosed as having schizophrenia. It describes the symptoms, causes and treatment and what can be done to help those with schizophrenia. It was written by psychiatric doctors.

The booklet describes in depth how a person with schizophrenia may behave and how they may seem to people who know them well. Some of the believed causes of schizophrenia are discussed and contributory factors such as stress are discussed. Treatment is generally explained and it is stressed that it must be continued even when a person feels they are well or recovered. Advice is given about how to support a person with schizophrenia. The booklet does not deal with the controversial opinions which surround diagnosis of schizophrenia. The English version includes addresses for the National Schizophrenia Fellowship around the country, other language versions do not and people may need to be given this information. This is an informative booklet which helps people understand more about what schizophrenia is considered to be.

The accompanying booklet, *Psychiatric diagnosis*, seeks to explain how mental health professionals come to make a diagnosis and why a diagnosis may sometimes change. It is densely typed and is only available in English. Issues involved in making a diagnosis when the health professional and patient do not share a common language or culture are not discussed.

The secret service: environmental health

FORMAT: Video, 20 mins

LANGUAGE: English, Gujarati, Urdu

TARGET AUDIENCE: General public, environmental health officers

PRICE: £15.00 inc.

PRODUCER: Gatehouse Television for Bolton Environmental Health Services, 1992

DISTRIBUTOR: Bolton Environmental Health Services

This video is for a general audience and aims to explain the role of environmental health services.

A tongue-in-cheek dramatised sequence about an environmental health service officer as a secret service agent is used to explain the many areas which environmental health covers. The 'agent' follows in the footsteps of a couple through a typical day. Topics covered include noise and air pollution, trading standards, workplace health and safety, hygiene in kitchens, food poisoning, rodent control. The couple are stereotypical, the man is short and inadequate, the woman big and domineering and both are depicted as foolish. Some commentators have found this objectionable. However the video does give an overview of the kind of issues which environmental health departments can act upon.

Secrets

FORMAT: 24-page pack, illustrations

LANGUAGE: English

TARGET AUDIENCE: Health professionals, young people

PRICE: £5.25 + 25% p&p

PRODUCER: The Children's Society, 1989

DISTRIBUTOR: The Children's Society

This book for children and young people tells the story in words and pictures of a young woman who is sexually abused by her father. Written and drawn by a young woman who is a survivor of sexual abuse, it is available in two formats, one featuring a black family and one a white family. It was produced by The Children's Society.

The A4 book uses a comic-type format with two large colour drawings to a page and word bubbles forming the simple text. It tells the story of a young woman who is too afraid to tell about the abuse. Distress and fear are powerfully conveyed by facial expressions and words. The abuse stops when her younger brother is also abused and he tells their mother. In the story, the young people are believed, but this may often not be the case in real life – although the book does state, 'please tell – someone is bound to believe you'.

The book will be most relevant to young people and the author expresses the hope that it will help others in a similar position to tell and so stop the abuse. It may also be accessible to people with learning difficulties as it has a very visual storyline and may enable them to communicate what has happened to them. As it deals with a painful subject, it would need to be used carefully and is not the kind of book to be used without some preparation and follow-up. This is one of few resources produced on this topic for young people by young people.

Self defence? Common sense!

FORMAT: Video, 30 mins; with 6-page notes

LANGUAGE: English

TARGET AUDIENCE: Community workers, older people, women

PRICE: £40.00

PRODUCER: London Borough of Hammersmith and Fulham, 1992

DISTRIBUTOR: London Borough of Hammersmith and Fulham

This video about personal safety for pensioners was made by four older women who state that they made the video 'to show how common sense can be used to avoid danger'. It was produced by the London Borough of Hammersmith and Fulham Women's Services Department, Action Sports and the Community Safety Unit.

Four women feature in the video, three of whom are African-Caribbean. Divided into five sections the video takes the viewer through a safety/self-defence course. There are three exercise-based workshops – 'loosening up', breathing and voice, and relaxation – plus two role plays on location covering 'opening the

Self Defence?
Common Sense!
A Safety Video for Pensioners

door to strangers' and 'collecting your pension at the post office'. The workshop sessions are led by a tutor who takes the women through some gentle exercises which could easily be adapted for people who have limited mobility. The women are encouraged to trust their intuition, use common sense and be aware of what is happening around them to avoid danger. The role plays deal with common situations which some older women may worry about. They demonstrate practical steps people can take in both situations.

The video could be used with groups of older people wherever they meet. All the participants are women which will make it very accessible to women but men could also find it of interest. The sections are clearly delineated so it is easy for groups to discuss the content of each section and share views and experiences. The pace is relaxed and measured.

Information is presented clearly and important points are reinforced with written messages on the screen. There is enough material for several sessions on this topic and groups may wish to expand the exercise component. It may be helpful to have a trained exercise tutor present during the sessions. Brief notes accompany the video and reiterate learning points.

This is a good example of a multicultural resource which tackles a common anxiety in a practical manner. Older women are presented as in control and assertive, thus challenging stereotypes of what it is like to be older in our society. The women featured in the video were so enthusiastic about what they had learned in their self-defence class that they have trained as tutors themselves and now run courses for other pensioners.

Settling in the United Kingdom: a handbook for refugees from Vietnam

FORMAT: 35-page booklet

LANGUAGE: Cantonese, English, Vietnamese

TARGET AUDIENCE: Refugees, community workers, social workers

PRICE: £5.00 inc.

PRODUCER: Refugee Action, 1990

DISTRIBUTOR: Refugee Action

The handbook is for refugees from Vietnam who are coming to the United Kingdom or have just arrived. It is a brief introduction to life in the United Kingdom.

The booklet explains what a reception centre is and what happens there. Moving into the community, work and training, education, healthcare, rights, benefits and how to get help are all briefly described. The booklet is well laid out and easy to read with many black-and-white photographs of Vietnamese people in everyday situations such as visiting the doctor. Addresses of national organisations are

included. The booklet is a useful reference but needs to be supported with local information and would be enhanced by discussion with a community worker. Those newly arrived in the United Kingdom will find the booklet informative.

Sex education: the Muslim perspective

FORMAT: 36-page booklet

LANGUAGE: English

TARGET AUDIENCE: Parents, teachers, trainers

PRICE: £1.35

PRODUCER: Muslim Educational Trust, 1989

DISTRIBUTOR: Muslim Educational Trust

This booklet is for parents, educationalists and anyone who may be providing sex education to children and young people. It was produced by the Muslim Educational Trust, which is concerned with the educational needs of Muslim communities in the UK.

The booklet presents a Muslim viewpoint on sex education, outlining Islamic attitudes to sexual relationships and sexual behaviour. It includes a sample letter for parents to send to headteachers requesting specific information about the content of sex education in the school. It also discusses how sex education is taught in schools. This contains some inaccuracies (for example, that outside speakers are mostly responsible for sex education). The information in this section has now been overtaken by events such as the development of the National Curriculum, local management of schools and parents' rights to withdraw children from sex education lessons. Parents would need to be aware of these developments.

Shanti stress pack

FORMAT: Multimedia: with video, 45 mins; cassette, 60 mins; 11-page booklet

LANGUAGE: Bengali, English, Gujarati, Hindi, Punjabi, Urdu, with English subtitles

TARGET AUDIENCE: Women, community workers, trainers, primary healthcare teams, mental health teams

PRICE: £48.00 inc.

PRODUCER: Navigo Productions for Coventry Health Authority, 1991

DISTRIBUTOR: Shanti Asian Women and Stress Project

'Shanti' is a Hindi word meaning peace and inner harmony. The pack examines what stress is, the causes of stress, managing and dealing with stress and when to seek professional help. Women of different ages, in different work/family and home situations demonstrate stress and its effects. Several methods of dealing with stress are shown including deep breathing and relaxation techniques. The audio cassette consists of a progressive relaxation technique, one side of which is set to music. The booklet contains a transcript of the cassette to ensure the relaxation technique is fully understood.

The women in the video act out a variety of everyday situations which can cause stress – they are immediately recognisable and realistic. Stress is presented as part of all our lives and not as a personal failure. The techniques for dealing with stress are demonstrated clearly and simply. They are very practical (for example almost everyone can practice deep breathing). The video encourages women to acknowledge the stress in their lives and to find the best way for them to manage it.

The pack could be used by individuals or groups. The cassette is very useful for guiding women through the relaxation exercise. The video is broken down into sections which can be viewed separately, so allowing time for discussion. There is enough material for several sessions on stress management. This is an exceptional resource and although targeted at Asian women is of interest to anyone concerned with stress management. Asian communities in Coventry participated in making this video.

Sharaab: Asian language alcohol education trigger video

FORMAT: Video, 75 mins; with 21-page notes

LANGUAGE: English, Punjabi, Urdu

TARGET AUDIENCE: General public, trainers, primary healthcare teams, community workers

PRICE: £71.50

PRODUCER: I F Hyare for Aquarius, 1992

DISTRIBUTOR: Aquarius Education Unit

This video for adult Asian communities aims to trigger discussion, raise awareness and inform about alcohol and alcohol-related issues. It was made by Aquarius Action Projects and is the first in a series of planned health education resources about alcohol for Asian communities. It was funded by a number of local and national agencies including the Alcohol Education and Research Council, the Department of Health and the Health Education Authority.

The video consists of six sections, the first of which runs for 28 minutes and the others for approximately 8 to 10 minutes. There are four dramatic sections, each of which tell a story about alcohol use and contain some information about alcohol at the end. The first section is a complete run-through of all the sections and the last section is a review with sequences taken from each story, and information reinforced plus where to go for help. In order to ensure authenticity there are two sets of character names which are applicable in different language versions.

The settings and families are contemporary and will be familiar to many audiences. Similarly the story lines are realistic and show people in everyday situations, sometimes experiencing stress. Alcohol use and its potential problems are approached from a variety of angles such as peer pressure to drink in the pub, selling alcohol to under-age young people, drinking and driving and the effects of drinking on relationships. The accompanying notes suggest a variety of ways of using the video depending on the time available, with ideas for between one and six sessions. The aims of each section are stated with suggestions for trigger questions and ideas for discussion. Brief guidance is also given about group composition. The notes also recommend that local information about sources of help should be made available to participants. The resource has been designed to be used flexibly with groups. It does not directly tackle the issue of women and drinking as it was felt this might be offensive to some community leaders but the notes suggest that the issue is raised in discussion.

This video was the laureate winner at the Festival on Audiovisual Materials for the Health Education of the European Community in 1992. The acting and technical quality are comparable with TV soap operas and give the video a very professional feel. The video was part of a community-based education programme which is developing and evaluating appropriate and accessible methods of alcohol education in Asian communities.

Sickle cell anaemia

FORMAT: 26-page booklet

LANGUAGE: English

TARGET AUDIENCE: Healthcare professionals, primary healthcare teams, commissioners, service providers

PRICE: Free

PRODUCER: NHS Management Executive, 1993

DISTRIBUTOR: BAPS

This booklet for healthcare purchasers may also be of interest to providers and users of services. It addresses health services for people with sickle cell disorders. It is part of a series produced by the NHSME which aims to present users' views about current services and about what a quality service should consist of. The booklet was prepared with help from the Sickle Cell Society, people affected by sickle cell disorders and a lecturer in community genetic counselling.

The booklet briefly outlines what sickle cell anaemia is, its causes, symptoms and treatments. The responses of primary and acute healthcare services are outlined with suggestions for good practice. Difficulties that users experience with these services are noted.

Emphasis is placed on the role that specialist nurses can play, plus the importance of advocates for some users. Throughout, the booklet quotes from service users who highlight the issues raised, especially about the severity of pain during a crisis and the need for speedy pain relief. They particularly note the difficulties in persuading health professionals of the severity of their pain and the need for speedy pain relief. It is stressed that sickle cell can be a very serious and painful disorder. There is a checklist at the end to assist purchasers in examining how well their services are meeting the needs of people with sickle cell disorders.

This booklet is short enough to be read by everyone who may purchase or provide services for people with sickle cell disorders. It provides a useful basis for discussion about services and strongly states users' points of view.

Sickle wise

FORMAT: Video, 17 mins

LANGUAGE: English

TARGET AUDIENCE: Healthcare professionals, general public, primary healthcare teams

PRICE: £77.00

PRODUCER: Medical College of St Bartholomew's Hospital, 1984

DISTRIBUTOR: Educational Media Film and Video

This video aims to inform people with sickle cell anaemia and their families about the disease. It was designed to provide basic information about sickle cell disease to medical and paramedical staff.

The video uses a documentary style, combining interviews of people with sickle cell anaemia talking about how it affects them and their families, with explanations of the disease from doctors and graphic illustrations. It provides a clear and informative description of what sickle cell is, who it is likely to affect, what happens during 'crises' and how people can manage the illness. People featured include parents of a child with sickle cell anaemia who speak emotively of their initial distress but are now more optimistic. The overall message of the video is for people to be informed and to maintain a positive outlook on life.

It may be of most interest to those who are newly diagnosed. It would be useful if viewed with a health worker so that worries could be discussed and up-to-date information provided about treatment and local services. Although now several years old it benefits from being short and extremely informative.

Silent in the crowd

FORMAT: Video, 13 mins

LANGUAGE: English

TARGET AUDIENCE: Mental health teams, general public

PRICE: £60.00 + £2.00 p&p

PRODUCER: Webb Productions, 1991

DISTRIBUTOR: Cinenova

This video for a general audience is about the high rates of mental illness in black and minority ethnic groups. It was made by an independent producer, Monika Baker, and funded by the Arts Council.

The video has an unusual format featuring a Birmingham-based women's acapella group, Black Voices, who perform throughout the video using lyrics and freestyle dance.

A number of issues are raised – the high incidence of mental illness in black communities, differences in diagnosis and treatment of black and white people, lack of access to counselling and therapy and the effect of racism on a person's mental health. The performers sing, dance and dramatise the issues. Throughout, psychiatrists are quoted, commenting on these issues and noting research findings. It is a visually compelling video, the performers starkly reflect the feelings of people who are diagnosed as mentally ill and with the psychiatrists' comments this reinforces the view that racism is causing high rates of mental illness.

This short video can be used to trigger discussion about a range of issues to do with mental illness and black and minority ethnic groups. It can be difficult to hear at times as the singing often provides a background to the commentary, so it is probably not suitable for viewing in large groups. A number of worrying facts are presented which, combined with haunting lyrics, lead the viewer to question why black people have such high rates of mental illness and when ill are treated differently from white people.

Silent tears: an educational programme about female circumcision

FORMAT: Video, 20 mins; with 10-page booklet, 14-page information pack

LANGUAGE: English

TARGET AUDIENCE: Health professionals, women, community workers

PRICE: £10.00

PRODUCER: Tower Hamlets Health Promotion Service, 1990

DISTRIBUTOR: London Black Women's Health Action Project

This video and accompanying booklets aim to increase awareness of and provide information about female circumcision for communities where circumcision is practised and for people working with those communities.

The video explains what female circumcision is and the different types of circumcision practised, with the aid of animated graphics. A discussion follows about the reasons given for circumcision – physical, religious and economic. A doctor outlines the physical and mental effects it may have on women's health. Female circumcision is linked with the oppression of women to the advantage of men and links are made with other forms of oppression such as footbinding, some fashions and chastity belts. A group of women, many of whom have been circumcised themselves, express a range of views on circumcision and whether or not their daughters will be circumcised. The sound quality of this part of the video is poor. The accompanying booklet reiterates many of the points made and includes a brief bibliography.

The video is good trigger material, it presents a feminist viewpoint about female circumcision and the women's group reflects the difficulties communities face in challenging this practice. The producers hope the video will enable women to talk about circumcision and that it may also reach men in communities where circumcision is practised.

Smoking prevention for minority ethnic groups: a resource pack

FORMAT: 90-page manual and photocopiable handouts

LANGUAGE: Photocopiable handouts in Bengali, Cantonese, English, Gujarati, Punjabi, Turkish, Urdu

TARGET AUDIENCE: General public, health professionals, community workers

PRICE: £5.00 + p&p

PRODUCER: Health Education Authority Helios Project

DISTRIBUTOR: HEA Helios

This pack is for health professionals and others working in the field of health. It aims to support and encourage specific health promotion initiatives on smoking aimed at black and minority ethnic groups. It was funded by the Health Education Authority and the Department of Health and produced by the HEA Helios Project.

The pack addresses facts about smoking, smoking prevention, helping people to stop smoking and campaigning against smoking. A range of photocopiable handouts translated into community languages is included, containing information about smoking and tips on giving up. Guidance is given about translating health promotion materials. Examples of good practice and brief descriptions of health promotion campaigns targeting ethnic minority communities are included. The pack is illustrated with multiracial photographs of people and accompanied by quotes gathered by the Cities Research Unit Study. These voice the rarely canvassed opinions and viewpoints of people from black and minority ethnic groups about smoking and giving up.

This pack provides useful background material about smoking for health professionals aiming to work with different communities. The pack is a starting point with ideas about how to begin such work.

Snax teaching pack: activities and resources for secondary age pupils exploring healthy eating issues

FORMAT: Multimedia with video, 25 mins; 94-page workbook; photocards × 40, colour; leaflet; A2 poster, colour

LANGUAGE: English

TARGET AUDIENCE: Key Stage 3 (12–14), Key Stage 4 (14–16)

PRICE: £50.00 + £3.20 p&p

PRODUCER: St Patrick's Health Promotion Unit and South Birmingham Health Authority, 1992

DISTRIBUTOR: St Patrick's HP Department

An activity pack for secondary teachers of Key Stages 3 and 4 pupils which aims to inform about healthy eating and support young people in making healthy eating choices. It focuses on snacks – those which are healthy and those which are not so healthy. It was produced by St Patrick's Health Promotion Unit and South Birmingham Health Authority, funded by the Department of Health in conjunction with the Health Education Authority.

The workbook contains 36 activities which explore healthy eating issues, each activity is explained clearly and some contain photocopiable worksheets. Topics dealt with are: attitudes to health, self-image and healthy eating, surveying eating habits, the food around us, fat and sugar, advertising and

healthier snack production. The activities take account of a variety of diets and deal realistically with young people's eating habits (e.g. 'I like chips', 'choose low sugar fizzy drinks if possible', etc.). The activities are interesting and likely to appeal to young people, there are lots of quizzes, wordsearches, problem pages, etc., all designed to promote informed discussion. Activities can be selected according to time available and are designed to be incorporated across the curriculum.

The video takes the form of a young people's magazine programme with a fast-moving pace and catchy rap music. It includes jokes, a phone-in, a video box (a visual problem page), information from a dietitian, food demonstrations, a quiz and lots of young people talking about food. It can be used on its own or as a complement to the workbook either viewed right through or in sections matched with an appropriate activity from the workbook. The video script was written by a multi-disciplinary team consisting of teachers, a dietitian, actors and the young people taking part in it. Young people may decide they would like to make their own video too.

This teaching pack is flexible and fun, encouraging young people to find out more about nutrition. The multicultural approach recognises that people may have different diets but all of us can eat more healthily and all of us need more information about what healthy eating is. The ideas for the pack were developed as a result of a series of workshops for teachers, health promotion officers and representatives of school meals services.

Solvent abuse pack for retailers

FORMAT: 33-page guidance booklet; 36-page training booklet, illustrations; 4-page newsletter; 5-page guidelines; stickers; leaflet

LANGUAGE: Leaflet: English, Hindi, Punjabi, Urdu; guidelines: Bengali, English, Gujarati, Hindi, Punjabi , Urdu; newsletter and booklets: English

TARGET AUDIENCE: Environmental health officers

PRICE: Free

PRODUCER: Re-Solv, 1993

DISTRIBUTOR: Re-Solv

This pack is for retailers who may sell products which could be used for solvent abuse. It provides information about solvent abuse and guidelines on the sale and merchandising of 'sniffable' products.

Produced by Re-Solv, the Society for the Prevention of Solvent and Volatile Substance Abuse, the pack contains a leaflet which explains what solvent abuse is, plus suggestions for retailers about displaying and selling such products. Guidance is given about recognising potential abusers, refusing to sell products and avoiding conflict with customers. Retailers are reminded about the law regarding the supply of intoxicating substances. A set of stickers is included stating that solvents will be sold only at the counter or that sale of solvents may be restricted. The leaflet has been produced for use with a staff training video made by Re-Solv, but the video is not available in languages other than English. The pack is a useful support to retailers concerned about tackling the issue of sale of solvents and can be kept as a handy reference for staff.

A sound start for your baby

FORMAT: Video, 8 mins

LANGUAGE: English

TARGET AUDIENCE: Primary healthcare teams, parents

PRICE: £20.00 inc.

PRODUCER: Tower Hamlets Health Promotion Service, 1992

DISTRIBUTOR: East London & City HPS

This video was produced for an English-speaking multicultural community. It seeks to increase parents' awareness of hearing loss among infants in the first year of life and enable them to recognise some of the signs of hearing loss. It was made by East London and the City Health Promotion Service and funded by the City and East London Family Health Services and London Docklands Development Corporation.

Babies are shown at different stages (early weeks, 3 months, 6 months, 8 months and 1 year) and demonstrate the expected milestones in terms of response to sound and vocal responses. Parents are encouraged to consult health visitors and/or GPs if they have any worries about their babies' hearing. There are many shots of parents talking to their babies and babies cooing back with delight. The video features families from a wide range of different communities. The main points are repeated at the end.

The video is intended to be used by health visitors and doctors as part of the child health surveillance programme. The makers recommend parents see it when their baby is 2 to 3 months old and again at 7 to 8 months old. Health visitors may find it useful to view at home with parents as it is short, informative and interesting. The video was developed in response to requests from audiologists who were concerned that hearing loss was sometimes detected at later stages in children from some communities. The video was made with the involvement of parents and health professionals and the results of a pilot of the video with parents were very positive.

So you have diabetes!: how to eat for health

FORMAT: 10-page pack

LANGUAGE: Gujarati/English, Punjabi/English and Urdu/English

TARGET AUDIENCE: General public

PRICE: 35p + p&p under 100, 30p + p&p over 100

PRODUCER: Parkside Nutrition and Dietetic Services, 1993

DISTRIBUTOR: Central & North West London Health Promotion Unit

This booklet provides guidelines on healthy eating for people who have diabetes and their families. It was produced by Parkside Nutrition and Dietetic Services and Parkside Health Promotion Unit. The booklet was originally developed to accompany a video which is no longer available.

The booklet is written bilingually with the text of both languages side by side. It explains very simply what diabetes is. Advice is given about how to control diabetes with diet, suggesting foods and drinks to choose and those to avoid. This includes traditional foods, convenience foods, snacks and alcohol. There is also a bilingual pull-out diet card with a suggested meal plan for a day. Readers are advised to take regular exercise, keep weight within the normal range and consult their doctor if they experience problems. This booklet could be used to support information and advice from a health professional and may serve as a useful reminder of points discussed. Family members may also find it informative.

So you've been told you have diabetes?

FORMAT: Pack of 10 booklets

LANGUAGE: African-Caribbean, Bengali, Cantonese, Greek, Gujarati, Hindi, Punjabi, Turkish, Urdu, Vietnamese

TARGET AUDIENCE: Older people, health professionals

PRICE: £1.00

PRODUCER: Standing Conference of Ethnic Minority Senior Citizens, 1991

DISTRIBUTOR: SCEMSC

This A4-size booklet is for older people who have recently been diagnosed with (non-insulin dependent) diabetes. It gives some basic information about what diabetes is and how it can be managed. It was prepared by the Standing Conference of Ethnic Minority Senior Citizens and Age Concern with contributions from the British Diabetic Association. It was funded by the Department of Health.

The booklet begins with a first-person account by an older woman explaining how diabetes affects her and how she manages the illness. A brief explanation of diabetes follows with an address list for further information. The booklet opens into a poster which covers how diabetes may affect people and includes footcare, sight and hypoglycaemia. Advice is given on how to take care of yourself and what foods to eat. The text is quite small and may not be easily read as a poster. There are some small line drawings to accompany the text. This is a useful booklet for older people and their families.

Spanner in the works: education for racial equality and social justice in white schools

FORMAT: 100-page manual

LANGUAGE: English

TARGET AUDIENCE: Teachers, trainers

PRICE: £8.95

PRODUCER: Trentham Books, 1991

DISTRIBUTOR: CEDC

This manual is a record of initiatives taken in some nursery and primary schools in Cumbria which arose as part of a multicultural education project. It will be of interest to those teaching in predominantly white schools. The authors are teachers and all worked as advisers in Cumbria Education Authority's equal opportunities projects.

The manual is in eleven sections and describes a wide range of approaches for teaching about and promoting equality across the curriculum. Activities and projects are described and illustrated with examples of children's work. Any support material required is listed and suggestions for developing work further are included. The activities encourage children to value themselves, explore similarities and differences between themselves and others, express feelings honestly and develop strategies for dealing with conflict. They also help children discover more about their own culture, develop an understanding of power and enable them to begin to recognise oppression. A wide range of teachers and schools throughout Cumbria contributed to the book.

Surma: the gift that can be dangerous

FORMAT: Video, 20 mins (English) + 7 mins (Asian languages); with 5-page leaflet and 9-page notes

LANGUAGE: Video in English (with additional scenes in Gujarati, Hindi, Punjabi); leaflet in Bengali, English, Hindi, Punjabi, Urdu

TARGET AUDIENCE: Health professionals, general public

PRICE: £50.00 + VAT

PRODUCER: Black Box Productions, 1988

DISTRIBUTOR: Phil Swerdlow

This video aims to inform health professionals and organisations about the dangers of Surma, an Asian cosmetic which can contain very high quantities of lead. It was produced in association with Nottingham Health Authority and doctors from Nottingham University who have carried out research into lead in Asian cosmetics.

The documentary-style video begins by reporting the death of a 3-year-old from lead poisoning as a result of use of Surma. A consultant paediatrician and a community physician explain the symptoms and consequences of lead poisoning for children. Street interviews with people from Asian communities reflect a range of views about use of Surma and limited knowledge of its lead content. We are reminded that Surma is banned from sale in the UK but is often brought into the country as a gift by those returning from visits or pilgrimages. There is no substitute for Surma. This may have religious significance for some but there are safe alternatives. The community physician has sought to inform new parents of the dangers of Surma and also works with grandmothers so that they too are aware of its danger.

The video is suitable for individual or group viewing by health professionals or a general audience, and there are additional scenes in Gujarati, Hindi and Punjabi for a general audience. It is supported by a leaflet for group leaders which reiterates the main points made in the video. Another leaflet is available for Asian communities in community languages which informs people of the dangers.

Talk, play and learn

FORMAT: Video, 9 mins

LANGUAGE: English, Gujarati, Punjabi, Urdu

TARGET AUDIENCE: Parents, health professionals

PRICE: £19.00 inc.

PRODUCER: Mid-Downs Health Authority, 1991

DISTRIBUTOR: Horsham Hospital

This video for Asian parents stresses the importance of talking and playing in the development of young children and explains the speech therapy service. Scenes of parents and babies at home are used to illustrate communication between parent and child. A voice-over explains the importance of early communication and emphasises that children learn from play. Speech therapy services are explained with examples of the kind of speech problems to look out for. A speech therapy session is seen in action. The commentator states that it is important for a child to communicate effectively, but which language the child uses is not significant.

The video has a relaxed pace with simple commentary. Some parents may find the information limited. It does not comment on the language development of children from bilingual families or indicate any milestones in language development. Presenters may need to provide additional information about this and about how to contact local speech therapy services. The video may trigger discussion with parents about how they can support their child's language development. It is probably most useful in discussions with individual parents as speech therapy can be demonstrated and scenes of a child of the relevant age shown.

Taso: living positively with AIDS

FORMAT: 2 videos, 25 mins and 30 mins; with 32-page booklet

LANGUAGE: English

TARGET AUDIENCE: Community groups, counsellors, general public, trainers

PRICE: £45.00 inc., £25.00 inc. for charitable and educational organisations

PRODUCER: Small World Productions, 1990

DISTRIBUTOR: TALC

This two-part video and booklet is about the care, support and counselling of people who are living with HIV. It is appropriate for general and professional audiences but may be most relevant to those who are living with HIV and/or providing care and services to people living with HIV. It was made by Taso (Aids Support Organisation, Uganda) with financial assistance from the World Health Organization's Global Programme on Aids.

Part 1, The Taso Story, outlines how Taso developed from a few committed volunteers and now provides help for over 2000 people.

The work of Taso is explained through case studies and we see support groups in action, counselling sessions in progress, home visits, exercise classes and social events. The philosophy of living positively is encouraged with equal emphasis on physical and mental wellbeing. Taso counsellors, many of whom are HIV positive, support people to plan their lives and think about how their families, especially children, will cope when they die. The video is not about HIV transmission but deals with the importance of support and practical help for people who are HIV positive. The video does not use actors nor does it avoid acknowledging that people may become very ill and will die. Yet it is an uplifting video, as people come to terms with being HIV positive and support each other.

Part 2, AIDS Counselling, presents Taso's approach to counselling through three case studies and the work of three experienced counsellors. The skills and attitudes required to become a counsellor are explained and a Taso training course for volunteers is seen in action. We see counselling sessions in progress dealing with typical but very challenging situations such as talking with someone newly diagnosed HIV positive and discussing making a will with a young mother who is dying. Professionals talk of how stressful they find this work at times and of the importance of making counselling available to people.

The accompanying booklet contains more information about the work of Taso, for example describing the children's clinic and providing support for counsellors who are 'burnt out'. There are several testimonies from people who are HIV positive explaining how the virus has affected their lives. A brief outline of the four-day induction courses Taso organises for volunteers is also included, with guidelines for counselling practice. The videos are designed to be viewed separately and with the booklet.

This resource will be of particular interest to health and social workers, community groups and voluntary agencies. Although HIV and AIDS are the main focus of this resource the information about counselling skills is applicable to any situation where counselling may take place and provides a clear demonstration of those skills in action. The video was made with the involvement of clients, counsellors, workers and volunteers at Taso.

A taste of health

FORMAT: Video, 20 mins; with 5-page leaflet

LANGUAGE: Bengali, English, Hindi

TARGET AUDIENCE: Parents, health professionals

PRICE: £26.50 inc.

PRODUCER: Royal Society of Medicine, 1986

DISTRIBUTOR: Healthcare Productions

This video for Asian communities seeks to inform about a healthy diet. It was made as part of the Asian Mother and Baby Campaign which was supported by the Department of Health. The video was sponsored by Seven Seas and the Milk Marketing Board.

The video is presented by Geetha Bala who explains that a traditional diet is healthy and reinforces healthy eating messages in between dramatised sequences. Two families are seen shopping and discussing what to buy, often disagreeing (for example, children wanting more sweets than parents would wish). The presenter advises how to eat less fat, sugar and salt and combines this with tips about food selection, preparation and cooking. Viewers are also advised to eat more whole grains and pulses, fruit and vegetables. Vitamin supplements are mentioned (vitamin D in particular) and brand-named products shown. Viewers are advised to buy over-the-counter vitamins if they think they need a supplement.

The video is accompanied by a leaflet for health professionals who may need some help in advising people from Asian communities about diet and nutrition. The video can be used in group settings or viewed at home. Health professionals may find it a useful way of triggering discussion about diet and stressing that a traditional diet is healthy.

Teaching for equality: educational resources on race and gender

FORMAT: 118-page pack

LANGUAGE: English

TARGET AUDIENCE: Teachers, lecturers

PRICE: £4.95 + 10% p&p

PRODUCER: Runnymede Trust, 1987

DISTRIBUTOR: CEDC

This book, for teachers and educationists, provides a resource list of policies, practices and classroom resources for race and gender equality in schools. The list was developed from a Department of Education and Science sponsored regional course in Berkshire. It is published by Runnymede Trust and was partly funded by the British Council of Churches.

The book contains 660 entries covering background material, policy development, evaluation and assessment; also local education authority documents relating to equality. Material is included for teachers in general, for classroom use and in relation to specific subjects. It contains examples of good practice and material selected for classroom use has a strong visual element. Some resources were produced by young people or community organisations. Each entry lists author, title, publisher, language if relevant, ISBN and supplier, with a brief sentence describing the resource.

The book is well laid out with an easy-to-use index. The authors suggest it should be used as a starting point rather than considered as a definitive guide. It was published in 1987, predating the National Curriculum, and new resources have been produced since then which readers will wish to be aware of. However it provides a good background to the development of equality in educational settings and usefully links race and gender.

Teeth for life

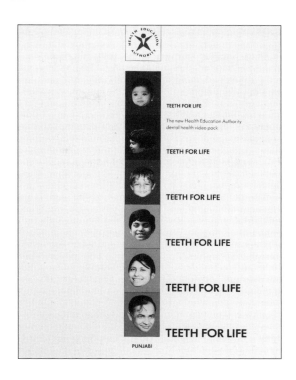

FORMAT: 2 videos, 13 mins and 19 mins; with 95-page trainers' booklet

LANGUAGE: Bengali, Punjabi or Urdu with English subtitles

TARGET AUDIENCE: General public, health professionals

PRICE: £20.00 + p&p + VAT

PRODUCER: Health Education Authority, 1993

DISTRIBUTOR: Concord Film and Video Council

This trigger video pack is for health professionals and lay workers and aims to help them promote oral/dental health education among Asian communities. It consists of a video in two parts and an accompanying booklet of notes for trainers. The pack was developed as a response to research findings about Asian communities' experiences of dental health services. It was developed by the Health Education Authority with joint funding from the Department of Health.

Drama is used to explore issues about oral health. Part one opens with a family returning from a party. The children brush their teeth properly, but their parents have some problems which lead to them making appointments with the dentist. In part two the parents visit the dentist for the first time. Anxieties people may have about dental visits are addressed and what to expect during a visit is covered. Animated sequences are used to explain gingivitis and periodontal disease. Photographs of various dental treatments 'before and after' are shown.

The booklet for trainers covers aims, objectives and points to consider when planning sessions. There are thirteen suggested sessions covering a range of issues, which can be used flexibly according to time available and audience interest. The pack has been designed for use by a wide range of people and the booklet notes that only two of the sessions would need the involvement of a health professional. The pack does not deal with dental decay or diet related to dental health and suggests other resources can be used to deal with these topics. This pack is unusual because it deals with topics not often addressed, such as anxieties about going to the dentist and worries about cost. Sessions are designed to encourage informed discussion and to take account of people's religious, cultural and spiritual values. For example, one session suggests points for discussion for a Muslim audience about dental treatment during Ramadan. Although designed for use in a group setting there may be occasions when it is appropriate for home viewing by individuals, perhaps with a health professional (for example, to reassure someone about what to expect at the dentist). Each language version of the video has been filmed separately with different actors so that dress, names, etc. reflect the cultural group more accurately. The pack was developed in consultation with members of Asian communities.

Thalassaemia major and me

FORMAT: 16-page booklet, illustrations, mostly colour

LANGUAGE: Bengali, Cantonese, English, Greek, Gujarati, Hindi, Punjabi, Turkish and Urdu

TARGET AUDIENCE: Key Stage 2 (8–12), Key Stage 3 (12–14), parents, teachers

PRICE: 25p inc.

PRODUCER: United Kingdom Thalassaemia Society, 1992

DISTRIBUTOR: UK Thalassaemia Society

This booklet for children (Key Stages 2 and 3) explains thalassaemia major in a simple and reassuring manner. It was produced by the Thalassaemia Society and sponsored by the Department of Health.

The full-colour booklet uses words and pictures to tell the story of a boy who has thalassaemia major. The reader learns about blood, white blood cells, iron, transfusions and medication given by pump at night. The information is basic and presented in a matter of fact way. The boy is shown enjoying everyday life and playing actively with friends; he says the pump helps him 'have a great time playing and doing all my favourite things'. At the end is space for writing a list of new words learnt and four pages for colouring in.

This is a pleasant and useful booklet which children will enjoy. It can be used as a way of explaining to a child what thalassaemia is and helping a child to talk about the condition. The book can be used with siblings, friends and class groups to explain about thalassaemia to them too.

Think safe, be safe

FORMAT: Video, 20 mins

LANGUAGE: Bengali, English, Hindi/Urdu

TARGET AUDIENCE: Older people, community workers

PRICE: £25.00 inc.

PRODUCER: Coventry Environmental Services Department, 1991

DISTRIBUTOR: Coventry Environmental Services Department

This video is for older people from black and minority ethnic groups. It aims to raise awareness of, and provide information about, safety and accident prevention in the home. The video uses a voice-over to inform about potential hazards and sensible precautions to take as we watch several older people in their own homes demonstrating the advice given. This makes the video realistic as we see older people coping with everyday life and potential hazards in their own surroundings. A wide range of older people is shown from different racial groups and different family structures, including people living alone. There are a few short clips of people talking about accidents but they don't give any information about the circumstances leading up to the accident or precautions to ensure it doesn't happen again.

The advice given in the voice-over is extensive and because there is so much becomes difficult to remember. The video could be used with groups of older people to promote discussion about accident prevention. It would benefit from being used in small sections so that people have time to think and discuss their own situation and how they could best use the information; this could be done easily as the film uses a room by room approach to safety.

Towards racial equality in education

FORMAT: Video, 23 mins

LANGUAGE: English

TARGET AUDIENCE: Teachers, parents

PRICE: £40.78 inc.

PRODUCER: Berkshire Education Department, 1991

DISTRIBUTOR: Dramatic Distribution

This video is for teachers, governors, parents and students and aims to identify strategies to challenge and counteract racism in schools. It was produced by Berkshire Education Department Resources Unit.

The video consists of twenty-six 30-second trigger sequences which are set in schools and are all based on real incidents. It is split into five sections each of which explores a different theme – multicultural education, racist incidents, curriculum, stereotypes and language. The accompanying presenters' notes suggest a format for workshop discussion of the triggers. This covers exploring the incident from the viewpoints of all involved (including the effect on the rest of the school), identifying action which could be taken and evaluating ideas and action arising from the discussion. The notes suggest a mixture of role plays and group activities which can be selected appropriately according to time available and composition of the group. Similarly the video can be used to examine a particular issue or each theme may be worked through as part of the course.

This resource could be used as part of teacher training and in-service training. It may be particularly useful for schools and colleges in the process of developing anti-racist policies. The video includes several triggers involving parents which make it accessible to governor and parent groups, so providing opportunities for parents and teachers to discuss these issues.

Training: implementing racial equality at work

FORMAT: 28-page pack

LANGUAGE: English

TARGET AUDIENCE: Trainers

PRICE: £4.02

PRODUCER: Commission for Racial Equality, 1991

DISTRIBUTOR: Lavis Marketing

This guide is an overview of the basic elements of good practice in the provision and development of racial equality training in employment. It is designed for use by senior managers, trainers, equal opportunity and personnel officers and those providing training. It was produced by the Commission for Racial Equality and is intended to build on an earlier CRE publication, *Training: the implementation of equal opportunities at work*, volumes 1 and 2.

The guide identifies some basic principles, strategies and conditions for the success of training and highlights key questions to be answered before training programmes are set up. Common elements of training for all staff are listed in terms of essential learning elements and outputs (the skills and experience staff should acquire as a result of the training). Sections are included for different staff (e.g. senior managers, recruitment staff) and more specific learning elements and outputs identified for the roles. The guide does not examine how to deliver training but focuses on the outcomes which can be achieved through racial equality training. This practical document will be of interest to those involved in training on racial equality issues. It is concise and clear, identifying tangible and measurable targets for organisations to work towards when developing training on racial equality issues.

Travelling people

FORMAT: Video, 50 mins

LANGUAGE: English

TARGET AUDIENCE: Travellers, community workers, health professionals, service providers, primary healthcare teams

PRICE: £25.00 inc.

PRODUCER: Northern Visions, 1993

DISTRIBUTOR: Northern Visions

This documentary explores the experiences of travelling people in Ireland, their culture, language and way of life and the discrimination they face daily. It was made by Northern Visions in close cooperation with traveller activists and the Dublin Travellers Education Development Group.

Throughout the video travellers emphasise that they see themselves as an ethnic group and that discrimination against travellers is racism. Covert filming shows travellers being refused a drink in a pub and being verbally abused. Interviews with people in the street reflect prejudice and ignorance. Health, housing, education and politics are all explored from travellers' experiences. The lack of services and adequate sites for caravans is documented and stereotypes of travellers challenged. Although the video describes the situation in Ireland it is also relevant to Britain and gives travellers a voice. The video ends with scenes of a unique housing development which has been developed by a local authority in consultation with the traveller community it will house.

The video is suitable for general viewing by any group. It may be appropriate for service providers in raising awareness about traveller communities and meeting the needs of all sections of the community. It could also be used with traveller groups to explore how to gain access to services and challenge inequality.

Understanding schizophrenia

FORMAT: 9-page booklet

LANGUAGE: Bengali, English, Gujarati, Hindi, Punjabi, Urdu

TARGET AUDIENCE: Mental health teams, general public

PRICE: 32p inc.

PRODUCER: West Birmingham Health Authority, Health Education Unit, 1990

DISTRIBUTOR: Northern Birmingham Community HPS

This booklet is for people who have been diagnosed as having schizophrenia and their families. It aims to explain what is meant by the term schizophrenia. It was developed from the series *Understanding Schizophrenia* which was written in English. The Department of Health in conjunction with the Health Education Authority funded the translations.

The booklet explains in clear language what health professionals usually mean by the term schizophrenia, including symptoms and behaviour. Treatments and what to expect from hospital and community services are generally described. Readers are encouraged to discuss treatments with their doctor, especially if side effects are experienced. A section on sources of help with useful addresses is included. The booklet notes that the symptoms of schizophrenia may be viewed and treated differently in other cultures.

The booklet is informative and reassuring. Some people may wish to ask questions and discuss the information further with a health professional. A linkworker or interpreter may be needed to facilitate this. The booklet was developed with the assistance of communities in West Birmingham.

Visit to the X-ray department Reporting a racist incident

FORMAT: Video, 14 mins and 7 mins; with 35-page teachers' notes

LANGUAGE: English

TARGET AUDIENCE: Teachers, lecturers

PRICE: £25.00 inc.

PRODUCER: Northampton Health Authority, Video Communication Services

DISTRIBUTOR: Northampton College

This two-part video and accompanying teaching notes were developed as support materials for teaching English to speakers of other languages (ESOL). The video was produced by Northampton Health Authority for NATECLA with financial assistance from the Ruth Hayman Trust.

Part one was filmed in a hospital X-ray department and realistically illustrates a hospital environment. It follows a woman through the procedure for a chest X-ray and barium meal X-ray. We see signs and notices commonly seen in hospitals, with staff asking questions and giving directions. Part two contains a home interview with a woman reporting a racist incident to a police officer. The officer is calm and sympathetic, the woman explains the incident clearly, but also states she is frightened by what has happened. The teaching notes contain transcripts, suggested lesson plans, pictures for language cues, copies of notices translated into Gujarati, Punjabi and Cantonese and a copy of a hospital letter.

These materials were developed because ESOL staff found that these topics featured heavily in their classes but they were unable to find appropriate teaching materials. Although the video illustrates 'perfect' situations it provides a wide range of material with which students can practise English. The notes recommend it is used flexibly to suit the needs of students. This is a practical and useful resource which students and teachers will find interesting.

Voices from Eritrea, Kurdistan and Somalia

FORMAT: Pack, with 4 booklets

LANGUAGE: English

TARGET AUDIENCE: Key Stage 2 (8–12), Key Stage 3 (12–14), Key Stage 4 (14–16), teachers

PRICE: £7.95

PRODUCER: Minority Rights Group, 1991

DISTRIBUTOR: Minority Rights Group

This pack is a collection of autobiographical, bilingual writing by young refugees from Eritrea, Kurdistan and Somalia. Also included are notes for teachers on integrating refugee children into schools.

For use in schools, it can support work at Key Stages 2, 3, and 4, in English and geography. It is also for use in teaching English to speakers of other languages in schools and adult education settings. The pack was produced by the Minority Rights Group with funding from a large number of charitable organisations and commercial companies.

Each booklet contains accounts by children and young people from one of the countries. The accounts are written bilingually in English with the relevant language on the facing page. They describe life in their countries of origin and what they can remember of life before they became refugees. The accounts are about leaving their country, the journey, arrival in the UK and what life has been like since then. The booklets are illustrated with maps and photographs and drawings by the younger children. The children and young people describe and make sense of what they have seen and experienced in everyday language. Background information about each country is included for teachers. The booklets could be used in small and large group work.

The teachers' notes aim to give a better understanding of the psychological needs of refugee children so that they can be more successfully integrated into British schools. This covers some of the insights provided by psychotherapeutic work carried out with refugees and may help teachers in their work with refugee pupils. The material and further reading in the notes may be helpful to individual teachers and schools and could be used to inform training in this area with a wide range of professionals who are concerned with children's welfare.

Weaning: an information pack for those working with Asian communities

FORMAT: Video, 10 mins; leaflets × 12; 34-page pack

LANGUAGE: Leaflets: English, Gujarati, Urdu; video: Hindi and English versions on one tape

TARGET AUDIENCE: Parents, health visitors, dietitians, health professionals

PRICE: £4.99 inc.

PRODUCER: Bolton Health Authority, 1989

DISTRIBUTOR: Bolton Centre for Health Promotion

The pack aims to provide general information about weaning babies from Asian families. The loose-leaf information folder is targeted primarily at health visitors and dietitians, but is also of interest to other health professionals. The video is targeted at mothers.

Weaning practices and problems and how these may affect Asian communities are described briefly. It is stressed that the problems are not because Asian diets are deficient, but may be caused by inappropriate advice from health workers, social disadvantage, pressure from advertising to adopt Western foods, and poor communication of health education messages. Information is provided about weaning generally, including worries and problems parents may have. The main Asian religions are described briefly and Asian food and eating habits outlined. It is emphasised that these are general descriptions and health workers are encouraged not to view Asian families as a homogenous group. Lists of sugar-free and animal-product-free manufactured baby foods are included and may be useful for quick reference.

WEANING

An information pack for those working with asian communities.

The video follows baby Saajid being weaned. It covers preparation of first foods, including family foods, avoidance of salt, sugar and strong spices, finger foods, vitamin supplements and manufactured baby foods (showing a range of different brand names). It is short enough to be viewed with the health visitor during a home visit so that viewpoints can be shared and questions answered. It could also be shown in waiting areas such as clinics and in groups where mothers meet. The leaflets are simply laid out with black-and-white drawings and short text. Use of family foods is encouraged and one leaflet is a collection of Asian recipes suitable for young babies. The leaflet about iron explains why iron is needed and which foods supply it. The leaflets can be used to support the video and/or supplement information from a health worker.

The pack was developed by the Food in the Community Resource Group made up of health visitors and dietitians who met to share experiences of weaning and nutrition-related problems.

A welcome break: the shared care scheme

FORMAT: Video, 30 mins

LANGUAGE: English, Punjabi

TARGET AUDIENCE: Carers, parents, social workers

PRICE: £20.00 + p&p + VAT

PRODUCER: Birmingham Social Services, 1990

DISTRIBUTOR: Shared Care Team

This video describes a shared care scheme (also known as respite care) which supports families with children with disabilities. The parents and carers are from a range of different cultures, backgrounds and family structures.

The video consists of interviews with parents and carers talking frankly about their experiences. Parents explain what life is like for a family of a child with a disability and how the shared care scheme offers all family members, including the child 'a welcome break'. Carers describe how they became involved in the scheme including the assessment procedure, training and support for carers. We see shared care in action in different families with children who have a wide range of disabilities. The importance of a child's cultural background is acknowledged with shared care links being made between families of similar cultural backgrounds. The benefits of the scheme are described by parents and carers as are some of their initial anxieties.

This video gives a glimpse of what the scheme is about and will be of interest to parents considering using a scheme or potential carers. Service providers may find it a useful trigger when considering how well services meet the needs of all sections of the community. The video was made with the involvement of parents, carers and children from Birmingham.

Welcome to primary school

FORMAT: Video, 16 mins; with booklet

LANGUAGE: English

TARGET AUDIENCE: Parents, teachers

PRICE: £40.78 inc.

PRODUCER: Berkshire Education Department Resources Unit, 1987

DISTRIBUTOR: Dramatic Distribution

This video is for parents from Asian communities and aims to show how they can contribute to their children's primary education. It seeks to give parents a clearer picture of what children do at school.

The video visits a number of primary schools. Multiracial groups of children are seen learning in a child-centred environment, which we are told may be very different from the kind of education experienced by the children's parents. There are good examples of how schools have welcomed and involved parents.

Teachers demonstrate bilingual teaching and talk about support of the child's home language and culture. School governors discuss recognising and valuing the culture and background of all children. Parents are encouraged to consider standing as school governors and the importance of communication between governors and parents is emphasised. The accompanying booklet notes key points from the video and suggests discussion questions linked to these.

This video may be used in group settings with parents to trigger discussion about how parents can become involved in school activities. It could also be viewed by parents at home. The video may also be useful in training settings to prompt teachers and others to consider how to welcome, encourage and enable parents to become more involved in the school.

What is cancer? Questions and answers about cancer

FORMAT: Cassette, 17 mins; with 4-page and 8-page factsheets

LANGUAGE: Bengali (Sylheti), Cantonese, Gujarati, Hindi, Punjabi, Urdu, English for an African-Caribbean audience

TARGET AUDIENCE: General public

PRICE: £3.00 inc.

PRODUCER: CancerLink, 1992

DISTRIBUTOR: CancerLink

This audio cassette and accompanying factsheets describe the service CancerLink offers to anyone whose life is affected by cancer

and answers some common questions about cancer. It was made by CancerLink which is associated with the Cancer Relief Macmillan Fund.

The cassette begins with an introduction to the support CancerLink provides, especially the phonelines. A simple and clear explanation of cancer and treatments is given, accompanied by a question-and-answer session. Common worries are covered such as tests which will be necessary, side effects of treatments, pain control, complementary or holistic treatments, myths about cancer and whether people will survive cancer.

Information given is general and reassuring. Advice is also given about healthy living such as diet, giving up smoking, regular cervical screening and being breast-aware. The cassettes create an informal atmosphere yet provide information in a knowledgeable manner. The Asian language and Cantonese cassettes include a section at the end of common terms (in English) which people will hear when cancer is being discussed.

The factsheets are entitled 'Cancer and treatments' and 'Are you having problems eating?' They provide basic information in community languages which support the cassettes. The eating factsheet has been designed to reflect the traditional diets of each community. The cassette for an African-Caribbean audience is in English and uses actors from various African-Caribbean communities. The cassettes and factsheets are not detailed, but do encourage people to ask questions and provide details of how to get more information, in community languages if necessary. Family and friends may also find them helpful.

What to do about headlice

FORMAT: Video, 4 mins

LANGUAGE: Bengali, English

TARGET AUDIENCE: Parents

PRICE: £15.00 inc.

PRODUCER: Tower Hamlets Health Promotion Service, 1989

DISTRIBUTOR: East London & City HPS

This video is for Bengali communities and aims to inform parents about the detection, treatment and prevention of headlice.

The video uses a voice-over and assures viewers that most children will have headlice at sometime. It is stressed that parents should not feel ashamed about this and we are told research has indicated that headlice prefer clean hair. The detection, treatment and prevention of headlice are clearly demonstrated by a mother of three children. Advice is given about where to get appropriate lotions and shampoos, with several common brands shown. The viewer is reminded that if their child has headlice the whole family should be treated. It is also helpful to tell the school and parents of the child's friends. The video is short and informative. It is suitable for home viewing and may be a way of starting discussion on this sensitive topic.

The video was produced in response to requests from school nurses for more information on this subject for parents.

'What we have to say...' Asian youth speak out about being black in Britain in the 1990s

FORMAT: Video, 29 mins

LANGUAGE: English

TARGET AUDIENCE: Key Stage 3 (12–14), Key Stage 4 (14–16), young people (16-plus), youth workers, teachers

PRICE: £20.00 (maximum: prices vary according to purchaser)

PRODUCER: Newton Street Youth Association, 1991

DISTRIBUTOR: Asian Community Media

This video is for a general audience and is about the experiences of young men from Asian communities growing up in Britain today. It was produced by a group of young Pakistani men (aged 13 upwards) who attend a local youth centre in the Greater Manchester area. North West Arts and Tameside Metropolitan Borough Council provided financial support.

The video focuses on racism and the young men's experiences of it. A mix of interviews, group discussions and a reconstruction of a racist attack are used to document their accounts. Racial abuse at school and on the streets is described including abuse from teachers. Racial attacks are something all the young men have experienced, and some feel they have to protect their families. The limited and uninterested reaction of the police is discussed. The young men talk of the support and understanding they have received from other members of the youth centre.

The video was made by the young men themselves. What it lacks in technical quality is more than made up for by the content. It would be useful as a trigger for discussion about racism and its effects. It could be used with young people in group settings and for training professionals such as youth workers and teachers.

Where it really matters: developing anti-racist education in predominantly white primary schools

FORMAT: 73-page book

LANGUAGE: English

TARGET AUDIENCE: Teachers/lecturers

PRICE: £4.95

PRODUCER: Development Education Centre, 1990

DISTRIBUTOR: Development Education Centre

This book is for all those working in predominantly white primary schools from class teachers to headteachers. It aims to encourage recognition by teachers, schools and teacher trainers of the need to develop anti-racist education and support them to take it on.

The book makes a clear and unequivocal case for anti-racist education as essential in predominantly white schools. It examines what happens in the school with suggestions for classroom work, implications for staff development, and involvement of the whole school including parents and governors. It is illustrated and contains many examples of classroom practice and pupils' work. One section covers planning, evaluation, assessment and resourcing anti-racist work in the classroom. The book predates many documents about the National Curriculum but does indicate how the work may be incorporated into the curriculum.

The book can be read as a whole or used to help plan staff meetings about anti-racist work and to raise awareness. It may also be useful in teacher training and in-service training. A reference section of other resources and relevant documents is included. A large number of children and teachers were involved in contributing to the book.

Where to from here? A handbook for Chinese carers

FORMAT: 60-page manual

LANGUAGE: Cantonese

TARGET AUDIENCE: Health professionals, carers, primary healthcare teams

PRICE: £2.50 + 80p p&p

PRODUCER: Health Education Authority, 1992

DISTRIBUTOR: Health Education Authority

This manual for Chinese carers aims to provide useful information about services which exist to help carers and to advise how to approach service providers. It is a companion to the handbook for professionals *Working with Chinese carers*. It was commissioned by the King's Fund Centre and produced with financial and editorial support from the Health Education Authority.

The manual has ten sections providing practical information on a range of issues such as financial assistance, medical and health services, death and dying, and personal support for the carer. Appendices include lists of national organisations and Chinese organisations in the UK. There is also a glossary outlining the role of professionals and common services which carers may come into contact with. There is also a sample letter in English for carers to send to service providers. This requests a meeting with an interpreter present to discuss services available and the carers' needs. There is no English translation of the manual. It would be helpful if a carer could discuss the information provided with a professional (with the assistance of a linkworker or interpreter if necessary) as more local and specific information can then be provided. Many carers will find this booklet a

useful introduction to services supporting carers.

While you are pregnant: safe eating and how to avoid infection from food and animals

FORMAT: 13-page booklet

LANGUAGE: Bengali, Cantonese, English, Greek, Gujarati, Hindi, Punjabi, Turkish, Urdu

TARGET AUDIENCE: Parents, women

PRICE: Free

PRODUCER: Department of Health and Central Office of Information, 1993

DISTRIBUTOR: BAPS

This booklet for pregnant women contains the most recent advice from the Department of Health about preventing infection from food or animals.

The booklet identifies some of the infections which may be passed to a pregnant woman through food or contact with animals. The reader is advised about foods to avoid during pregnancy, preparation and cooking methods to use to minimise the possibility of infection and tips about handling animals and hygiene. It is easy to read and the information is clear. The booklet can stand alone but women may wish to discuss the information with a health professional. Pregnant women and their families will find this a useful and reassuring booklet which can be referred to quickly. It will be of most use if women receive it early in their pregnancy.

White awareness: handbook for anti-racism training

FORMAT: 211-page manual

LANGUAGE: English

TARGET AUDIENCE: Trainers

PRICE: £8.50

PRODUCER: University of Oklahoma Press, 1989

DISTRIBUTOR: EDS

This manual aims to help white people understand personal, cultural and institutional racism and to take responsibility for challenging racist attitudes and behaviours. The manual was written by a consultant researcher and teacher, specialising in issues of oppression.

The six-stage programme explores racism comprehensively. It aims to enable participants to identify various forms of racism, confront personal fears and feelings about racism, define how personal attitudes and behaviours are representative of racism and develop strategies to challenge racism on a personal and institutional level. Each stage consists of an introduction to the issue, rationale and method, followed by a series of activities suitable for use with groups. These can be used selectively according to time available, group composition, etc. There is enough material for a 45-hour course.

This manual has become well known for presenting the view that racism is a white problem which must be tackled by white people. While much of the material is about the USA it is easily transferable to the situation in the UK and is equally applicable. Those involved in race equality training may find this a useful resource with many ideas about how to explore the complexity of racism with groups.

White lies

FORMAT: Video, 23 mins; with 15-page notes; A2 poster and A3 poster

LANGUAGE: English

TARGET AUDIENCE: Key Stage 3 (12–14), Key Stage 4 (14–16), young people (16-plus), teachers, youth workers

PRICE: £35.00

PRODUCER: Swingbridge Video, 1987

DISTRIBUTOR: Swingbridge Video

This resource was produced for young white people in North East England. It aims to initiate discussion about racism and encourage young people to take responsibility for challenging it. It was produced in consultation with an advisory group of representatives from youth organisations, community groups, anti-fascist groups, local authorities, teachers and the Community Relations Council in the Newcastle area.

The video has nine short sequences, each dealing with an aspect of racism. These are linked by a rap. Young people (from white, African-Caribbean and Asian communities) are interviewed and give their views on racism. There are also some dramatised sections. For example an Asian person is seen being turned down for a job by a white employer. The young people are forthright in their views and challenge the viewer to consider facts about racism. The accompanying notes are designed to be used with the video and to provide further information for discussion. They consist mainly of quotes from other sources which are linked to each sequence in the video. There are also two posters, one featuring a football scene with the slogan 'United against racism and fascism', and the other promoting the video.

The video is lively and suitable for use in informal settings such as youth centres and job clubs. It is probably best viewed sequence by sequence, with time for discussion in between each one. The video was produced as a result of concern by youth workers in the North East that racist ideas, beliefs and practices were common among many of the young white people that they worked with. The video was commissioned as one part of an anti-racist strategy.

Whose image? Anti-racist approaches to photography and visual literacy

FORMAT: Pack; with 22-page booklet and A1 poster

LANGUAGE: English

TARGET AUDIENCE: Teachers, youth workers, community workers

PRICE: £5.00 inc.

PRODUCER: Building Sights, 1989

DISTRIBUTOR: Building Sights

This booklet and poster aim to encourage discussion and exploration of how photographs structure understanding of information about other cultures. They have been designed for use inside and outside classroom settings. The pack was produced by Building Sights, a community education and photography project in Birmingham and funded by the Arts Council.

The booklet consists of four contributions (one interview and three essays) about how photographs are socially constructed. It questions the motives and interests of those who produce photographic images. The reader is reminded of how powerful visual images are in maintaining stereotypes, of how pervasive visual images are and of their use as a source of information. A resource list of further reading and useful addresses is included. There are suggested activities for use in the classroom which encourage students to examine photographs critically and question the

message portrayed. The accompanying poster illustrates some of these activities.

The booklet is probably of most interest to teachers, youth workers and community workers. The activities could be used with some adaptation for many groups (including adults) either within schools or other group settings. Those involved in resource production may find this of interest too as it raises questions about ownership of images.

Why you need to know about thalassaemia

FORMAT: Video, 10 mins

LANGUAGE: Bengali, English, Gujarati, Punjabi, Urdu

TARGET AUDIENCE: General public

PRICE: £25.00

PRODUCER: Penumbra for UK Thalassaemia Society, 1990

DISTRIBUTOR: UK Thalassaemia Society

This video aims to inform people about thalassaemia, especially people who may be carriers of thalassaemia trait. The video mainly targets Asian communities.

It encourages people who have origins in Bangladesh, India, Pakistan, the Middle East and the Mediterranean to have a blood test to find out whether or not they carry thalassaemia trait. It was funded by the Department of Health.

Actors play all the main parts and the script is based on true stories. It opens with a young couple visiting the doctor because one of them has thalassaemia trait. There are interviews with parents who have children with thalassaemia trait and thalassaemia major and a student explains how having the illness has affected his education. Parents talking about their children with visual images of small children having blood transfusions in hospital makes powerful viewing. The distress thalassaemia can cause for individuals and families is evident. When both partners have the trait a test is advised early in pregnancy to establish if the baby is affected. Termination of pregnancy is suggested as a possibility if the baby has thalassaemia major, but there is no discussion of this. This could be a controversial area for some viewers. Presenters need to enable a sensitive discussion of this.

The video recommends viewers also read the booklet *All you need to know about thalassaemia trait* (see earlier entry). The UK Thalassaemia Society offers advice, but recommends the family doctor as the first point of contact. It is an informative video suitable for use in group settings or viewing at home. It would probably be most helpful if people saw it before conceiving. It could also be used in training to raise awareness among medical staff of the seriousness of thalassaemia and of the need for screening.

Women's health: where to get help

FORMAT: Cassette, 12 mins; with 6-page script

LANGUAGE: Sylheti

TARGET AUDIENCE: Women

PRICE: £1.50 inc.

PRODUCER: Culture Waves for Bloomsbury and Islington Health Authority, 1992

DISTRIBUTOR: Camden and Islington Health Promotion Department

This audio cassette is for women from Bengali (Sylheti-speaking) communities. It aims to inform about sources of help for women's health problems. The cassette is the second in a series of three health information tapes for women from Bengali communities.

The cassette adopts a radio drama approach and we hear two women, Sufia and Aisha, talking about some of their health problems. They briefly explain their symptoms (pelvic pain, missed periods, vaginal discharge) and agree it is difficult to consult with their male GP about such personal problems. The community health worker calls on Sufia to discuss the health of her child. As she is also Bengali the women feel they can discuss their own health with her too. She confirms it is wise to consult a doctor, explaining where they can see a woman doctor and how to arrange an interpreter if needed. She tells the women that shyness can also be a problem for health workers as they may not be able to understand what is wrong with a patient. The women comment that husbands may not understand women's health problems either and this can cause difficulties in the relationship.

The cassette does not attempt to diagnose the women's problems but stresses the need to consult a doctor and provides practical information about how to get help. Sources of help suggested are local to Bloomsbury and Islington. As this information is also printed on the cassette sleeve it could easily be replaced with relevant local information. The cassettes are designed to be available, free of charge, in lending libraries, GPs' surgeries, clinics and community centres. They may be a useful trigger for discussion in women's groups but many women may prefer to listen to them in the privacy of their own homes. The cassette is good value for money. It was produced in close consultation with local Bengali communities.

Working with black adult learners: a practical guide

FORMAT: 159-page manual

LANGUAGE: English

TARGET AUDIENCE: Lecturers, trainers

PRICE: £9.95 inc.

PRODUCER: National Institute of Continuing Adult Education, 1993

DISTRIBUTOR: NIACE

This manual is for education professionals at all levels (from tutors to managers and governors), who are involved in providing education and training to black adult learners. It aims to identify key issues and good practice in the delivery of education and training, address anti-racist strategies and provide a focus for training education professionals. It was produced as a result of a conference held by the Ethnic Minorities Education Policy Committee in 1991 and subsequent workshops.

The manual examines pre-course issues, recruitment and selection and on-course issues in three sections. Within each section a range of topics is explored such as outreach work, staffing issues, ethnic monitoring and language support. Introductory comments to each issue summarise current views and identify good practice. A checklist of key issues for students, practitioners or managers (as appropriate) is followed by a resource list and useful contact addresses. The manual is well laid out and easy to read. It contains model policy documents and useful extracts from a variety of sources to illustrate points and good practice.

The manual will be useful to education professionals as it clearly identifies good practice and provides guidance on how to achieve it. It could be used in a variety of training settings, for in-service training and initial training. It is equally useful for course teams or working parties and lends itself to flexible use as issues of concern or relevance can be selected and worked upon individually.

Working with Chinese carers: a handbook for professionals

FORMAT: 51-page pack

LANGUAGE: English

TARGET AUDIENCE: Social workers, health professionals, primary healthcare teams

PRICE: £2.50 + 80p p&p

PRODUCER: King's Fund Centre with Health Education Authority

DISTRIBUTOR: Health Education Authority

This book is for those who wish to work with or who are already working with Chinese carers. It aims to provide practical advice on identifying carers, meeting their needs and enlisting the help of support services.

The book is based upon research undertaken among Chinese carers in Liverpool, which the authors state is applicable anywhere in Britain as Chinese communities often share the same background and occupation, etc. The history and present situation of Chinese communities in Britain is described, and information provided about the research findings, including several case studies.

In general, Chinese carers were receiving little or no support and were often unaware of their rights or any sources of help and support. How to contact Chinese carers is explored with practical advice about the most appropriate and effective ways of contacting people. There are suggestions about how to organise services to meet the needs of Chinese carers and how to work with other services (voluntary and statutory) to do this. The book stresses that many Chinese carers are very isolated because of language barriers, unsocial working hours, a widely dispersed population and cultural differences. Those seeking to reach Chinese carers will find this book identifies practical steps which can be taken to reach people. A wide range of professionals and organisations working with Chinese communities contributed to the booklet.

Your baby's hearing

FORMAT: Video, 10 mins; with 4-page notes

LANGUAGE: Bengali with or without English subtitles

TARGET AUDIENCE: Parents, primary healthcare teams

PRICE: £16.17

PRODUCER: Tower Hamlets Health Promotion Service

DISTRIBUTOR: East London & City HPS

This video is for parents from Bengali communities. It aims to increase parents' awareness of hearing loss among infants in the first year of life and enable them to recognise some of the signs of hearing loss. It was made by Tower Hamlets Health Promotion Unit and funded by the City and East London Family Health Service and London Docklands Development Corporation.

Babies are shown at different stages (early weeks, 3 months, 6 months, 8 months and 1 year) and demonstrate the expected milestones in terms of response to sound and vocal responses. There are lots of shots of parents (mostly mothers) talking to their babies and babies cooing back with delight. Parents are encouraged to consult health visitors and/or GPs if they have any worries about their babies' hearing. The main points are repeated at the end.

The video is intended to be used by health visitors and doctors as part of the child health surveillance programme. The makers recommend parents see it when their baby is 2 to 3 months old and again at 7 to 8 months old. Health visitors may find it useful to view at home with parents as it is short, informative and interesting. The video was developed in response to requests from audiologists who were concerned that hearing loss was sometimes detected at later stages in children

from Bengali communities. The video was made with the involvement of parents and health workers from Bengali communities and the results of a 6-week pilot of the video with parents were very positive.

Your children's teeth

FORMAT: Video, 7 mins; with 3-page script

LANGUAGE: Bengali without subtitles, Punjabi or Urdu with subtitles, English

TARGET AUDIENCE: Parents, health professionals

PRICE: £12.75

PRODUCER: Tower Hamlets Health Promotion Service

DISTRIBUTOR: East London & City HPS

This video is for Bengali communities and aims to inform parents about how to care for their children's teeth.

The video uses a voice-over and stresses the need to care for infants' first teeth. The role of sugar in dental decay is explained by displaying the amount of sugar in various common items such as a chocolate biscuit. Low sugar items are shown and advised as the healthier option. The video features a range of common brand-named products. Low sugar foods for babies are also covered in the video, which advises savoury rather than sweet manufactured products. Parents are encouraged to use traditional family foods. The importance of correct brushing is emphasised and we see mothers helping to brush babies' and children's teeth. Parents are advised to consult their health visitor for further help and to ensure their children visit the dentist from an early age.

The video is suitable for viewing at home or in group settings. It would benefit from the presence of a health professional or community worker to enable further discussion and sharing of views. The video was made in consultation with local Bengali communities.

Your guide to diabetes

FORMAT: 30-page pack

LANGUAGE: Bengali, English, Gujarati, Punjabi, Urdu

TARGET AUDIENCE: General public, health professionals, carers

PRICE: £15.00 inc.

PRODUCER: Preston Health Authority

DISTRIBUTOR: Preston HPU

This pack aims to provide information in community languages about diabetes and its management for people from Asian communities. It was produced by Preston Health Authority and was sponsored by Lancashire Family Health Services Authority and two commercial companies.

The pack consists of an A4 ring binder with 6 pages of information about diabetes in each community language. Pages are photocopiable stiff card and so are durable. Diabetes is explained and how diet can help control. diabetes is covered in some detail. The dietary information is reflective of Asian diets, reference is made to the exchange system for carbohydrate, advice is given about alcohol and fasting is mentioned. Information is given about hypoglycaemia, general health care and sources of help.

The pack is a useful way of providing some basic information for people with diabetes, their families and carers and could support health professionals who are advising people about diabetes management. It may be useful to adapt the sources of help section to include local addresses and phone numbers. The pack was produced by health professionals to support health education work within Asian communities.

Your guide to family planning

FORMAT: 21-page booklet, illustrations

LANGUAGE: Bengali, Gujarati, Hindi, Punjabi and Urdu (with bilingual text in English)

TARGET AUDIENCE: General public

PRICE: Free

PRODUCER: Family Planning Association

DISTRIBUTOR: Family Planning Association

This booklet produced for Asian communities aims to provide information to both men and women on the basic facts needed to make choices relating to contraceptives. It was produced by the Family Planning Association with funding from the Department of Health and the Health Education Authority.

The booklet has several sections: 'Introduction to family planning', 'How the reproductive system works', 'Methods of contraception', 'Information on AIDS and safer sex', 'Women's health checks', 'How to get more advice'. The format is bilingual with the Asian text predominant and English alongside. Eleven methods of contraception are covered: the combined pill, progestogen-only pill, injectable contraceptives, intrauterine device (IUD), diaphragm or cap and spermicide, sponge, condom, natural methods, female sterilisation, male sterilisation, emergency methods. A description of each method is given, how it works, possible side effects, its suitability for some women, some information on how to use the different methods.

The information is clearly laid out with photographic-type illustrations to support the information regarding each method. It can be used as a stand-alone resource or as a useful reference point after a consultation with a health professional. The bilingual format makes it accessible to members of Asian communities and health professionals. The booklet stresses that it only outlines the basic facts about family planning. Also, since the booklet was produced several new methods of contraception have become available so further information will be necessary to support this resource. Extensive research prior to the development of the booklet confirmed the need for such a resource and it was piloted with target communities. The booklet received a Plain English Campaign Crystal Mark Award.

Your move

FORMAT: Video, 12 mins

LANGUAGE: Dialogue in Hindi with narration available in Bengali, English, Gujarati, Hindi, Sylheti or Urdu

TARGET AUDIENCE: Parents

PRICE: £9.95 inc.

PRODUCER: Endboard Productions for Sandwell Road Safety Unit, 1991

DISTRIBUTOR: Sandwell Road Safety Unit

This video for Asian communities aims to raise awareness among parents of how and why children are hurt on the road and inform parents about how to protect them.

A dramatised sequence is used to illustrate potential dangers to children on the roads and show what parents can do to ensure their children are safe. A family with three children (of 11 years, 7 years and pre-school age) are moving into a new house. The bustle of unpacking leaves the children unattended outside. The video emphasises how children do not appreciate the dangers of traffic and that parents must exercise care by ensuring children have safe places to play. When unpacking is complete, the family visit a funfair and the journey there provides the parents with opportunities to show the children how to cross roads safely and use safe crossing places. Parents will recognise many of the situations in the video as family life is portrayed in a realistic manner and the urban setting will be familiar to most.

This video could be used in group settings or viewed by families at home. It is useful trigger material and could lead to discussions among parents about issues, such as where children can play safely (for example the family in the video live in a house but some families will live in flats), and whether anything can be done to make residential areas safer such as traffic calming measures. Discussion of what and how to teach children about road safety may also be welcome.

Your right to health

FORMAT: Video, 20 mins; with 6-page notes and 12-page transcript

LANGUAGE: Cantonese

TARGET AUDIENCE: General public

PRICE: £29.90 inc.

PRODUCER: Penumbra Productions for Department of Health, 1988

DISTRIBUTOR: CFL Vision

This video is for Cantonese-speaking Chinese communities and is targeted at both sexes and all age groups. It aims to inform about the National Health Service and encourage people to make use of it. It was made by the Department of Health and is the first in a series of planned health education materials directed at Chinese communities.

A commentary accompanies visuals of services interspersed with dramatic sketches about common situations such as registering with a GP, finding out about a family planning clinic, seeking medical help in an emergency. It covers a range of health care services from pregnancy and birth through to old age. Leaflets and booklets in Cantonese about health services, benefits and health promotion are also mentioned.

Services are described generally rather than specifically and people may want further information about what actually happens. Health and safety at work are also discussed. The difficulties of communicating are noted and advice is given about how to seek help with interpreting if needed. The overall message of the video is that the NHS is for everyone.

The video has been designed for use by community groups as well as health professionals and is suitable for viewing in a group setting or by individuals and families at home. It may be appropriate to arrange separate viewings for men and women if services such as family planning or cervical screening are to be discussed to avoid any potential embarrassment.

Two information sheets accompany the video, one provides some background information about Chinese people in Britain and health in Chinese communities. The other is a brief checklist of points to consider before showing the video such as checking relevant local information is available and identifying key members of the community who could be invited to the session. There is also a national address list of organisations which may be useful points of contact within Chinese communities.

Your rights to health care

FORMAT: Video, 15 mins; with 4-page notes

LANGUAGE: Somali and dubbed English

TARGET AUDIENCE: General public, primary healthcare teams, refugees

PRICE: £11.92

PRODUCER: Tower Hamlets Health Promotion Service, 1992

DISTRIBUTOR: East London & City HPS

Made for Somali people who are resident or refugees in Britain, this video seeks to inform them about healthcare services and their right to use them. It was made by Tower Hamlets Health Promotion Unit in conjunction with City and East London Family Health Services and with the involvement of local Somali communities and health professionals.

The video features Somali people using various health services and this usefully illustrates a wide range of settings as well as a wide spectrum of people using the services (for example, single people, parents with children). Health services are shown to be modern and health professionals welcoming. The role of the GP and the procedure for finding and registering with a doctor is explained clearly. It is stressed that the GP is usually the first point of contact for healthcare and that treatment is free.

The video is broken up into six sections: 'Your rights to healthcare'; 'What is a family doctor'; 'How to get treatment from a family doctor'; 'What a family doctor can do'; 'Services you can use directly'; 'Advice and support'. The video ends with a brief recap of the main points.

This video would benefit from being viewed with a health professional or community worker so that the different services could be discussed further and local information about GPs, health centres, dentists, etc. could be given. Linkworkers and interpreters are briefly mentioned and it may be helpful to explain this further. It is also suitable for individual viewing and in this way may reach other members of the family and community. The video was made as a result of a consultation exercise with local Somali communities and health workers who identified information about and access to health services as a priority.

You're talking to me now?

See *Counselling and sexuality*

Zara dhyan dein

FORMAT: Video, 35 mins

LANGUAGE: Hindi with English subtitles

TARGET AUDIENCE: General public

PRICE: £35.00 + VAT + £5.00 p&p (prices for public sector; phone for details of prices for private sector)

PRODUCER: Thames Television, 1991

DISTRIBUTOR: Academy Television

This series of eight 5-minute programmes for general audiences were originally shown on television. They seek to raise awareness among Hindi-speaking communities about a range of issues related to health. They were made by Health Wise Productions for Yorkshire Television.

The series is presented by a doctor who discusses the issue with professionals and members of the community. The videos are technically good and the information is presented concisely. They are short enough to trigger discussion as well as provide information. They could be used in a variety of settings, with groups or even in waiting areas. Some need additional information to ensure they are up to date but others can stand alone.

Programme 1 deals with paan chewing. The viewer is informed that it is associated with oral cancer and gum disease, advice is given about how to give up.

Programme 2 covers screening for handicap including tests available and genetic counselling. Newer tests have been developed since the programme was made and viewers would need to be made aware of this. It is stated that all handicap can be detected with screening and viewers need to be informed that this is incorrect.

Programme 3 emphasises the importance of immunisation and explains which diseases can be prevented. The immunisation schedule has now changed so this would need updating. It does not mention that some children should

not be immunised and parental concerns about side effects are not really dealt with.

Programme 4 discusses postnatal depression, the symptoms women may experience and explains how this is different from 'baby blues'. Early recognition and treatment is advised. A mother describes how women may feel after the birth of a baby.

Programme 5 is about child safety at home and demonstrates what parents can do to make the home safe for small children; potential hazards are identified and made safe.

Programme 6 aims to encourage more Asian people and families to consider fostering. Foster parents explain why they chose to do it and talk about what it is like to be a foster parent. Advice is given about how to become a foster parent.

Programme 7 is about domestic violence and covers what women can do if they are subject to violence at home. A GP suggests talking with the couple alone and together and if the problem is still unresolved recommends counselling. This programme does not fully reflect the options open to women or recognise the reality of life for women living with a violent partner.

Programme 8 encourages everyone to consider taking some form of regular exercise, perhaps a sport, exercise class or just walking more often. An exercise trainer demonstrates some gentle exercises for viewers to try at home.

APPENDIX 1:
POSTERS AND MODELS

Afro-Caribbean pack

FORMAT: Pack; 29 pieces of artificial food

TARGET AUDIENCE: Healthcare professionals, primary healthcare teams

PRICE: £190.06 inc.

PRODUCER: Replica Foods, 1991

DISTRIBUTOR: Replica Foods

CONTAINS: Callaloo leaf × 6, plantain, okra, hard dough bread, hard dough bread slice, paw-paw half, pomegranate third, breadfruit, breadfruit section, akee portion (10 pcs), ginger root, pumpkin wedge, yam, sweet potato slice × 2, sweet potato section, prawn king size, bream, red mullet, avocado, banana, grapefruit, lime, mango, orange, pineapple, aubergine, carrot + leaves, green pepper, red pepper, turnip, lantern pepper

AIDS

FORMAT: Poster, 42 × 42 cms, colour

LANGUAGE: Bengali, Cantonese, English, Somali, Vietnamese

TARGET AUDIENCE: General public

CONTENTS: Facts about HIV/AIDS

PRICE: 50p

PRODUCER: Tower Hamlets Health Promotion Service

DISTRIBUTOR: East London & City HPS

AIDS does not discriminate. Today it's someone else's problem; tomorrow it could be yours

FORMAT: Poster, A2

LANGUAGE: English

TARGET AUDIENCE: General public

PRICE: £1.00 inc. (5+ copies 75p each)

PRODUCER: Blackliners, 1992

DISTRIBUTOR: Blackliners

Black by popular demand … d.condom

FORMAT: Poster, A2, colour

LANGUAGE: English

TARGET AUDIENCE: General public

CONTENTS: Safer sex information

PRICE: Free

PRODUCER: Health First, 1993

DISTRIBUTOR: Health First

Can you afford not to know about sickle cell and thalassaemia?

FORMAT: Poster, A2, colour

LANGUAGE: English

TARGET AUDIENCE: General public

PRICE: Free

PRODUCER: Birmingham Sickle Cell and Thalassaemia Centre, 1993

DISTRIBUTOR: Birmingham Sickle Cell and Thalassaemia Centre

Community poster: HIV/AIDS

FORMAT: Poster, A3, black-and-white

LANGUAGE: Captioned in Bengali, Cantonese, English, Gujarati, Hindi and Urdu

TARGET AUDIENCE: General public

PRICE: £3.60

PRODUCER: East Birmingham Health Promotion Service

DISTRIBUTOR: East Birmingham HPS

Don't think about it: use it!

FORMAT: Poster, A3 (safer sex)

LANGUAGE: Bengali, English, Gujarati, Hindi, Punjabi, Turkish, Urdu

TARGET AUDIENCE: General public

PRICE: £1.95

PRODUCER: The Naz Project, 1992

DISTRIBUTOR: Naz Project

Fact: you're never too old to enjoy sex

FORMAT: Poster, 43 × 21 cms, colour

LANGUAGE: English

TARGET AUDIENCE: Older people

PRICE: £2.00

PRODUCER: Age Concern Lewisham, 1993

DISTRIBUTOR: Age Concern England

Fireworks safety campaign: it is a criminal offence to sell fireworks to anyone aged under 16

FORMAT: Poster, A4

LANGUAGE: Bengali, English, Gujarati, Punjabi, Urdu, Welsh

TARGET AUDIENCE: General public

PRICE: Free

PRODUCER: DTI, 1992

DISTRIBUTOR: Department of Trade and Industry

Give yourself a chance: eat more healthy food

FORMAT: Poster, A2, colour

LANGUAGE: Bengali

TARGET AUDIENCE: General public

PRICE: £1.00 inc.

PRODUCER: Tower Hamlets Health Authority Department of Nutrition and Dietetics

DISTRIBUTOR: East London & City HPS

Heart burn

FORMAT: Poster, A3, colour

LANGUAGE: Bengali/English, Gujarati/English, English, Hindi/English, Punjabi/English, Urdu/English

TARGET AUDIENCE: General public

CONTENTS: Highlights the connection between smoking and coronary heart disease.

PRICE: 35p (minimum order £2.50)

PRODUCER: Health Education Authority and Cleanair, 1991

DISTRIBUTOR: Cleanair

If a blood sample is being taken . . .

FORMAT: Poster

LANGUAGE: Captioned in Arabic, Bengali, Cantonese, English, Greek, Gujarati, Hindi, Punjabi, Turkish and Urdu

TARGET AUDIENCE: Women

CONTENTS: Information for women about anonymous HIV testing

PRICE: Free

PRODUCER: Central Office of Information and Department of Health, 1993

DISTRIBUTOR: BAPS

If you or your baby are having a blood or urine test

FORMAT: Poster, A1, colour

LANGUAGE: Captioned in Arabic, Bengali, Cantonese, English, Greek, Gujarati, Hindi, Punjabi, Turkish and Urdu

TARGET AUDIENCE: Parents

CONTENTS: Details of anonymous HIV testing

PRICE: Free

PRODUCER: Central Office of Information and Department of Health, 1990

DISTRIBUTOR: BAPS

Imran Khan says: protect your children against childhood disease. Ask your doctor, health visitor or clinic about immunisation now

FORMAT: Poster, A1, colour

LANGUAGE: Captioned in Bengali, English, Gujarati, Hindi, Punjabi and Urdu

TARGET AUDIENCE: Parents

PRICE: Free

PRODUCER: HEA, 1991

DISTRIBUTOR: Health Education Authority

National AIDS Helpline

FORMAT: Poster, A1, colour

LANGUAGE: Captioned in Arabic, Bengali, Cantonese, Gujarati, Hindi, Punjabi, Urdu and Turkish

TARGET AUDIENCE: General public

CONTENTS: Promotes the NAH minority language telephone lines.

PRICE: Free

PRODUCER: HEA, 1990

DISTRIBUTOR: Health Education Authority

Nutrition education posters (Asian diet)

FORMAT: Poster, A2, colour × 6

LANGUAGE: English

TARGET AUDIENCE: General public

PRICE: £3.50 inc. set

PRODUCER: Leicester Health Authority Nutrition and Dietetic Service, 1989

DISTRIBUTOR: Fosse Health Trust

Replica Asian foods

FORMAT: Pack, 17 pieces of artificial food

TARGET AUDIENCE: Healthcare professionals, primary healthcare teams

PRICE: £57.88

PRODUCER: British Diabetic Association, 1993

DISTRIBUTOR: British Diabetic Association

CONTAINS: portion of white rice, 2 portions of brown rice, portion of chick pea dhal, portion of mung bean dhal, small mixed salad, 2 sweetmeats, piece of white pitta bread, piece of wholemeal pitta bread, 3 chapattis (assorted sizes), pot of plain yoghurt, pot of fruit yoghurt, 1 aubergine and 1 mango

Safer sex is good sex (use a condom)

FORMAT: Poster, A3

LANGUAGE: Bengali, English, Gujarati, Hindi, Punjabi, Turkish, Urdu

TARGET AUDIENCE: General public

PRICE: £1.95 inc.

PRODUCER: The Naz Project, 1993

DISTRIBUTOR: Naz Project

Safer sex: think about it: talk about it: enjoy it! HIV and AIDS affects us all

FORMAT: Poster, 60 × 42 cms, black-and-white

LANGUAGE: English

TARGET AUDIENCE: General public

CONTENTS: For African-Caribbean communities

PRICE: £4.00 inc. (statutory bodies), £2.00 inc. (voluntary/community groups)

PRODUCER: Newham Council, 1993

DISTRIBUTOR: Newham Council

Safer sex: time to start talking. HIV and AIDS affects us all

FORMAT: Poster, 60 × 42 cms, black-and-white

LANGUAGE: English

TARGET AUDIENCE: General public

CONTENTS: Silhouette of an Asian couple talking

PRICE: £4.00 inc. (statutory bodies), £2.00 (voluntary/community groups)

PRODUCER: Newham Council, 1993

DISTRIBUTOR: Newham Council

Teach-a-bodies playpeople

FORMAT: Pack; 4 dolls, 2 adults (55 cm) and 2 children (46 cm); available as a black, brown or white family

TARGET AUDIENCE: People with learning difficulties, health professionals, counsellors, social workers

PRICE: £195.00

PRODUCER: Learning Development Aids, 1991

DISTRIBUTOR: Learning Development Aids

All dolls have fingers, tongues, mouths, anal openings, facial features, nipples and navels. Adult dolls have pubic and underarm hair. Male dolls have uncircumcised penises. Female dolls have vaginal openings and clitorises.

The adult male doll has underwear, clothes and condom. The adult female doll has underwear, clothes, tampon, sanitary towel (permanently attached to panties), and in utero baby boy with attached umbilical cord and placenta. The male and female child dolls have underwear and clothes.

Stamp out racism
Together we can push out racism
Why shouldn't I go for that job?
Why shouldn't I go out with him?

FORMAT: 4 posters, A2, colour. With 12-page notes

LANGUAGE: English

TARGET AUDIENCE: 14- to 16-year-olds, 16- to 19-year-olds

PRICE: £7.16

PRODUCER: Youth Clubs UK, 1993

DISTRIBUTOR: Youth Clubs UK

What's so tough and manly about risking your partner's life? Love safely – use a condom

FORMAT: Poster, A2

LANGUAGE: English

TARGET AUDIENCE: General public

PRICE: £1.00 inc.

PRODUCER: Blackliners, 1992

DISTRIBUTOR: Blackliners

APPENDIX 2: LATE AND FORTHCOMING RESOURCES

The following resources have not been reviewed because they were received too late or were not yet available at the time of going to press. However all resources listed here should be nationally available by the time this publication is in print. Brief information about the resource, as provided by the producers, has been included.

Alcohol and sexual health video for Asian communities

FORMAT: Video, 45 mins

LANGUAGE: English, Gujarati, Punjabi, Urdu

PRICE: Contact distributor

PRODUCER: I F Hyare for Aquarius, early 1995

DISTRIBUTOR: Aquarius

CONTENTS: A three-part trigger video for adult audiences to raise awareness and promote discussion of issues related to alcohol and sexual health. It can be used in community settings or in training professionals and others about how to raise and work with these issues. It uses two programmes adapted from another source, *Sharaab*, plus another programme. Issues presented are the effects of alcohol on personal relationships, sexual behaviour and sexual health.

All about twins

FORMAT: 24-page manual, illustrations

LANGUAGE: English/Urdu

PRICE: £1.00 inc.

PRODUCER: Multiple Births Foundation, 1992

DISTRIBUTOR: Multiple Births Foundation

CONTENTS: Deals with care during the antenatal and postnatal period.

A big night out

FORMAT: Video, 22 mins

LANGUAGE: English

PRICE: Contact distributor

PRODUCER: I F Hyare for Aquarius, 1994

DISTRIBUTOR: Aquarius Education Unit

CONTENTS: A three-part trigger video for use with young people in formal and informal settings. It features young people from a range of cultural backgrounds and centres on a Friday night out. The video presents a number of issues for exploration – alcohol, sexism, racism, prejudice and sexual health. Designed for use with a facilitator.

Caring for young smiles

FORMAT: Video, 7 mins

LANGUAGE: English, Bengali, Cantonese, Gujarati, Turkish, Somali

PRICE: Contact distributor

PRODUCER: Oral Health Promotion Team, 1993

DISTRIBUTOR: City & East London FHSA

CONTENTS: The video aims to inform parents

and carers about how to care for children's teeth. It explains tooth decay, advises how to reduce sugar in the diet and how to identify sugar-free foods. Each language version has been filmed and scripted separately.

Damage caused to the body by diabetes

FORMAT: Video, 8 mins

LANGUAGE: Bengali, with and without English subtitles

PRICE: £15.00 inc.

PRODUCER: East London and The City Health Promotion Service, 1994

DISTRIBUTOR: East London & City HPS

CONTENTS: Looks at how people can reduce or eliminate the risk of damage from their diabetes. It focuses on risk to eyes, kidneys, feet, and the risk of heart attack or stroke, and emphasises the importance of keeping diabetes well under control.

Doing the right thing

FORMAT: 12-page booklet

LANGUAGE: English

PRICE: Free

PRODUCER: The Naz Project, 1993

DISTRIBUTOR: Naz Project

CONTENTS: HIV/AIDS awareness and prevention

Driving and diabetes Travel and diabetes

FORMAT: Two video programmes on one video tape, $3^1/_2$ and 4 mins

LANGUAGE: Bengali, with and without English subtitles

PRICE: £15.00 inc.

PRODUCER: East London and The City Health Promotion Service, 1994

DISTRIBUTOR: East London & City HPS

CONTENTS: *Driving and diabetes* explains legal responsibilities and procedures for people with diabetes who drive, and gives simple precautions to follow. *Travel and diabetes* advises on how to plan for overseas travel. It looks at precautions which should be taken for the journey, and during the visit.

Food photopacks: Afro – Caribbean

FORMAT: Cardset, 16 cards, A5, colour

LANGUAGE: English

PRICE: £12.00 inc.

PRODUCER: Bedford County Council Education Service

DISTRIBUTOR: Multicultural Education Resources

CONTENTS: 1. A selection of fruit and vegetables; 2. Yam; 3. Green bananas; 4. Sugar-cane; 5. Pepper, ginger, garlic; 6. Mangoes; 7. Cassava; 8. Breadfruit; 9. Breadfruit; 10. Christophene, Cohocho (Jamaica); 11. Tania, Coco (Jamaica); 12. Sweet potatoes; 13. Pumpkin; 14. Dasheen; 15. Melon; 16. Plantain.

Food photopacks: Asian – Gujarati

FORMAT: Cardset, 24 cards, A5, colour

LANGUAGE: Gujarati, English and phonetic

PRICE: £12.00 inc.

PRODUCER: Bedford County Council Education Service

DISTRIBUTOR: Multicultural Education Resources

CONTENTS: 1. Ladies' fingers; 2. Mangoes; 3. Radish; 4. Rhubarb; 5. Bitter-melon; 6. Mixed vegetables; 7. Pumpkin; 8. Marrow; 9. Gourd; 10. Chillies; 11. Bulbous roots; 12. Ghosby.

Food photopacks: Asian – Urdu

FORMAT: Cardset, 16 cards, A5, colour

LANGUAGE: Urdu, English and phonetic

PRICE: £12.00 inc.

PRODUCER: Bedford County Council Education Service

DISTRIBUTOR: Multicultural Education Resources

CONTENTS: 1. Crisp cake made of pulse; 2. Fresh and dried red chilli; 3. Chick peas and pulses; 4. Pop corn and ground rice; 5. Mix masala or ingredients; 6. Mix masala or ingredients; 7. Pulse and vermicellies; 8. Betel – loaf ingredients; 9. Cake and biscuit; 10. Methi; 11. Karaila; 12. Basmati rice; 13. Flour; 14. Pure and vegetable ghee; 15. Dhunia; 16. Ginger, garlic, onion, pepper (green); 17. Green and red chillies; 18. Ladies' fingers; 19. Pomegrante; 20. Aubergine; 21. Cake and biscuit; 22. Food and drinks; 23. Grocer's shop; 24. Fruits and vegetables.

Hypoglycaemia
Coping with diabetes during illness

FORMAT: Two video programmes ($2^{1}/_{2}$ mins each) on one videotape

LANGUAGE: Bengali with and without English sub-titles

PRICE: £15.00 inc.

PRODUCER: East London and The City Health Promotion Service, 1994

DISTRIBUTOR: East London & City HPS

CONTENTS: *Hypoglaecemia* looks at the causes, the warning signs, and the treatment of 'hypos'. *Coping with diabetes during illness*

explains the effect of illness on blood sugar level and gives a set of guidelines to follow.

It covers treatment, testing, diet, medicine, and in what circumstances a doctor should be consulted.

Insulin injections for diabetes
Blood testing for diabetes

FORMAT: Two video programmes ($2^{1}/_{2}$ mins and 6 mins) on one videotape

LANGUAGE: Bengali with and without English sub-titles

PRICE: £15.00 inc.

PRODUCER: East London and The City Health Promotion Service, 1992

DISTRIBUTOR: East London & City HPS

CONTENTS: *Insulin injections for diabetes* describes the equipment needed for injecting insulin, demonstrates the correct procedure for injecting and shows safe needle disposal. *Blood testing for diabetes* explains the importance of blood testing and demonstrates the procedure using BM Test 1–44.

Quiet strength

FORMAT: Video, 13 mins

LANGUAGE: English

PRICE: Contact distributor

PRODUCER: Preeya Lal for African-Caribbean Mental Health Project, 1992

DISTRIBUTOR: African-Caribbean Mental Health Project

CONTENTS: The video is about one person's experiences of psychiatric services, with contributions and comments from other users of mental health services. The video was made by service users and presents their points of view.

Recipe book

FORMAT: 24-page pack, illustrations

LANGUAGE: English

PRICE: £2.00 inc.

PRODUCER: Bedford County Council Education Service

DISTRIBUTOR: Multicultural Education Resources

CONTENTS: Easy-to-cook recipes originally from South Asia.

Sex education, values and morality

FORMAT: 47-page pack

LANGUAGE: English

PRICE: £4.99 + 80p p&p

PRODUCER: Health Education Authority, 1994

DISTRIBUTOR: Health Education Authority

CONTENTS: Practical issues involved in developing school sex education policies.

Tablets for diabetes
Urine testing for diabetes

FORMAT: Two video programmes (2 mins and 5 mins) on one videotape

LANGUAGE: Bengali with and without English sub-titles

PRICE: £15.00 inc.

PRODUCER: East London and The City Health Promotion Service, 1992

DISTRIBUTOR: East London & City HPS

CONTENTS: *Tablets for diabetes* briefly shows the range of tablets available, how they work and general advice on taking tablets. *Urine testing for diabetes* explains the importance of urine testing and demonstrates the procedure using Diastix.

Travellers' health series 1: Food

FORMAT: Video, 19 mins (one of six separate videos, available only as a set)

LANGUAGE: English

PRICE: £65.00 inc. (set of six videos)

PRODUCER: Eastern Health Board, 1986

DISTRIBUTOR: Dr Steevens Hospital

CONTENTS: Features women from the travelling community in a studio discussion about nutrition. The 'expert' advice is clearly communicated, identifying balanced diet, appropriate cooking methods, food groups. Displays of food help to convey effective visual messages.

Travellers' health series 2: Needles (1)

FORMAT: Video, 10 mins (one of six separate videos, available only as a set)

LANGUAGE: English

PRICE: £65.00 inc. (set of six videos)

PRODUCER: Eastern Health Board, 1986

DISTRIBUTOR: Dr Steevens Hospital

CONTENTS: A women traveller filmed on a site narrates this film. She talks about diphtheria, tetanus, polio and whooping cough and says more travellers' children suffer from these than 'settled' people. Immunisation is explained and why booster sessions are needed. A baby is shown being immunised. The explanations are clear.

Travellers' health series 3: Ante-natal care

FORMAT: Video, 18 mins (one of six separate videos, available only as a set)

LANGUAGE: English

PRICE: £65.00 inc. (set of six videos)

PRODUCER: Eastern Health Board, 1986

DISTRIBUTOR: Dr Steevens Hospital

CONTENTS: A studio discussion featuring women from the travelling community and a health professional is used to explain what antenatal care is and why it is important. A piece of 'archived' film is then used to show a woman visiting the doctor to confirm her pregnancy and she is seen attending her first antenatal appointment.

Travellers' health series 4: Needles (2)

FORMAT: Video, 7 mins (one of six separate videos, available only as a set)

LANGUAGE: English

PRICE: £65.00 inc. (set of six videos)

PRODUCER: Eastern Health Board, 1986

DISTRIBUTOR: Dr Steevens Hospital

CONTENTS: This video is filmed on a travellers' site and features a young male traveller explaining to a young girl why it is important to be immunised against measles, rubella and tuberculosis.

Travellers' health series 5: Chest infection

FORMAT: Video, 10 mins (one of six separate videos, available only as a set)

LANGUAGE: English

PRICE: £65.00 inc. (set of six videos)

PRODUCER: Eastern Health Board, 1986

DISTRIBUTOR: Dr Steevens Hospital

CONTENTS: This video features a section in a studio with two women travellers and a doctor explaining the importance of knowing about chest infections, causes, prevention and treatment. Women from travelling communities are also filmed on site talking about the same issues.

Travellers' health series 6: Gastro-enteritis

FORMAT: Video, 9 mins (one of six separate videos, available only as a set)

LANGUAGE: English

PRICE: £65.00 inc. (set of six videos)

PRODUCER: Eastern Health Board, 19XX

DISTRIBUTOR: Dr Steevens Hospital

CONTENTS: This video features a studio discussion introduced by women travellers. The vulnerability of young children to this condition is stressed, as is the need for prevention. Women travellers are filmed on site talking about the condition and a health professional is filmed reinforcing this message.

Zara dhyan dein: series 2

FORMAT: Video, 40 mins

LANGUAGE: Hindi with English subtitles

PRICE: £35.00 + VAT + £5.00 p&p (prices for public sector; phone for details of prices for private sector)

PRODUCER: Thames Television, 1993

DISTRIBUTOR: Academy Television

CONTENTS: Health and social issues affecting Asian families in Britain: bed wetting, sensible eating, head lice, snoring, antenatal care, kitchen hygiene, skin care, child car seats.

Zara dhyan dein: series 3

FORMAT: Video, 50 mins

LANGUAGE: Hindi with English subtitles

PRICE: £35.00 + VAT + £5.00 p&p (prices for public sector; phone for details of prices for private sector)

PRODUCER: Thames Television, 1993

DISTRIBUTOR: Academy Television

CONTENTS: Health and social issues affecting Asian families in Britain: you and your GP, hospital services, family planning, having a baby, postnatal advice, child development, child dental health, depression, smoking, alcohol, drug abuse.

APPENDIX 3: CRITICAL READERS

Frances Presley
Information Officer, SHARE, King's Fund Centre

Phil Sealy and the staff of
Standing Conference of Ethnic Minority Senior Citizens (SCEMSC)

Poonam Jagota
Project Worker, South Manchester Health Promotion Unit

Ziba Nadimi
Health Promotion Officer, East London & The City Health Promotion Service

Fauzia Ahmad
Health Promotion Officer, Lewisham and North Southwark Health Promotion Unit

Kirat Randhawa
Trainee Health Promotion Officer, Camden and Islington Health Promotion Unit

Kiran Kumar
Senior Health Promotion Officer, North Bedfordshire Health Promotion Unit

Gulab Singh
Deputy District Health Promotion Officer, Preston Health Promotion Unit

Ghulam Shabbir
Environmental Health Officer, Environmental Health/Road Safety Department, Cambridgeshire County Council

Rose Das
Health Adviser, GUM Clinic, Newcastle General Hospital

Pami Bal
Project Manager, Staff Training and Development Centre, North Mersey Community NHS Trust

APPENDIX 4: QUESTIONNAIRE

Your name

Title of the resource

Are you familiar with this resource?   Yes   No

After reading the review could you comment on the following:

Was enough information given to enable you to decide if this resource was something you might use and/or purchase?

Do you feel you now have a sense of what this resource is about, who it is for and how it might be used?

What was the most useful part of the review?

What was the least useful part of the review?

Do you think there is anything else the review could have commented on?

Was it easy to read?

If this is a review of a resource you are not familiar with has the review made you want to see it?

OR

If this is a review of a resource you are familiar with do you think it is a fair and accurate description of it?

Any other comments?

Please return to Mary Ryan, Health Promotion Information Centre, Health Education Authority, Hamilton House, Mabledon Place, London WC1H 9TX

APPENDIX 5: DIRECTORIES

Accident Prevention Materials

TYPE OF RESOURCE: Catalogue of health resources for ESOL students

LANGUAGE: Resources in English

PRODUCER: HEAL Project, South Birmingham Health Authority

ADDRESS: HEAL Project, St Patricks Centre for Health Promotion, Highgate Street, Birmingham B12 0YA

TEL: 021 446 4747

PRICE: approx. £3

Department of Health Literature

TYPE OF RESOURCE: List of free leaflets and posters

LANGUAGE: Resources in English and some in community languages

PRODUCER: Department of Health

ADDRESS: Department of Health, Skipton House, 80 London Road, London SE1 6LW

TEL: 071 972 5262

PRICE: Free

Directory of Community Interpreting Services and Resources in the Greater London Area

TYPE OF RESOURCE: Directory, 80 pp. + tables

LANGUAGE: Directory in English

PRODUCER: London Interpreting Project

ADDRESS: London Interpreting Project, 20 Compton Terrace, London N1 2UN

TEL: 071 359 6798

PRICE: approx. £8.50

Ethnic Minority Health Information: a catalogue of health education videos and leaflets

TYPE OF RESOURCE: Catalogue, 77 pp.

LANGUAGE: Catalogue and resources in English, Hindi, Punjabi, Urdu, Gujarati, Bengali

PRODUCER: Department of Health and N Films

ADDRESS: N Films, 78 Holyhead Road, Handsworth, Birmingham B21 0LH

TEL: 021 507 0341

PRICE: £13.25 inc.

Information Leaflets in Community Languages

TYPE OF RESOURCE: List, 46 pp.

LANGUAGE: Resources in many languages, including Swahili, Somali, Amharic, Armenian, Farsi

PRODUCER: Leicestershire County Council Libraries and Information Service

ADDRESS: Publications Department, Leicestershire Libraries and Information Service, Thames Tower, 99 Burleys Way, Leicester LE1 3TZ

TEL: 0533 538921

PRICE: £15 inc. (cheques to Leicestershire County Council)

Mental Health in Translation

TYPE OF RESOURCE: List

LANGUAGE: Resources in Bengali, Cantonese, English, Gujarati, Hindi, Polish, Punjabi, Turkish, Urdu, Vietnamese

PRODUCER: MIND (National Association for Mental Health)

ADDRESS: 22 Harley Street, London W1N 2ED

TEL: 071 637 0741

PRICE: Free

APPENDIX 6: DISTRIBUTORS

Academy Television
104 Kirkstall Road
Leeds
LS3 1JS
Tel 0532 461528

Acer Centre
Wyvil School
Wyvil Road
London
SW8 2TJ
Tel 071 627 2662

African-Caribbean Mental Health Project
Zion Community Health & Resource Centre
Zion Crescent
Hulme
Manchester
M15 5BY
Tel 061 226 9562

Age Concern England
Astral House
1268 London Road
London
SW16 4ER
Tel 081 679 8000

Age Exchange
11 Blackheath Village
London
SE3 9LA
Tel 081 318 9105

Albany Video
Albany Video Distribution
Battersea Studios
Television Centre
Thackeray Road
London
SW8 3TW
Tel 071 498 6811

AMS Educational
Woodside Trading Estate
Low Lane
Horsforth
Leeds
LS18 5NY
Tel 0532 580309

Aquarius
32 Essex Street
Birmingham
B5 4TR
Tel 021 666 6711

Aquarius Education Unit
6th Floor
The White House
111 New Street
Birmingham
B2 4EU
Tel 021 632 4727

Arthritis Care
18 Stephenson Way
London
NW1 2HD
Tel 071 916 1500

Asian Community Media
c/o Black Issues in Community Arts
Hyde Youth and Community Centre
Lower Bennett Street
Hyde
Cheshire
SK14 1PP
Tel 061 368 7401

BAPS
BAPS Health Publications Unit
Heywood Stores
Manchester Road
Heywood
Lancs
OL10 2PZ
Tel 0706 366287

BBC Educational Developments
PO Box 50
Wetherby
West Yorkshire
LS23 7EZ
Tel 0937 541001

BBC for Business
PO Box 77
Wetherby
West Yorkshire
LS23 7HN
Tel 0937 541133

BBC Videos for Education and Training
BBC Training Videos
Woodlands
80 Wood Lane
London
W12 0TR
081 576 2415

Berkshire Design and Technology Centre
Brakenhale School
Bracknell
RG12 7BA
Tel 0344 861671

Birmingham FHSA
Birmingham Family Health Services Authority
Aston Cross
50 Rocky Lane
Aston
Birmingham
B6 5RQ
Tel 021 333 4444 ext 2180

Birmingham Maternity Hospital
Health Promotion
Birmingham Maternity Hospital
Queen Elizabeth Medical Centre
Edgbaston
Birmingham
B15 2TG

Birmingham Road Safety Unit
Road Safety Unit
Birmingham City Council
1 Lancaster Circus
Queensway
Birmingham
B4 7DQ
Tel 021 235 7457

Birmingham Sickle Cell and Thalassaemia Centre
Ladywood Health Centre
395 Ladywood Middleway
Ladywood
Birmingham
B1 2TP
Tel 021 454 4262

A. & C. Black
Sales & Distribution Centre
PO Box 19
Eaton Socon
Huntingdon
Cambridgeshire
PE19 3SF
Tel 0480 212666

Black HIV/AIDS Network
BCM BHAN
London WC1N 3XX
Tel 081 749 2828

Blackburn Hyndburn and Ribble Valley HPU
Blackburn Hyndburn and Ribble Valley
Health Promotion Unit
53 James Street
Blackburn
B1 6BE
Tel 0254 582946

Blackliners
49 Effra Road
Brixton
London
SW2 1BZ
Tel 071 738 7468

Bolton Environmental Health Services
Weston House
Weston Street
Bolton
BL3 2AR
Tel 0204 364656

Bolton Centre for Health Promotion
Bolton Health Authority
3 Chorley New Road
Bolton
BL1 4QR
Tel 0204 371353

Bournemouth English Book Centre
PO Box 1496
Poole
Dorset
BH12 3YD
Tel 0202 715555

British Diabetic Association
10 Queen Anne Street
London
W1M 0BD
Tel 071 323 1531

British Red Cross
Supply Department
British Red Cross National Headquarters
9 Grosvenor Crescent
London
SW1X 7EJ
Tel 071 235 5454

British Youth Council
57 Chalton Street
London
NW1 1HU
Tel 071 387 7559/5882

Brook Advisory Centres
Education and Publications Unit
153a East Street
London
SE17 2SD
Tel 071 708 1234

BSS (Mosaic)
PO Box 7
London
W3 6XJ
Tel 081 992 5522

Building Sights
Tindal School
Tindal Street
Balsall Heath
Birmingham
B12 9QS
Tel 021 440 1582

Cambridgeshire Road Safety
Cambridgeshire County Council
Road Safety Section
5 York Road
Millfield
Peterborough
PE1 1BP
Tel 0733 892697

Camden and Islington Health Authority
Health Promotion Department
St Pancras Hospital
4 St Pancras Way
London
NW1 0PE
Tel 071 387 1908

CancerLink
17 Britannia Street
London
WC1X 9JN
Tel 071 833 2451

CEDC
Community Education Development Centre
Lyng Hall
Blackberry Lane
Coventry
CV2 3JS
Tel 0203 638660

Ceddo Film/Video
Ceddo Film/Video Ltd
63–5 Coburg Road
Wood Green
London
N22 6UB
Tel 081 889 2105

Central and North West London HPU
Central and North West London Health
Promotion Unit
Grace Ward
Northwick Park Hospital
Watford Road
Harrow
Middlesex
HA1 3UJ
Tel 081 869 3643

Central Television
Video Resources Centre
Central TV
Central House
Broad Street
Birmingham
B1 2JP
Tel 021 643 9898

CFL Vision
PO Box 35
Wetherby
West Yorkshire
LS23 7EX
Tel 0937 541010

Child 2000
11–13 Clifton Terrace
London
N4 3SR
Tel 071 272 7774

Children's Society
The Children's Society
Edward Rudolph House
Margery Street
London
WC1X 0JL
Tel 071 837 4299

Cinenova
Film and Video Distribution
113 Roman Road
London
E2 0HU
Tel 081 981 6828

City & East London FHSA
City & East London Family Health Services
Authority
St Leonard's
Nuttall Street
London
N1 5LZ
Tel 071 739 6566

City of Bradford Metropolitan Council
Strategic Personnel
Chief Executive's Office
City of Bradford Metropolitan Council
6th Floor
Metrochange House
61 Hall Ings
Bradford
BD1 5SG
Tel 0274 752048

Cleanair
33 Stillness Road
London
SE23 1NG
Tel 081 690 4649

Concord Video and Film Council
201 Felixstowe Road
Ipswich
IP3 9BJ
Tel 0473 726012

Confederation of Indian Organisations
5 Westminster Bridge Road
London
SE1 7XW
Tel 071 928 9889

Coventry Environmental Services Department
Broadgate House
Broadgate
Coventry
CV1 1NH
Tel 0203 833333

Cygnet
Cygnet Limited
PO Box 273
High Wycombe
Bucks
P12 3XE
Tel 0494 450541

Cystic Fibrosis Research Trust
Alexandra House
5 Blyth Road
Bromley
Kent
BR1 3RS
Tel 081 464 7211

Department of Trade and Industry
Room 313
10–18 Victoria Street
London
SW1H 0NN
Tel 071 215 5000

Derbyshire FHSA
Derbyshire Family Health Services Authority
Derwent Court
Stuart Street
Derby
DE1 2FZ
Tel 0332 290445

Development Education Centre
Development Education Centre Ltd
Gillett Centre
998 Bristol Road
Selly Oak
Birmingham
B29 6LE
Tel 021 472 3255

Dewsbury Health Authority
Dental Services Manager
Health Centre
Greenside
Cleckheaton
West Yorkshire
BD19 5AP
Tel 0274 873501

Dorset Health Commission
Victoria House
Princes Road
Ferndown
Dorset
Tel 0202 893000

Down's Syndrome Association
155 Mitcham Road
London
SW17 9PG
Tel 081 682 4012

Dramatic Distribution
79 London Street
Reading
Berkshire
RG1 4QA
Tel 0734 394170

Dr Steevens Hospital
Room G19
Dr Steevens Hospital
Dublin 8
Ireland
Tel 010 353 1 679 0700

East Birmingham HPS
East Birmingham Health Promotion Service
102 Blakesley Road
Yardley
Birmingham
B25 8RN
Tel 021 783 3358

East London & City HPS
East London & The City Health Promotion
Service
Bow House
153–9 Bow Road
London
E3 2SE
Tel 081 983 1141

EDS
3 Henrietta Street
London
WC2E 8LU
Tel 071 240 0856

Educational Media Film and Video
Educational Media Film and Video Ltd
235 Imperial Drive
Rayners Lane
Harrow
Middlesex
HA2 7HE
Tel 081 868 1908

Ethnic Study Group
Coordinating Centre for Community and
Health Care
2(B) Lessingham Avenue
Tooting
London
SW17 8LU
Tel 081 682 0216

Family Planning Association
27–35 Mortimer Street
London
W1N 7RJ
Tel 071 636 7866

Fosse Health Trust
Director of Nutrition and Dietetics
Fosse Health Trust
c/o Glenfield Hospital
Groby Road
Leicester
LE3 9QP
Tel 0533 871471 ext 3377

Foundation for Women's Health
FORWARD
38 King Street
London
WC2E 8JT
Tel 071 379 6889

**Greater Manchester Community Work
Training Group**
23 Newmount Street
Manchester
M4 4DE
Tel 061 953 4117

Greater Manchester County Fire Service
146 Bolton Road
Swinton
Manchester
M27 2US
Tel 061 736 5866 ext 2088

Greenwich Education Services
2nd Floor
Riverside House
Woolwich High Street
London
SE18 6DF
Tel 081 854 8888

HEA HELIOS
Health Education Authority HELIOS Project
University of the West of England
Redland Hill
Bristol
BS6 6UZ
Tel 0272 238317

Health and Ethnicity Programme
North East and North West Thames RHA
40 Eastbourne Terrace
London
W2 3QR
Tel 071 262 8011 ext 3176

Healthcare Productions
Healthcare Productions Limited
2 Stucley Place
Camden Lock
London
NW1 8NS
Tel 071 267 8757

Health Education Authority
Marston Book Services
Customer Services Department
PO Box 87
Oxford
OX2 0DT
Tel 0865 204745

Health First
Mary Sheridan House
15 St Thomas Street
London
SE1 8RY
Tel 071 955 4366

Health Visitors Association
50 Southwark Street
London
SE1 1UN
Tel 071 378 7255

Health Wise Productions
9 Batley Enterprise Centre
513 Bradford Road
Batley
West Yorkshire
WF17 8JY
Tel 0924 474374

Herts Family Health
14 Parliament Square
Hertford
SG14 1ED
Tel 0992 552841

Horsham Hospital
Speech Therapy Managers' Office
Horsham Hospital
Hurst Road
Horsham
West Sussex
RH12 2DR
Tel 0403 250155 ext 2203

Hygia Communications
Hygia Communications Ltd
1 Regent Street
London
SW1Y 4NR
Tel 071 734 7665

Institute of Child Health
30 Guilford Street
London
WC1N 1EH
Tel 071 242 9789

International Planned Parenthood Federation
PO Box 759
Inner Circle
Regent's Park
London
NW1 4LQ
Tel 071 486 0741

Keep Warm, Keep Well
Freepost (SE 2851)
London
SE99 7XU
Tel 0800 289404 (freephone),
0800 269626 (freephone Minicom)

King's Healthcare
94–104 Denmark Hill
London
SE5 8RX
Tel 071 738 6181

Lambeth Women and Children's Health Project
Unit 8, Holles House
Angell Town Estate
Overton Road
London
SW9 7JN
Tel 071 737 7151

Lancashire FHSA
Caxton Road
Fulwood
Preston
PR2 4ZZ
Tel 0772 704141

Language and Skills Unit
Clarence Street Centre
Clarence Street
Bolton
BL1 2ET
Tel 0204 25500 ext 215

Language Alive
Chandos Junior Infant School
Vaughton Road South
Highgate
Birmingham
B12 0YN
Tel 021 446 4301

Lavis Marketing
73 Lime Walk
Headington
Oxford
OX3 7AD
Tel 0865 67575

Learning Development Aids
Duke Street
Wisbech
Cambridgeshire
PE13 2AE
Tel 0945 63441

Leicester Council for Voluntary Services
Market Centre Offices
11 Market Place
The Jetty
Leicester
LE1 5GG
Tel 0533 513999

Leicestershire Education Committee
Centre for Multicultural Education
Rushey Mead Centre
Harrison Road
Leicester
LE4 6RB
Tel 0533 665451

Leicestershire HA Video Unit
Leicestershire Health Authority
Health Education Video Unit
Clinical Sciences Building
Leicester Royal Infirmary
PO Box 65
Leicester
LE2 7LX
Tel 0533 550461

Local Government Management Board
Publications Section
Local Government Management Board
Arndale House
Arndale Centre
Luton
LU1 2TS
Tel 0582 451166

London Black Women's Health Action Project
Neighbourhood Building
1 Cornwall Avenue
London
E2 0HW
Tel 081 980 3503

London Borough of Hammersmith and Fulham
The Video and AV Unit
London Borough of Hammersmith and Fulham
Hammersmith Town Hall
Room 1
King Street
London
W6 9JU
Tel 081 748 3020 ext 2170

Macmillan Magazines
Macmillan Magazines Ltd
4 Little Essex Street
London
WC2R 3LF
Tel 071 836 0533

Manchester Council for Community Relations
4th Floor
Peter House
2–14 Oxford Street
Manchester
M1 5AG
Tel 061 228 0710

Maternity Links
The Old Co-op
42 Chelsea Road
Easton
Bristol
BS5 6AF
Tel 0272 558495

Minority Rights Group
379 Brixton Road
London
SW9 7DE
Tel 071 978 9498

Mitcham Community Centre
North East Mitcham Community Centre
Woodland Way
Mitcham
Surrey
CR4 2DZ
Tel 081 648 9939

Mount Vernon Hospital NHS Trust
Rickmansworth Road
Northwood
Middlesex
HA6 2RN
Tel 0895 278494

Multicultural Education Resources
County Service
Northern Base
66 Cedar Road
Bedford
MK42 0JE
Tel 0234 364475

Multiple Births Foundation
Queen Charlotte's and Chelsea Hospital
Goldhawk Road
London
W6 0XG
Tel 081 748 4666

Muslim Educational Trust
130 Stroud Green Road
London
N4 3RZ
Tel 071 272 8502

NACRO (National Association for the Care and Resettlement of Offenders)
169 Clapham Road
London
SW9 0PU
Tel 071 582 6500

Nakayoshi Kai
The Japanese Friendship Group
PO Box 2185
Barnet
Herts
EN5 5RB

National Association of Race Equality Advisers
c/o Birmingham City Council
Race Relations Unit
Central Executive Department
Congreve House
3 Congreve Passage
Birmingham
B3 3DA
021 235 2627

National Asthma Campaign
Information Department
National Asthma Campaign
Providence House
Providence Place
London
N1 0NT
Tel 071 226 2260

National Children's Bureau
8 Wakley Street
London
EC1V 7QE
Tel 071 278 9441

National Committee on AIDS Control
European Project: AIDS and Mobility
Polderweg 92
NL-1093 KP
Amsterdam
The Netherlands
Tel 010 31 20 693 9444

National Extension College
18 Brooklands Road
Cambridge
CB2 2HN
Tel 0223 316644

National Schizophrenia Fellowship Midlands
National Schizophrenia Fellowship
Midlands Regional Office
9 St Michael's Court
Victoria Street
West Bromwich
B70 8EZ
Tel 021 500 5988

National Sickle Cell Programme
PO Box 322
London
SE25 4BW
Tel 081 771 4365

Naz Project
The Naz Project
Palingswick House
241 King Street
London
W6 9LP
Tel 081 563 0191

Newham Council
Social Services Department
Newham Council
Room 115
99 The Grove
Stratford
London
E15 1HR
Tel 081 534 4545 ext 25617

N Films
78 Holyhead Road
Handsworth
Birmingham
B21 0LH
Tel 021 507 0341

NIACE
Publications Sales
National Institute of Adult Continuing
Education
198 De Montfort Street
Leicester
LE1 7GE
Tel 0533 551451

North East & North West Thames RHA
Communications Unit
North East & North West Thames Regional
Health Authority
40 Eastbourne Terrace
London
W2 3QR
Tel 071 725 3200

Northampton College
ESOL
Northampton College
Open Campus
Military Road
Northampton
NN1 3ET
Tel 0604 734170

Northern Birmingham Community HPS
Northern Birmingham Community Health
Promotion Service
Resource Section
Carnegie Centre for Health Promotion
Hunters Road
Hockley
Birmingham
B19 1DR
Tel 021 554 3899

Northern Visions
4 Donegall Street Place
Belfast
BT1 2FN
Tel 0232 245495

Oldham Resource and Information Centre
7–8 Commercial Road
Oldham
OL1 1DP
Tel 061 626 4130

Organon
Organon Laboratories Ltd
Cambridge Science Park
Milton Road
Cambridge
CB4 4FL
Tel 0223 423445

Out on a Limb
Battersea Studios
Television Centre
Thackeray Road
London
SE8 3TW
Tel 071 498 9643

Outreach
43 Dalrymple Road
London
SE4 2BQ
Tel 081 692 0761

Partnership Project
Braybrook Professional Centre
Amos Lane
Wednesfield
Wolverhampton
WV11 1ND

Pavilion Publishing
8 St George's Place
Brighton
East Sussex
BN1 4GB
Tel 0273 623222

Phil Swerdlow
19 Roland Avenue
Nuthall
Nottingham
NG16 1BB
Tel 0602 278 588

Positively Women
5 Sebastian Street
London
EC1V 0HE
Tel 071 490 5501

Pre-school Playgroups Association
45–9 Union Road
Croydon
CR0 2XU
Tel 081 684 9542

Preston HPU
Preston Health Promotion Unit
Watling Street Road
Fulwood
Preston
PR2 4DX
Tel 0772 711215

Refugee Action
The Offices
The Cedars
Oakwood
Derby
DE2 4FY
Tel 0332 833310

Replica Foods
Replica Foods Ltd
Block G
Carkers Lane
53–79 Highgate Road
London
NW5 1TL
Tel 071 485 3485

Re-Solv
30a High Street
Stone
Staffordshire
ST15 8AW
Tel 0785 817885

Royal College of Nursing
External Affairs Department
20 Cavendish Square
London
W1M 0AB
Tel 071 409 3333

St Patricks Health Promotion Department
Centre for Community Health
Highgate Street
Birmingham
B12 0YA
Tel 021 446 4747

St Thomas's Hospital
Director of Midwifery
St Thomas's Hospital
Lambeth Palace Road
London
SE1 7EH
Tel 071 928 9292

Salford Health Promotion Centre
Salford Health Authority
3rd Floor
Peel House
Albert Street
Eccles
Salford
M30 0NJ
Tel 061 787 0304

Sandwell HPU
Sandwell Health Promotion Unit
8 Grange Road
West Bromwich
West Midlands
B70 8PD
Tel 021 525 5363

Sandwell Road Safety Unit
Technical and Development Services
Department
Wigmore
Pennyhill Lane
West Bromwich
West Midlands
B71 3RZ
Tel 021 569 4270

Save the Children
Education Unit
Public Affairs Department
Mary Datchelor House
17 Grove Lane
London
SE5 8RD
Tel 071 703 5400

SCEMSC
Standing Conferences of Ethnic Minority
Senior Citizens
55A Westminster Bridge Road
London
SE1 7XW
Tel 071 928 0095

Shanti Asian Women and Stress Project
Health Promotion Services
Coventry Health Authority
Coventry and Warwickshire Hospital
Stoney Stanton Road
Coventry
CV1 4FH
Tel 0203 844092

Shared Care Team
Birmingham Social Services
Ladywood Area Office
23 All Saints Road
Hockley
Birmingham
B18 5QB
Tel 021 523 4361

Sickle Cell Society
54 Station Road
London
NW10 4UA
Tel 081 961 7795

South Birmingham Health Authority
Springfields Centre for Health Promotion
Raddlebarn Road
Selly Oak
Birmingham
B29 6JB
Tel 021 627 8230

South Buckinghamshire NHS Trust
Dental Health Education Department
Castlefield Community Health Centre
Chiltern Avenue
High Wycombe
Buckinghamshire
HP12 3UR
Tel 0494 437841

South Glamorgan HA
Health Promotion Centre
South Glamorgan Health Authority
Carville House
Rockwood Hospital
Fairwater Road
Llandaff
Cardiff
CF5 2YN
Tel 0222 578767

Southampton Council of Community Services
18 Oxford Street
Southampton
Hants
SO1 1DJ
Tel 0703 228291

Southern Derbyshire NHS Trust
Information Department
Community Health Services NHS Trust
Southern Derbyshire
Wilderslowe
121 Osmaston Road
Derby
DE1 2GA
Tel 0332 363371

Steven Bywater
4 James Dee Close
Quarry Bank
Dudley
West Midlands
DY5 1DH
Tel 03845 72456

Survivor Speakout
34 Osnaburgh Street
London NW3
Tel 071 916 5472/5473

Swingbridge Video
Norden House
41 Stowell Street
Newcastle upon Tyne
NE1 4YB
Tel 091 232 3762

TALC
PO Box 49
St Albans
Herfordshire
AL1 4AX
Tel 0727 853869

Threshold Housing Advice
Hammersmith Centre
126 Uxbridge Road
London
W12 8AA
Tel 081 749 2927

20th Century Vixen
13 Aubert Park
London
N5 1TL
Tel 071 359 7368

UK Thalassaemia Society
United Kingdom Thalassaemia Society
107 Nightingale Lane
London
N8 7QY
Tel 081 348 0437

Venture Press
16 Kent Street
Birmingham
Tel 021 622 3911

Verité à Tous
147 Heathfield Road
Lozells
Birmingham
B19 1HL
Tel 021 507 1090

VOLCUF
Voluntary Organisations Liaison Council for
Under Fives
77 Holloway Road
London
N7 8JZ
Tel 071 607 9573

West Lambeth Community Care
West Lambeth Community Care (NHS) Trust
Whittington Centre
11–13 Rutford Road
Streatham
London
SW16 2DQ
Tel 081 677 7415

West Midlands Fire Service
Fire Service Headquarters
Leicester Circus
Queensway
Birmingham
B4 7DE
Tel 021 380 6713

Wolverhampton Health Promotion
Wolverhampton Health Promotion
Department
Sheldon Langley Ward
The Royal Hospital
Cleveland Road
Wolverhampton
WV2 1BT
Tel 0902 644853

**Working Group against Racism in
Children's Resources**
460 Wandsworth Road
London
SW8 3LX
071 627 4594

Youth Clubs UK
Youth Clubs UK Publications
11 St Bride Street
London
EC4A 4AS
Tel 071 353 2366